WHY WERE OUR REFORMERS BURNED?

J. C. Ryle

THE BANNER OF TRUTH TRUST

THE BANNER OF TRUTH TRUST

Head Office
3 Murrayfield Road
Edinburgh, EH12 6EL
UK

North America Office
PO Box 621
Carlisle, PA 17013
USA

banneroftruth.org

© The Banner of Truth Trust 2022
First published 2022

*

ISBN
Print: 978 1 80040 243 0
Epub: 978 1 80040 244 7
Kindle: 978 1 80040 245 4

*

Typeset in 10.5/13.5 pt Adobe Garamond Pro at
The Banner of Truth Trust

Printed in the UK by
Buchanan McPherson Ltd.,
Hamilton

The chapter contained in this booklet is taken from J. C. Ryle's
Five English Reformers. *It also appears in the larger volume*
Light from Old Times. *Both these titles are also published by
the Banner of Truth Trust.*

INTRODUCTION

THROUGH his courageous writings Bishop J. C. Ryle has given to the church a generously large gift. For more than a century now the value of his writings has not diminished in the slightest. From his pen we have many treasured books and articles that bless, inform and challenge. Ryle's writings had a cutting edge for those who read them when they were first published in the latter half of the nineteenth century. Men and women, and young people too, who read Ryle's reprints in the twenty-first century continue to feel the sharpness and relevance of what he had to say despite the passing of the years. *Why Were Our Reformers Burned?* is a prime example of that.

Today's tide of secularism is invasive. It pressurizes Christians, intimidating many of them into silence with respect to the glorious truths we hold dear. Feeling backed into a corner, Christians have sometimes been tempted to unite with anyone with whom we feel we have a modicum of agreement. But no matter how worthy the motive, we dare not blur, compromise, or even sacrifice the foundational truths of our Christian faith. To remain faithful to the word of God in this generation will invite others to accuse us of being dogmatic, intolerant, and even extremist. This booklet reminds us of the vital importance of holding fast to the basic truths of the Christian gospel.

Ringing through the centuries are the courageous words of Hugh Latimer, spoken to his fearful fellow martyr Nicholas Ridley as they were about to be burned at the stake in Oxford: 'Be of good cheer, Master Ridley, and play the man. We shall this day light such a candle, by God's grace, in England, as I trust shall never be put out.' Yet today that candle is flickering almost to the extent of being extinguished. Recent archbishops and church leaders have addressed the Pope as 'Your holiness,' referring to him as the 'greatest evangelist,' describing the Reformation as a big mistake, and even saying that the Roman Catholic Church is 'the bearer of the message of salvation.' Others feel that, as there are Roman Catholics who possess the same spiritual gifts as they do themselves, doctrinal differences between the Church of Rome and the churches of the Reformation can be ignored.

Therefore, to ask and answer the question, 'Why were our Reformers burned?' could not be more pertinent. It is the question Ryle addresses in the introductory chapter of his book 'Five English Reformers,' first published a decade before his death in 1900. As a Bible-believing Christian, I love the Lord, I believe the gospel, and I trust every word and every truth revealed in Scripture. It pains me that the sufficiency and simplicity of the finished work of Christ, who died bearing sin in his own body and rose triumphantly from the grave, should be distorted, diminished, or supplemented. I feel grief for the millions of individuals who are led away from confident trust in Jesus alone for salvation. I passionately believe that heaven is not a reward, nor is righteousness earned, but are gifts of God's free grace to be received by the empty hand of faith alone.

This booklet, read carefully and prayerfully, will not lead anyone to smug self-righteousness or complacency. Understanding the error of a theological system should stir compassion and winsome boldness towards those who are caught up in it. We will find ourselves seeking to 'save [them] with fear, pulling them out of the fire, hating even the garment defiled by the flesh.' I feel deeply grateful to God for those who lived and laid down their lives for the truth of the gospel. The world was not worthy of them: they took up the cross and followed their Saviour. We need to understand why they did it, and in our times have a similar, costly commitment to the truth of the gospel.

Here J. C. Ryle opens his heart and reveals to us his great concern. He writes from a very definite Church of England position, but, nevertheless, this little booklet is a *must-read* for all Christians. I also commend to you the book from which it is extracted, *Five English Reformers* (which is available from the Banner of Truth Trust). It contains short biographies of five English martyrs: John Hooper (Bishop of Gloucester), Rowland Taylor (Rector of Hadleigh in Suffolk), Hugh Latimer (Bishop of Worcester), John Bradford (Prebendary of St Paul's), and Nicholas Ridley (Bishop of London). Their lives and deaths will deepen your understanding of the vital importance of the great Reformation of the sixteenth century.

ROGER CARSWELL
Evangelist, based in Yorkshire

WHY WERE OUR REFORMERS BURNED?

THERE are certain facts in history which the world tries hard to forget and ignore. These facts get in the way of some of the world's favourite theories, and are highly inconvenient. The consequence is that the world shuts its eyes against them. They are either cut dead as vulgar intruders, or passed by as tiresome bores. Little by little they sink out of sight of the students of history, like ships in a distant horizon, or are left behind like a luggage train in a siding. Of such facts the subject of this paper is a vivid example: 'The Burning of our English Reformers; and the Reason why they were Burned.'

It is fashionable in some quarters to deny that there is any such thing as certainty about religious truth, or any opinions for which it is worthwhile to be burned. Yet, 300 years ago, there were men who were certain they had found out truth, and were content to die for their opinions. It is fashionable in other quarters to leave out all the unpleasant things in history, and to paint everything with a rose-coloured hue. A very popular history of our English Queens hardly mentions the martyrdoms of Queen Mary's days! Yet Mary was not called 'Bloody Mary' without reason, and scores of Protestants were burned in her reign. Last, but not least, it is thought very bad taste in many quarters to say anything which throws discredit on the Church of Rome. Yet it is as certain that the Romish Church burned our English Reformers as it is that William the Conqueror won the battle of Hastings. These difficulties meet me face to face as I walk up to the subject which I wish to unfold in this paper. I know their magnitude, and I cannot evade them. I only ask my readers to give me a patient and indulgent hearing.

After all, I have great confidence in the honesty of Englishmen's minds. Truth is truth, however long it may be neglected. Facts are facts, however long they may lie buried. I only want to dig up some old facts which the sands of time have covered over, to bring to the light of day some old English monuments which have been long neglected, to unstop some old wells which the prince of this world has been diligently filling with earth. I ask my readers to give me their attention for a few minutes, and I trust to be able to show them that it is good to examine the question, 'Why were our Reformers Burned?'

I. The *broad facts* of the martyrdom of our Reformers are a story well known and soon told. But it may be useful to give a brief outline of these facts, in order to supply a framework to our subject.

Edward VI, 'that incomparable young prince,' as Bishop Burnet justly calls him, died on 6 July 1553. Never, perhaps, did any royal personage in this land die more truly lamented, or leave behind him a fairer reputation. Never, perhaps, to man's poor fallible judgment, did the cause of God's truth in England receive a heavier blow. His last prayer before death ought not to be forgotten, 'O Lord God, defend this realm from Papistry, and maintain thy true religion.' It was a prayer, I believe, not offered in vain.

After a foolish and deplorable effort to obtain the crown for Lady Jane Grey, Edward was succeeded by his eldest sister, Mary, daughter of Henry VIII, and his first Queen, Catherine of Aragon, and best known in English history by the ill-omened name of 'Bloody Mary.' Mary had been brought up from her infancy as a rigid adherent of the Romish Church. She was, in fact, a very Papist of Papists, conscientious, zealous, bigoted, and narrow-minded in the extreme. She began at once to pull down her brother's work in every possible way, and to restore Popery in its worst and most offensive forms. Step by step she and her councillors marched back to Rome, trampling down one by one every obstacle, and as *thorough* as Lord Strafford in going straight forward to their mark.[1] The Mass was restored; the English service was taken away; the works of Luther, Zwingli, Calvin, Tyndale, Bucer, Latimer, Hooper, and Cranmer were proscribed. Cardinal Pole was invited to England. The foreign Protestants resident in England were banished. The leading divines of the Protestant Church of England were deprived of their offices, and, while some escaped to the Continent, many were put in prison. The old statutes against heresy were once more brought forward, primed and loaded. And thus by the beginning of 1555 the stage was cleared, and that bloody tragedy, in which Bishops Bonner and Gardiner played so prominent a part, was ready to begin.

For, unhappily for the credit of human nature, Mary's advisers were not content with depriving and imprisoning the leading English Reformers. It was resolved to make them abjure their principles, or to put them to death. One by one they were called before special Commissions, examined about their religious opinions, and called upon to recant, on pain of death if they refused. No third course, no alternative was left to them. They were either to give up Protestantism and receive Popery, or else they were to be burned alive. Refusing to recant, they were one by one handed over to the secular power, publicly brought out and chained to stakes, publicly surrounded with faggots, and publicly sent out of the world by that most cruel and painful of deaths, the death by fire. All these are broad facts which all the apologists of Rome can never gainsay or deny.

It is a broad fact that during the four last years of Queen Mary's reign no less than 288 persons were burnt at the stake for their adhesion to the Protestant faith.

---

[1] A reference to Thomas Wentworth, Earl of Strafford, a leading figure in the 'Personal Rule' of Charles I (1629–40), when he acted as Lord Deputy of Ireland. Along with William Laud and others, he formed part of the inner circles which advised the King. They were known as the 'Thorough Party.'—*Publisher*.

>   In 1555 there were burnt 71
>   In 1556 there were burnt 89
>   In 1557 there were burnt 88
>   In 1558 there were brunt 40
>   ___
>   288[2]

Indeed, the faggots never ceased to blaze whilst Mary was alive, and five martyrs were burnt in Canterbury only a week before her death. Out of these 288 sufferers, be it remembered, one was an archbishop, four were bishops, twenty-one were clergymen, fifty-five were women, and four were children.

It is a broad fact that these 288 sufferers were not put to death for any offence against property or person. They were not rebels against the Queen's authority, caught red-handed in arms. They were not thieves, or murderers, or drunkards, or unbelievers, or men and women of immoral lives. On the contrary, they were, with barely an exception, some of the holiest, purest, and best Christians in England, and several of them the most learned men of their day.

I might say much about the gross injustice and unfairness with which they were treated at their various examinations. Their trials, if indeed they can be called trials, were a mere mockery of justice. I might say much about the abominable cruelty with which most of them were treated, both in prison and at the stake. But you must read Fox's *Martyrs* on these points. I make no comment on the stupid impolicy of the whole persecution. Never did Rome do herself such irreparable damage as she did in Mary's reign. Even unlearned people, who could not argue much, saw clearly that a Church which committed such horrible bloodshed could hardly be the one true church of Christ![3] But I have no time for all this. I

---

[2] These numbers are given by Soames, in his *History of the Reformation*, 4:587, and are taken from Strype. Some historians give higher numbers.

[3] A lady in high position told Bonner in a letter, after Philpot's death, that his cruelty had lost the hearts of 20,000 Papists in twelve months.

must conclude this general sketch of this part of my subject with two short remarks.

For one thing, I ask my readers never to forget that for the burning of our Reformers the Church of Rome is wholly and entirely responsible. The attempt to transfer the responsibility from the Church to the secular power is a miserable and dishonest subterfuge. The men of Judah did not slay Samson; but they delivered him bound into the hands of the Philistines! The Church of Rome did not slay the Reformers; but she condemned them, and the secular power executed the condemnation! The precise measure of responsibility which ought to be meted out to each of Rome's agents in the matter is a point that I do not care to settle. Miss Strickland, in her *Lives of the Queens of England,* has tried in vain to shift the blame from unhappy Mary. With all the zeal of a woman, she has laboured hard to whitewash her character. The reader of her biography will find little about martyrdoms. But it will not do. Mr Froude's volume tells a very different tale. The Queen, and her Council, and the Parliament, and the popish bishops, and Cardinal Pole, must be content to share the responsibility among them. One thing alone is very certain. They will never succeed in shifting the responsibility off the shoulders of the Church of Rome. Like the Jews and Pontius Pilate, when our Lord was crucified, all parties must bear the blame. THE BLOOD is upon them all.

For another thing, I wish my readers to remember that the burning of the Marian martyrs is an act that the Church of Rome has never repudiated, apologized for, or repented of, down to the present day. There stands the huge blot in her escutcheon; and there stands the huge fact side by side, that she has never made any attempt to wipe it away. Never has she repented of her treatment of the Vaudois and the Albigenses; never has she repented of the wholesale murders of the Spanish Inquisition; never has she repented of the massacre of St Bartholomew; never has she repented of the burning of the English Reformers. We should make a note of that fact, and let it sink down into our minds. Rome never changes. Rome will never admit that she has made mistakes. She burned our English Reformers 300 years ago. She tried hard to stamp out by violence the Protestantism which she could not prevent spreading by arguments. If Rome had only the power, I am not sure that she would not attempt to play the whole game over again.

II. The question may now arise in our minds, *Who were the leading English Reformers* that were burned? What were their names, and what were the circumstances attending their deaths? These are questions which may very properly be asked, and questions to which I proceed at once to give an answer.

In this part of my paper I am very sensible that I shall seem to many to go over old ground. But I am bold to say that it is ground which ought often to be gone over. I, for one, want the names of our martyred Reformers to be 'household words' in every Protestant family throughout the land. I shall, therefore, make no apology for giving the names of the nine principal English martyrs in the chronological order of their deaths, and for supplying you with a few facts about each of them. Never, I believe, since Christ left the world, did Christian men ever meet a cruel death with such glorious faith, and hope, and patience, as these Marian martyrs. Never did dying men leave behind them such a rich store of noble sayings, sayings which deserve to be written in golden letters in our histories, and handed down to our children's children.

(1) The first leading English Reformer who broke the ice and crossed the river, as a martyr in Mary's reign, was *John Rogers,* a London minister, Vicar of St Sepulchre's, and Prebendary and Reader of Divinity at St Paul's. He was burned in Smithfield on Monday, 4 February 1555. Rogers was born at Deritend, in the parish of Aston, near Birmingham. He was a man who, in one respect, had done

more for the cause of Protestantism than any of his fellow sufferers. In saying this I refer to the fact that he had assisted Tyndale and Coverdale in bringing out a most important version of the English Bible, a version commonly known as Matthews' Bible. Indeed, he was condemned as 'Rogers, *alias* Matthews.' This circumstance, in all human probability, made him a marked man, and was one cause why he was the first who was brought to the stake.

Rogers' examination before Gardiner gives us the idea of his being a bold, thorough Protestant, who had fully made up his mind on all points of the Romish controversy, and was able to give a reason for his opinions. At any rate, he seems to have silenced and abashed his examiners even more than most of the martyrs did. But arguments, of course, went for nothing. 'Woe to the conquered!' If he had the word, his enemies had the sword.[4]

On the morning of his martyrdom he was roused hastily in his cell in Newgate, and hardly allowed time to dress himself. He was then led forth to Smithfield on foot, within sight of the Church of St Sepulchre, where he had preached, and through the streets of the parish where he had done the work of a pastor. By the wayside stood his wife and ten children (one a baby) whom the diabolical cruelty of Bishop Bonner had flatly refused him leave to see in prison. He just saw them, but was hardly allowed to stop, and then walked on calmly to the stake, repeating the 51st Psalm. An immense crowd lined the street, and filled every available spot in Smithfield. Up to that day men could not tell how English Reformers would behave in the face of death, and could hardly believe that Prebendaries and

---

[4] Rogers' prophetical words in prison, addressed to Day, printer of Fox's *Acts and Monuments,* are well worth quoting: 'Thou shalt live to see the alteration of this religion, and the gospel freely preached again. Therefore, have me commended to my brethren, as well in exile as here, and bid them be circumspect in displacing the Papists and putting good ministers into churches, or else their end will be worse than ours.' Fox, 3:309, 1684 edition.

Dignitaries would actually give their bodies to be burned for their religion. But when they saw John Rogers, the first martyr, walking steadily and unflinchingly into a fiery grave, the enthusiasm of the crowd knew no bounds. They rent the air with thunders of applause. Even Noailles, the French Ambassador, wrote home a description of the scene, and said that Rogers went to death 'as if he was walking to his wedding.' By God's great mercy he died with comparative ease. And so the first Marian martyr passed away.

(2) The second leading Reformer who died for Christ's truth in Mary's reign was *John Hooper,* Bishop of Gloucester. He was burned at Gloucester on Friday, 9 February 1555.

Hooper was a Somersetshire man by birth. In many respects he was, perhaps, the noblest martyr of them all. Of all Edward VI's bishops, none has left behind him a higher reputation for personal holiness, and diligent preaching and working in his diocese. None, judging from his literary remains, had clearer and more scriptural views on all points in theology. Some might say that Edward VI's Bishop of Gloucester was too Calvinistic; but he was not more so than the Thirty-nine Articles. Hooper was a far-sighted man, and saw the danger of leaving nest-eggs for Romanism in the Church of England. In his famous dispute with Cranmer and the other bishops about wearing Romish vestments at his consecration, it has been, I know, the fashion to condemn him as too stiff and unbending. I say boldly that the subsequent history of our Church makes it doubtful whether we ought not to reverse our verdict. The plain truth is, that in principle Hooper was right, and his opponents were wrong.

A man like Hooper, firm, stern, not naturally genial, unbending and unsparing in his denunciation of sin, was sure to have many enemies. He was one of the first marked for destruction as soon as Popery was restored. He was summoned to London at a very early stage of the Marian persecution, and, after lingering eighteen months in prison, and going through the form of examination by

Bonner, Gardiner, Tunstall, and Day, was degraded from his office, and sentenced to be burned as a heretic.

At first it was fully expected that he would suffer in Smithfield with Rogers. This plan, for some unknown reason, was given up, and to his great satisfaction Hooper was sent down to Gloucester, and burnt in his own diocese, and in sight of his own cathedral. On his arrival there, he was received with every sign of sorrow and respect by a vast multitude, who went out on the Cirencester Road to meet him, and was lodged for the night in the house of a Mr Ingram, which is still standing, and probably not much altered. There Sir Anthony Kingston, whom the good bishop had been the means of converting from a sinful life, entreated him, with many tears, to spare himself, and urged him to remember that 'Life was sweet, and death was bitter.' To this the noble martyr returned this memorable reply, that 'Eternal life was more sweet, and eternal death was more bitter.'

On the morning of his martyrdom he was led forth, walking, to the place of execution, where an immense crowd awaited him. It was market day; and it was reckoned that nearly 7,000 people were present. The stake was planted directly in front of the western gate of the Cathedral Close, and within 100 yards of the deanery and the east front of the cathedral. The exact spot is marked now by a beautiful memorial at the east end of the churchyard of St Mary-de-Lode. The window over the gate, where popish friars watched the bishop's dying agonies, stands unaltered to this day.

When Hooper arrived at this spot, he was allowed to pray, though strictly forbidden to speak to the people. And there he knelt down, and prayed a prayer which has been preserved and recorded by Fox, and is of exquisitely touching character. Even then a box was put before him containing a full pardon, if he would only recant. His only answer was, 'Away with it; if you love my soul, away with it!' He was then fastened to the stake by an iron round his waist, and fought his last fight with the king of terrors. Of all the martyrs, none perhaps, except Ridley, suffered more than Hooper did. Three times the faggots had to be lighted, because they would not burn properly. Three quarters of an hour the noble sufferer endured the mortal agony, as Fox says, 'neither moving backward, forward, nor to any side,' but only praying, 'Lord Jesus, have mercy on me; Lord Jesus, receive my spirit'; and beating his breast with one hand till it was burned to a stump. And so the good Bishop of Gloucester passed away.

(3) The third leading Reformer who suffered in Mary's reign was *Rowland Taylor,* Rector of Hadleigh, in Suffolk. He was burned on Aldham Common, close to his own parish, the same day that Hooper died at Gloucester, on Friday, 9 February 1555.

Rowland Taylor is one of whom we know little, except that he was a great friend of Cranmer, and a doctor of divinity and canon law. But that he was a man of high standing among the Reformers is evident, from his being ranked by his enemies with Hooper, Rogers, and Bradford; and that he was an exceedingly able and ready divine is clear from his examination, recorded by Fox. Indeed, there is hardly any of the sufferers about whom the old Martyrologist has gathered together so many touching and striking things. One might think he was a personal friend.

Striking was the reply which he made to his friends at Hadleigh, who urged him to flee, as he might have done, when he was first summoned to appear in London before Gardiner:—

> What will ye have me to do? I am old, and have already lived too long to see these terrible and most wicked days. Fly you, and do as your conscience leadeth you. I am fully determined, with God's grace, to go to this bishop, and tell him to his beard that he doth naught. I believe before God that I shall never be able to do for my God such good service as I may do now.[5]

[5] Fox, *Acts and Monuments,* 3:138.

Striking were the replies which he made to Gardiner and his other examiners. None spoke more pithily, weightily, and powerfully than did this Suffolk incumbent.

Striking and deeply affecting was his last testament and legacy of advice to his wife, his family, and parishioners, though far too long to be inserted here, excepting the last sentence:

> For God's sake beware of Popery: for though it appear to have in it unity, yet the same is vanity and Antichristianity, and not in Christ's faith and verity.[6]

He was sent down from London to Hadleigh, to his great delight, to be burned before the eyes of his parishioners. When he got within two miles of Hadleigh, the Sheriff of Suffolk asked him how he felt. 'God be praised, Master Sheriff,' was his reply, 'never better. For now I am almost at home. I lack but just two stiles to go over, and I am even at my Father's house.'

As he rode through the streets of the little town of Hadleigh, he found them lined with crowds of his parishioners, who had heard of his approach, and came out of their houses to greet him with many tears and lamentations. To them he only made one constant address, 'I have preached to you God's word and truth, and am come this day to seal it with my blood.'

On coming to Aldham Common, where he was to suffer, they told him where he was. Then said he, 'Thank God, I am even at home.'

When he was stripped to his shirt and ready for the stake, he said, with a loud voice, 'Good people, I have taught you nothing but God's holy word, and those lessons that I have taken out of the Bible; and I am come hither to seal it with my blood.' He would probably have said more, but, like all the other martyrs, he was strictly forbidden to speak, and even now was struck violently on the

---

[6] Fox, *Acts and Monuments,* 3:144.

head for saying these few words. He then knelt down and prayed, a poor woman of the parish insisting, in spite of every effort to prevent her, in kneeling down with him. After this, he was chained to the stake, and repeating the 51st Psalm, and crying to God, 'Merciful Father, for Jesus Christ's sake, receive my soul into thy hands,' stood quietly amidst the flames without crying or moving, till one of the guards dashed out his brains with a halberd. And so this good old Suffolk incumbent passed away.

(4) The fourth leading Reformer who suffered in Mary's reign was *Robert Ferrar,* Bishop of St David's, in Wales. He was burned at Carmarthen on Friday, 30 March 1555. Little is known of this good man beyond the fact that he was born at Halifax, and was the last Prior of Nostel, in Yorkshire, an office which he surrendered in 1540. He was also Chaplain to Archbishop Cranmer and to the Protector Somerset, and to this influence he owed his elevation to the episcopal bench. He was first imprisoned for various trivial and ridiculous charges on temporal matters, in the latter days of Edward VI, after the fall of the Protector Somerset, and afterwards was brought before Gardiner, with Hooper, Rogers, and Bradford, on the far more serious matter of his doctrine. The articles exhibited against him clearly show that in all questions of faith he was of one mind with his fellow martyrs. Like Hooper and Taylor, he was condemned to be burned in the place where he was best known, and was sent down from London to Carmarthen. What happened there at his execution is related very briefly by Fox, partly, no doubt, because of the great distance of Carmarthen from London in those pre-railways days; partly, perhaps, because most of those who saw Ferrar burned could speak nothing but Welsh. One single fact is recorded which shows the good bishop's courage and constancy in a striking light. He had told a friend before the day of execution that if he saw him once stir in the fire from the pain of his burning, he need not believe the doctrines he had taught. When the awful

time came, he did not forget his promise, and, by God's grace, he kept it well. He stood in the flames holding out his hands till they were burned to stumps, until a bystander in mercy struck him on the head, and put an end to his sufferings. And so the Welsh bishop passed away.

(5) The fifth leading Reformer who suffered in Mary's reign was *John Bradford,* Prebendary of St Paul's, and Chaplain to Bishop Ridley. He was burned in Smithfield on Monday, 1 July 1555, at the early age of thirty-five. Few of the English martyrs, perhaps, are better known than Bradford, and none certainly deserve better their reputation. Strype calls Bradford, Cranmer, Ridley, and Latimer, the 'four prime pillars' of the Reformed Church of England. He was by birth a Manchester man, and to the end of his life retained a strong interest in the district with which he was connected. At an early age his high talents commended him to the notice of men in high quarters, and he was appointed one of the six royal chaplains who were sent about England to preach up the doctrines of the Reformation. Bradford's commission was to preach in Lancashire and Cheshire, and he seems to have performed his duty with singular ability and success. He preached constantly in Manchester, Liverpool, Bolton, Bury, Wigan, Ashton, Stockport, Prestwich, Middleton, and Chester, with great benefit to the cause of Protestantism, and with great effect on men's souls. The consequence was what might have been expected. Within a month of Queen Mary's accession Bradford was in prison, and never left it until he was burned. His youth, his holiness, and his extraordinary reputation as a preacher, made him an object of great interest during his imprisonment, and immense efforts were made to pervert him from the Protestant faith. All these efforts, however, were in vain. As he lived, so he died.[7]

---

[7] Bradford seems to have had a very strong feeling about the causes for which God permitted the Marian persecution. Writing to his mother from prison, he says: 'Ye all know there never was more knowledge of God, and less godly

On the day of his execution he was led out from Newgate to Smithfield about nine o'clock in the morning, amid such a crowd of people as was never seen either before or after. A Mrs Honeywood, who lived to the age of ninety-six, and died about 1620, remembered going to see him burned, and her shoes being trodden off by the crowd. Indeed, when he came to the stake the Sheriffs of London were so alarmed at the press that they would not allow him and his fellow sufferer, Leaf, to pray as long as they wished. 'Arise,' they said, 'and make an end; for the press of the people is great.'

'At that word,' says Fox, 'they both stood up upon their feet, and then Master Bradford took a faggot in his hands and kissed it, and so likewise the stake.' When he came to the stake he held up his hands, and, looking up to heaven, said, 'O England, England, repent thee of thy sins! Beware of idolatry; beware of false Antichrists! Take heed they do not deceive you!' After that he turned to the young man Leaf, who suffered with him, and said, 'Be of good comfort, brother; for we shall have a merry supper with the Lord this night.' After that he spoke no more that man could hear, excepting that he embraced the reeds, and said, 'Strait is the gate, and narrow is the way, that leadeth to eternal life, and few there be that find it.' 'He embraced the flames,' says Fuller, 'as a fresh gale of wind in a hot summer day.' And so, in the prime of life, he passed away.

(6, 7) The sixth and seventh leading Reformers who suffered in Mary's reign were two whose names are familiar to every Englishman, *Nicholas Ridley,* Bishop of London, and *Hugh Latimer,* once Bishop of Worcester. They were both burned at Oxford, back to back, at one stake, on 16 October 1555. Ridley was born at Willimondswike, in Northumberland, on the borders. Latimer was born at Thurcaston, in Leicestershire. The history of these two great English Protestants is so well known to most people that I need not say much about

---

living and true serving of God. God, therefore, is now come, and because he will not damn us with the world he punisheth us.' Fox, 3:255.

it. Next to Cranmer, there can be little doubt that no two men did so much to bring about the establishment of the principles of the Reformation in England. Latimer, as an extraordinary popular preacher, and Ridley, as a learned man and an admirable manager of the metropolitan diocese of London, have left behind them reputations which never have been surpassed. As a matter of course, they were among the first that Bonner and Gardiner struck at when Mary came to the throne, and were persecuted with relentless severity until their deaths.

How they were examined again and again by Commissioners about the great points in controversy between Protestants and Rome, how they were shamefully baited, teased, and tortured by every kind of unfair and unreasonable dealing, how they gallantly fought a good fight to the end, and never gave way for a moment to their adversaries, all these are matters with which I need not trouble my readers. Are they not all fairly chronicled in the pages of good old Fox? I will only mention a few circumstances connected with their deaths.

On the day of their martyrdom they were brought separately to the place of execution, which was at the end of Broad Street, Oxford, close to Balliol College. Ridley arrived on the ground first, and seeing Latimer come afterwards, ran to him and kissed him, saying, 'Be of good heart, brother; for God will either assuage the fury of the flames, or else strengthen us to abide it.' They then prayed earnestly, and talked with one another, though no one could hear what they said. After this they had to listen to a sermon by a wretched renegade divine named Smith, and, being forbidden to make any answer, were commanded to make ready for death.

Ridley's last words before the fire was lighted were these, 'Heavenly Father, I give thee most hearty thanks that thou hast called me to a profession of thee even unto death. I beseech thee, Lord God, have mercy on this realm of England, and deliver the same from all her enemies.' Latimer's last words were like the blast of a trumpet, which rings even to this day, 'Be of good comfort, Master Ridley, and play the man; we shall this day, by God's grace, light such a candle in England as I trust shall never be put out.'

When the flames began to rise, Ridley cried out with a loud voice in Latin, 'Into thy hands, O Lord, I commend my spirit: Lord, receive my spirit,' and afterwards repeated these last words in English. Latimer cried as vehemently on the other side of the stake, 'Father of heaven, receive my soul.'

Latimer soon died. An old man, above eighty years of age, it took but little to set his spirit free from its earthly tenement. Ridley suffered long and painfully, from the bad management of the fire by those who attended the execution. At length, however, the flames reached a vital part of him, and he fell at Latimer's feet, and was at rest. And so the two great Protestant bishops passed away. 'They were lovely and beautiful in their lives, and in death they were not divided.'

(8) The eighth leading English Reformer who suffered in Mary's reign was *John Philpot*, Archdeacon of Winchester. He was burned in Smithfield on Wednesday, 18 December 1555. Philpot is one of the martyrs of whom we know little comparatively, except that he was born at Compton, in Hampshire, was of good family, and well connected, and had a very high reputation for learning. The mere fact that at the beginning of Mary's reign he was one of the leading champions of Protestantism in the mock discussions which were held in Convocation, is sufficient to show that he was no common man. The relentless virulence with which he was persecuted by Gardiner is easily accounted for, when we remember that Gardiner, when he was deposed from his See in Edward VI's time, was Bishop of Winchester, and would naturally regard his successor, Bishop Ponet, and all his officials, with intense hatred. A popish bishop was not likely to spare a Protestant archdeacon.

The thirteen examinations of Philpot before the popish bishops are given by Fox at great length, and fill no less than one hundred and forty pages of one of the Parker Society volumes. The length to which they were protracted shows plainly how anxious his judges were to turn him from his principles. The skill with which the archdeacon maintained his ground, alone and unaided, gives a most favourable impression of his learning, no less than of his courage and patience.

The night before his execution he received a message, while at supper in Newgate, to the effect that he was to be burned next day. He answered at once, 'I am ready: God grant me strength and a joyful resurrection.' He then went into his bedroom, and thanked God that he was counted worthy to suffer for his truth.

The next morning, at eight o'clock, the sheriffs called for him, and conducted him to Smithfield. The road was foul and muddy, as it was the depth of winter, and the officers took him up in their arms to carry him to the stake. Then he said, merrily, alluding to what he had probably seen at Rome, when travelling in his early days, 'What, will you make me a pope? I am content to go to my journey's end on foot.'

When he came into Smithfield, he kneeled down and said, 'I will pay my vows in thee, O Smithfield.' He then kissed the stake and said, 'Shall I disdain to suffer at this stake, seeing my Redeemer did not refuse to suffer a most vile death on the cross for me?' After that, he meekly repeated the 106th, 107th, and 108th Psalms; and being chained to the stake, died very quietly. And so the good archdeacon passed away.

(9) The ninth and last leading Reformer who suffered in Mary's reign was *Thomas Cranmer,* Archbishop of Canterbury. He was burned at Oxford, on 21 March 1556. Cranmer was born at Aslacton, in Nottinghamshire. There is no name among the English martyrs so well known in history as his. There is none certainly in the list of our Reformers to whom the Church of England, on the whole, is so

much indebted. He was only a mortal man, and had his weaknesses and infirmities, it must be admitted; but still, he was a great man, and a good man.

Cranmer, we must always remember, was brought prominently forward at a comparatively early period in the English Reformation, and was made Archbishop of Canterbury at a time when his views of religion were confessedly half-formed and imperfect. Whenever quotations from Cranmer's writings are brought forward by the advocates of semi-Romanism in the Church of England, you should always ask carefully to what period of his life those quotations belong. In forming your estimate of Cranmer, do not forget his antecedents. He was a man who had the honesty to grope his way into fuller light, and to cast aside his early opinions and confess that he had changed his mind on many subjects. How few men have the courage to do this!

Cranmer maintained an unblemished reputation throughout the reigns of Henry VIII and Edward VI, although frequently placed in most delicate and difficult positions. Not a single man can be named in those days who passed through so much dirt, and yet came out of it so thoroughly undefiled.

Cranmer, beyond all doubt, laid the foundation of our present Prayer-book and Articles. Though not perhaps a brilliant man, he was a learned one, and a lover of learned men, and one who was always trying to improve everything around him. When I consider the immense difficulties he had to contend with, I often wonder that he accomplished what he did. Nothing, in fact, but his steady perseverance would have laid the foundation of our Formularies.

I say all these things in order to break the force of the great and undeniable fact that he was the only English Reformer who for a time showed the white feather, and for a time shrank from dying for the truth! I admit that he fell sadly. I do not pretend to extenuate his fall. It stands forth as an everlasting proof that the best of men are only men at the best. I only want my readers to remember that if Cranmer failed as no other Reformer in England failed, he also had done what certainly no other Reformer had done.

From the moment that Mary came to the English throne, Cranmer was marked for destruction. It is probable that there was no English divine whom the unhappy Queen regarded with such rancour and hatred. She never forgot that her mother's divorce was brought about by Cranmer's advice, and she never rested till he was burned.

Cranmer was imprisoned and examined just like Ridley and Latimer. Like them, he stood his ground firmly before the Commissioners. Like them, he had clearly the best of the argument in all points that were disputed. But, like them, of course, he was pronounced guilty of heresy, condemned, deposed, and sentenced to be burned.

And now comes the painful fact that in the last month of Cranmer's life his courage failed him, and he was persuaded to sign a recantation of his Protestant opinions. Flattered and cajoled by subtle kindness, frightened at the prospect of so dreadful a death as burning, tempted and led away by the devil, Thomas Cranmer fell, and put his hand to a paper, in which he repudiated and renounced the principles of the Reformation, for which he had laboured so long.

Great was the sorrow of all true Protestants on hearing these tidings! Great was the triumphing and exultation of all Papists! Had they stopped here and set their noble victim at liberty, the name of Cranmer would probably have sunk and never risen again. But the Romish party, as God would have it, outwitted themselves. With fiendish cruelty they resolved to burn Cranmer, even after he had recanted. This, by God's providence, was just the turning point for Cranmer's reputation. Through the abounding grace of God he repented of his fall, and found mercy. Through the same abounding grace he resolved to die in the faith of the Reformation.

And at last, through abounding grace, he witnessed such a bold confession in St Mary's, Oxford, that he confounded his enemies, filled his friends with thankfulness and praise, and left the world a triumphant martyr for Christ's truth.

I need hardly remind you how, on 21 March, the unhappy archbishop was brought out, like Samson in the hands of the Philistines, to make sport for his enemies, and to be a gazingstock to the world in St Mary's Church, at Oxford. I need hardly remind you how, after Dr Cole's sermon he was invited to declare his faith, and was fully expected to acknowledge publicly his alteration of religion, and his adhesion to the Church of Rome. I need hardly remind you how, with intense mental suffering, the archbishop addressed the assembly at great length, and at the close suddenly astounded his enemies by renouncing all his former recantations, declaring the Pope to be Antichrist, and rejecting the popish doctrine of the real presence. Such a sight was certainly never seen by mortal eyes since the world began!

But then came the time of Cranmer's triumph. With a light heart, and a clear conscience, he cheerfully allowed himself to be hurried to the stake amidst the frenzied outcries of his disappointed enemies. Boldly and undauntedly he stood up at the stake while the flames curled around him, steadily holding out his right hand in the fire, and saying, with reference to his having signed a recantation, 'This unworthy right hand,' and steadily holding up his left hand towards heaven.[8]

Of all the martyrs, strange to say, none at the last moment showed more *physical* courage than Cranmer did. Nothing, in short, in all his life became him so well as the manner of his leaving it. Greatly

---

[8] Soames is my authority for this statement about Cranmer's left hand. I can find it nowhere else. He also mentions, what other historians record, that when the fire had burned down to ashes, Cranmer's heart was found unconsumed and uninjured. Soames, *History of the Reformation,* 4:544.

he had sinned, but greatly he had repented. Like Peter he fell, but like Peter he rose again. And so passed away the first Protestant Archbishop of Canterbury.

I will not trust myself to make any comment on these painful and interesting histories. I have not time. I only wish my readers to believe that the half of these men's stories have not been told them, and that the stories of scores of men and women less distinguished by position might easily be added to them, quite as painful and quite as interesting.[9] But I will say boldly, that the men who were burned in this way were not men whose memories ought to be lightly passed over, or whose opinions ought to be lightly esteemed. Opinions for which 'an army of martyrs' died ought not to be dismissed with scorn. To their faithfulness we owe the existence of the Reformed Church of England. Her foundations were cemented with their blood. To their courage we owe, in a great measure, our English liberty. They taught the land that it was worthwhile to die for free thought. Happy is the land which has had such citizens! Happy is the Church which has had such Reformers! Honour be to those who at Smithfield, Oxford, Gloucester, Carmarthen, and Hadleigh have raised stones of remembrance and memorials to the martyrs!

III. But I pass on to a point which I hold to be one of cardinal importance in the present day. The point I refer to is *the special reason why our Reformers were burned*. Great indeed would be our mistake if we supposed that they suffered for the vague charge of refusing submission to the Pope, or desiring to maintain the inde-

---

[9] The following martyrdoms are recommended to the special notice of all who possess Fox's *Book of Martyrs:* Laurence Saunders, burned at Coventry; William Hunter, at Brentwood; Rawlins White, at Cardiff; George Marsh, at Chester; Thomas Hawkes, at Coggeshall; John Bland, at Canterbury; Alice Driver, at Ipswich; Rose Allen, at Colchester; Joan Waste, at Derby; Richard Woodman, at Lewes; Agnes Prest, at Exeter; Julius Palmer, at Newbury; John Noyes, at Laxfield, in Suffolk.

pendence of the Church of England. Nothing of the kind! The principal reason why they were burned was because they refused one of the peculiar doctrines of the Romish Church. On that doctrine, in almost every case, hinged their life or death. If they admitted it, they might live; if they refused it, they must die.

The doctrine in question was the *real presence* of the body and blood of Christ in the consecrated elements of bread and wine in the Lord's Supper. Did they, or did they not believe that the body and blood of Christ were really, that is, corporally, literally, locally, and materially, present under the forms of bread and wine after the words of consecration were pronounced? Did they or did they not believe that the real body of Christ, which was born of the Virgin Mary, was present on the so-called altar so soon as the mystical words had passed the lips of the priest? Did they or did they not? That was the simple question. If they did not believe and admit it, they were burned.[10]

There is a wonderful and striking unity in the stories of our martyrs on this subject. Some of them, no doubt, were attacked about the marriage of priests. Some of them were assaulted about the nature of the Catholic Church. Some of them were assailed on other points. But all, without an exception, were called to special account about the real presence, and in every case their refusal to admit the doctrine formed one principal cause of their condemnation.

(1) Hear what Rogers said:

> I was asked whether I believed in the sacrament to be the very body and blood of our Saviour Christ that was born of the

---

[10] 'The Mass was one of the principal causes why so much turmoil was made in the Church, with the bloodshed of so many godly men.' Fox, Preface to vol. 3 of *Acts and Monuments*. 'The sacrament of the altar was the main touchstone to discover the poor Protestants. This point of the real, corporal presence of Christ in the sacrament, the same body that was crucified, was the compendious way to discover those of the opposite opinion.' Fuller, *Church History*, 3:399, Tegg's edition.

Virgin Mary, and hanged on the cross, really and substantially? I answered, 'I think it to be false. I cannot understand really and substantially to signify otherwise than corporally. But corporally Christ is only in heaven, and so Christ cannot be corporally in your sacrament.'[11]

And therefore he was condemned and burned.

(2) Hear what Bishop Hooper said:

Tunstall asked him to say, 'whether he believed the corporal presence in the sacrament,' and Master Hooper said plainly 'that there was none such, neither did he believe any such thing.' Whereupon they bade the notaries write that he was married and would not go from his wife, and that he believed not the corporal presence in the sacrament; wherefore he was worthy to be deprived of his bishopric.[12]

And so he was condemned and burned.

(3) Hear what Rowland Taylor said:

The second cause why I was condemned as a heretic was that I denied transubstantiation, and concomitation, two juggling words whereby the Papists believe that Christ's natural body is made of bread, and the Godhead by and by to be joined thereto, so that immediately after the words of consecration, there is no more bread and wine in the sacrament, but the substance only of the body and blood of Christ.

Because I denied the aforesaid Papistical doctrine (yea, rather plain, wicked idolatry, blasphemy, and heresy) I am judged a heretic.[13]

And therefore he was condemned and burned.

---

[11] Fox, *Acts and Monuments,* 3:101.
[12] Fox, *Acts and Monuments,* 3:123.
[13] Fox, *Acts and Monuments,* 3:141.

(4) Hear what was done with Bishop Ferrar. He was summoned to 'grant the natural presence of Christ in the sacrament under the form of bread and wine,' and because he refused to subscribe this article as well as others, he was condemned. And in the sentence of condemnation it is finally charged against him that he maintained that 'the sacrament of the altar ought not to be ministered on an altar, or to be elevated, or to be adored in any way.'[14] And so he was burned.

(5) Hear what holy John Bradford wrote to the men of Lancashire and Cheshire when he was in prison:

> The chief thing which I am condemned for as an heretic is because I deny in the sacrament of the altar (which is not Christ's Supper, but a plain perversion as the Papists now use it) to be a real, natural, and corporal presence of Christ's body and blood under the forms and accidents of bread and wine: that is, because I deny transubstantiation, which is the darling of the devil, and daughter and heir to Antichrist's religion.[15]

And so he was condemned and burned.

(6) Hear what were the words of the sentence of condemnation against Bishop Ridley:

> The said Nicholas Ridley affirms, maintains, and stubbornly defends certain opinions, assertions, and heresies, contrary to the word of God and the received faith of the Church, as in denying the true and natural body and blood of Christ to be in the sacrament of the altar, and secondarily, in affirming the substance of bread and wine to remain after the words of consecration.[16]

And so he was condemned and burned.

---

[14] Fox, *Acts and Monuments,* 3:178.

[15] Fox, *Acts and Monuments,* 3:260.

[16] Fox, *Acts and Monuments,* 3:426.

(7) Hear the articles exhibited against Bishop Latimer:

> That thou hast openly affirmed, defended, and maintained that the true and natural body of Christ after the consecration of the priest, is not really present in the sacrament of the altar, and that in the sacrament of the altar remaineth still the substance of bread and wine.

And to this article the good old man replied:

> After a corporal being, which the Romish Church furnisheth, Christ's body and blood is not in the sacrament under the forms of bread and wine.[17]

And so he was condemned and burned.

(8) Hear the address made by Bishop Bonner to Archdeacon Philpot:

> You have offended and trespassed against the sacrament of the altar, denying the real presence of Christ's body and blood to be there, affirming also material bread and material wine to be in the sacrament, and not the substance of the body and blood of Christ.[18]

And because the good man stoutly adhered to this opinion he was condemned and burned.

(9) Hear, lastly, what Cranmer said with almost his last breath, in St Mary's Church, Oxford:

> As for the sacrament, I believe, as I have taught in my book against the Bishop of Winchester, the which my book teacheth so true a doctrine, that it shall stand at the last day before the

---

[17] Fox, *Acts and Monuments,* 3:426.
[18] Fox, *Acts and Monuments,* 3:495.

judgment of God when the Papist's doctrine contrary thereto shall be ashamed to show her face.[19]

If anyone wants to know what Cranmer had said in this book, let him take the following sentence as a specimen:

> They (the Papists) say that Christ is corporally under or in the form of bread and wine. We say that Christ is not there, neither *corporally nor spiritually*; but in them that worthily eat and drink the bread and wine he is spiritually, and corporally in heaven.[20]

And so he was burned.

Now, were the English Reformers right in being so stiff and unbending on this question of the *real presence?* Was it a point of such vital importance that they were justified in dying before they would receive it? These are questions, I suspect, which are very puzzling to many unreflecting minds. Such minds, I fear, can see in the whole controversy about the real presence nothing but a logomachy, or strife of words. But they are questions, I am bold to say, on which no well-instructed Bible reader can hesitate for a moment in giving his answer. Such an one will say at once that the Romish doctrine of the real presence strikes at the very root of the gospel, and is the very citadel and keep of Popery. Men may not see this at first, but it is a point that ought to be carefully remembered. It throws a clear and broad light on the line which the Reformers took, and the unflinching firmness with which they died.

Whatever men please to think or say, the Romish doctrine of the *real presence,* if pursued to its legitimate consequences, obscures every leading doctrine of the gospel, and damages and interferes with the whole system of Christ's truth. Grant for a moment that the Lord's Supper is a sacrifice, and not a sacrament; grant that every time the

---

[19] Fox, *Acts and Monuments,* 3:562.

[20] Cranmer on the Lord's Supper, Parker Society edition, p. 54.

words of consecration are used the natural body and blood of Christ are present on the Communion table under the forms of bread and wine; grant that everyone who eats that consecrated bread and drinks that consecrated wine does really eat and drink the natural body and blood of Christ; grant for a moment these things, and then see what momentous consequences result from these premises. You spoil the blessed doctrine of *Christ's finished work* when he died on the cross. A sacrifice that needs to be repeated is not a perfect and complete thing. You spoil the *priestly office* of Christ. If there are priests that can offer an acceptable sacrifice to God besides him, the great High Priest is robbed of his glory. You spoil the scriptural doctrine of the *Christian ministry*. You exalt sinful men into the position of mediators between God and man. You give to the sacramental elements of bread and wine an honour and veneration they were never meant to receive, and produce an *idolatry* to be abhorred of faithful Christians. Last, but not least, you overthrow the true doctrine of *Christ's human nature*. If the body born of the Virgin Mary can be in more places than one at the same time, it is not a body like our own, and Jesus was not 'the second Adam' in the truth of our nature. I cannot doubt for a moment that our martyred Reformers saw and felt these things even more clearly than we do, and, seeing and feeling them, chose to die rather than admit the doctrine of the real presence. Feeling them, they would not give way by subjection for a moment, and cheerfully laid down their lives. Let this fact be deeply graven in our minds. Wherever the English language is spoken on the face of the globe this fact ought to be clearly understood by every Englishman who reads history. Rather than admit the doctrine of the real presence of Christ's natural body and blood under the forms of bread and wine, the Reformers of the Church of England were content to be burned.

IV. And now I must ask the special attention of my readers while I try to show *the bearing of the whole subject on our own position and on our own times*. I must ask you to turn from the dead to the living, to look away from England in 1555 to England in this present enlightened and advanced age, and to consider seriously the light which the burning of our Reformers throws on the Church of England at the present day.

We live in momentous times. The ecclesiastical horizon on every side is dark and lowering. The steady rise and progress of extreme Ritualism and Ritualists are shaking the Church of England to its very centre. It is of the very first importance to understand clearly what it all means. A right diagnosis of disease is the very first element of successful treatment. The physician who does not see what is the matter is never likely to work any cures.

Now, I say there can be no greater mistake than to suppose that the great controversy of our times is a mere question of vestments and ornaments; of chasubles and copes; of more or less church decorations; of more or less candles and flowers; of more or less bowings and turnings and crossings; of more or less gestures and postures; of more or less show and form. The man who fancies that the whole dispute is a mere aesthetic one, a question of taste, like one of fashion and millinery, must allow me to tell him that he is under a complete delusion. He may sit on the shore, like the Epicurean philosopher, smiling at theological storms, and flatter himself that we are only squabbling about trifles; but I take leave to tell him that his philosophy is very shallow, and his knowledge of the controversy of the day very superficial indeed.

The things I have spoken of are *trifles,* I fully concede. But they are pernicious trifles, because they are the outward expression of an inward doctrine. They are the skin disease which is the symptom of an unsound constitution. They are the plague spot which tells of internal poison. They are the curling smoke which arises from a hidden volcano of mischief. I, for one, would never make any stir about church millinery, or incense, or candles, if I thought they meant nothing beneath the surface. But I believe they mean a great deal of error and false doctrine, and therefore I publicly protest against them, and say that those who support them are to be blamed.

I give it as my deliberate opinion that the root of the whole Ritualistic system is the dangerous doctrine of the real presence of Christ's natural body and blood in the Lord's Supper under the forms of the consecrated bread and wine. If words mean anything, this *real presence* is what is the foundation principle of Ritualism. This *real presence* is what the extreme members of the Ritualistic party want to bring back into the Church of England.

And just as our martyred Reformers went to the stake rather than admit the real presence, so I hold that we should make any sacrifice and contend to the bitter end, rather than allow a materialistic doctrine about Christ's presence in the Lord's Supper to come back in any shape into our Communion.

I will not weary my readers with quotations in proof of what I affirm. They have heard enough, perhaps too much, of them. But I must ask permission to give two short extracts.

Observe what Dr Pusey says, in a sermon called 'Will ye also go away?'[21]:

> While repudiating any materialistic conceptions of the mode of the presence of our Lord in the Holy Eucharist, such as I believe is condemned in the term 'corporal presence of our Lord's flesh and blood,' i.e., as though his precious body and blood were present in any gross or carnal way, and not rather sacramentally, really, spiritually—I believe that in the Holy Eucharist the body and blood of Christ are sacramentally, supernaturally, ineffably, but verily and indeed present, 'under the forms of bread and wine'; and that 'where his body is, there is Christ.'

---

[21] Parker's, 1867.

Observe what Dr Littledale says, in a tract called 'The Real Presence':

> I. The Christian Church teaches, and has always taught, that in the Holy Communion, after consecration, the body and blood of the Lord Jesus Christ are 'verily and indeed' present on the altar under the forms of bread and wine.
>
> II. The Church also teaches that this presence depends on God's will, not on man's belief, and therefore that bad and good people receive the very same thing in communicating, the good for their benefit, the bad for their condemnation.
>
> III. Farther, that as Christ is both God and Man, and as these two natures are for ever joined in his one person, his Godhead must be wherever his body is, and therefore he is to be worshipped in his sacrament.
>
> IV. The body and blood present are that same body and blood which were conceived by the Holy Ghost, born of the Virgin Mary, suffered under Pontius Pilate, ascended into heaven, but they are not present in the *same manner* as they were when Christ walked on earth. He, as Man, is now naturally in heaven, there to be till the last day, yet He is *supernaturally,* and just as truly, present in the Holy Communion, in some way which we cannot explain, but only believe.

In both these quotations, we may observe, there is an attempt to evade the charge of maintaining a 'gross and carnal presence.' The attempt, however, is not successful. It is a very curious fact that the Romish controversialist Mr Harding, Bishop Jewel's opponent, said just as much 300 years ago. He said:

> Christ's body is present not after a corporal, or carnal, or naturally wise, but invisibly, unspeakably, miraculously, supernaturally, spiritually, Divinely, and in a manner by him known.[22]

---

[22] Harding's Reply to Jewel, p. 434, Parker Society edition.

In both cases we can hardly fail to observe that the very expressions which our martyrs steadily refused is employed, 'present under the forms of bread and wine.'

It is clear, to my mind, that if Dr Pusey and Dr Littledale had been brought before Gardiner and Bonner three hundred years ago, they would have left the court with flying colours, and, at any rate, would not have been burned.

I might refer my readers to other published sermons on the Lord's Supper by men of high position in our Church. I might refer them to several Ritualistic manuals for the use of Communicants. I might refer them to the famous book *Directorium Anglicanum*. I simply give it as my opinion that no plain man in his senses can read the writings of extreme Ritualists about the Lord's Supper and see any real distinction between the doctrine they hold and downright Popery. It is a distinction without a difference, and one that any jury of twelve honest men would say at once could not be proved.

I turn from books and sermons to churches, and I ask any reflecting mind to mark, consider, and digest what may be seen in any thorough-going Ritualistic place of worship. I ask him to mark the superstitious veneration and idolatrous honour with which everything within the chancel, and around and upon the Lord's table, is regarded. I boldly ask any jury of twelve honest and unprejudiced men to look at that chancel and communion table, and tell me what they think all this means. I ask them whether the whole thing does not savour of the Romish doctrine of the real presence, and the sacrifice of the Mass? I believe that if Bonner and Gardiner had seen the chancels and communion tables of some of the churches of this day, they would have lifted up their hands and rejoiced; while Ridley, Bishop of London, and Hooper, Bishop of Gloucester, would have turned away with righteous indignation and said, 'This communion table is not meant for the Lord's Supper on the Lord's board, but for counterfeiting the idolatrous popish Mass.'

I do not for a moment deny the zeal, earnestness, and sincerity of the extreme Ritualists, though as much might be said for the Pharisees or the Jesuits. I do not deny that we live in a singularly free country, and that Englishmen, nowadays, have liberty to commit any folly short of 'felo-de-se.'[23] But I do deny that any clergyman, however zealous and earnest, has a right to re-introduce Popery into the Church of England. And, above all, I deny that he has any right to maintain the very principle of the real presence, for opposing which the Reformers of his Church were burned.

The plain truth is, that the doctrine of the extreme Ritualistic school about the Lord's Supper can never be reconciled with the dying opinions of our martyred Reformers. The members of this school may protest loudly that they are sound Churchmen, but they certainly are not Churchmen of the same opinions as the Marian martyrs. If words mean anything, Hooper, and Rogers, and Ridley, and Bradford, and their companions, held one view of the real presence, and the ultra-Ritualists hold quite another. If they were right, the Ritualists are wrong. There is a gulf that cannot be crossed between the two parties. There is a thorough difference that cannot be reconciled or explained away. If we hold with one side, we cannot possibly hold with the other. For my part, I say, unhesitatingly, that I have more faith in Ridley, and Hooper, and Bradford, than I have in all the leaders of the ultra-Ritualistic party.

But what are we going to do? The danger is very great, far greater, I fear, than most people suppose. A conspiracy has been long at work for *unprotestantizing* the Church of England, and all the energies of Rome are concentrated on this little island. A sapping and mining process has been long going on under our feet, of which we are beginning at last to see a little. We shall see a good deal more by and by. At the rate we are going, it would never surprise me if within

---

[23] Suicide, lit. felon of himself.—*Publisher*.

fifty years the crown of England were no longer on a Protestant head, and High Mass were once more celebrated in Westminster Abbey and St Paul's. The danger, in plain words, is neither more nor less than that of our Church being unprotestantized and going back to Babylon and Egypt. We are in imminent peril of re-union with Rome.

Men may call me an alarmist, if they like, for using such language. But I reply, there is a cause. The upper classes in this land are widely infected with a taste for a sensuous, histrionic, formal religion. The lower orders are becoming sadly familiarized with all the ceremonialism which is the stepping-stone to Popery. The middle classes are becoming disgusted with the Church of England, and asking what is the use of it. The intellectual classes are finding out that all religions are either equally good or equally bad. The House of Commons will do nothing unless pressed by public opinion. We have no Pyms or Hampdens there now.[24] And all this time Ritualism grows and spreads. The ship is among breakers, breakers ahead and breakers astern, breakers on the right hand and breakers on the left. Something needs to be done, if we are to escape shipwreck.

The very life of the Church of England is at stake, and nothing less. Take away the gospel from a church and that church is not worth preserving. A well without water, a scabbard without a sword, a steam-engine without a fire, a ship without compass and rudder, a watch without a mainspring, a stuffed carcase without life, all these are useless things. But there is nothing so useless as a church without the gospel. And this is the very question that stares us in the face.

---

[24] John Pym (1584–1643) and John Hampden (c.1595–1643) were English parliamentarians who were critical of the policy of the Stuart monarchy, especially that of Charles I. They were among the Five Members whose attempted arrest by King Charles I in the House of Commons in 1642 sparked the English Civil War. Pym also brought the accusation against William Laud (the King's adviser) of trying to convert England back to Catholicism.

Is the Church of England to retain the gospel or not? Without it in vain shall we turn to our archbishops and bishops, in vain shall we glory in our cathedrals and parish churches. Ichabod will soon be written on our walls. The ark of God will not be with us. Surely something ought to be done.

One thing, however, is very clear to my mind. We ought not lightly to forsake the Church of England. No! so long as her Articles and Formularies remain unaltered, unrepealed, and unchanged, so long we ought not to forsake her. Cowardly and base is that seaman who launches the boat and forsakes the ship so long as there is a chance of saving her. Cowardly, I say, is that Protestant Churchman who talks of seceding because things on board our Church are at present out of order. What though some of the crew are traitors, and some are asleep! What though the old ship has some leaks, and her rigging has given way in some places! Still I maintain there is much to be done. There is life in the old ship yet. The great Pilot has not yet forsaken her. The compass of the Bible is still on deck. There are yet left on board some faithful and able seamen. So long as the Articles and Formularies are not Romanized, let us stick by the ship. So long as she has Christ and the Bible, let us stand by her to the last plank, nail our colours to the mast, and never haul them down. Once more, I say, let us not be wheedled, or bullied, or frightened, or cajoled, or provoked, into forsaking the Church of England.

In the name of the Lord let us set up our banners. If ever we would meet Ridley and Latimer and Hooper in another world without shame, let us 'contend earnestly' for the truths which they died to preserve. The Church of England expects every Protestant Churchman to do his duty. Let us not talk only, but act. Let us not act only, but pray. 'He that hath no sword, let him sell his garment and buy one.'

There is a voice in the blood of the martyrs. What does that voice say? It cries aloud from Oxford, Smithfield, and Gloucester,

'Resist to the death the popish doctrine of the real presence, under the forms of the consecrated bread and wine in the Lord's Supper!'

NOTE

The following quotations about the doctrine of the 'real presence' are commended to the special attention of all Churchmen in the present day:

(1) 'Whereas it is ordained in this Office for the Administration of the Lord's Supper, that the Communicants should receive the same kneeling; (which order is well meant, for a signification of our humble and grateful acknowledgment of the benefits of Christ therein given to all worthy Receivers, and for the avoiding of such profanation and disorder in the Holy Communion, as might otherwise ensue;) yet, lest the same kneeling should by any persons, either out of ignorance and infirmity, or out of malice and obstinacy, be misconstrued and depraved; It is hereby declared, That thereby no adoration is intended, or ought to be done, either unto the Sacramental Bread or Wine thereby bodily received, or unto any corporal presence of Christ's natural Flesh and Blood. For the Sacramental Bread and Wine remain still in their very natural substances, and therefore may not be adored; (for that were Idolatry, to be abhorred of all faithful Christians;) and the natural Body and Blood of our Saviour Christ are in Heaven, and not here; it being against the truth of Christ's natural Body to be at one time in more places than one.'—Rubric at the end of the Communion Service in the Book of Common Prayer.

(2) 'As concerning the form of doctrine used in this Church of England in the Holy Communion, that the Body and Blood of Christ be under the forms of bread and wine, when you shall show the place where this form of words is expressed, then shall you purge

yourself from that which in the meantime I take to be a *plain untruth*.'—Cranmer's Answer to Gardiner, pp. 52, 53, Parker edition.

(3) 'The real presence of Christ's most blessed Body and Blood is not to be sought for in the sacrament, but in the worthy receiver of the sacrament.'—R. Hooker, Eccles. Pol., Book 5, p. 67.

(4) 'The Church of England has wisely forborne to use the term of *real presence* in all the books set forth by her authority. We neither find it recommended in the Liturgy, nor the Articles, nor the Homilies, nor the Church Catechism, nor Nowell's Catechism. For though it be once in the Liturgy, and once more in the Articles of 1552, it is mentioned in both places as a phrase of the Papists, and rejected for their abuse of it. So that if any Church of England man use it, he does more than the Church directs him; if any reject it, he has the Church's example to warrant him.'—Dean Aldrich's Reply, p. 13, 1684. See 'Goode on Eucharist,' p. 38.

OTHER BOOKS BY J. C. RYLE

PUBLISHED BY THE TRUST

BOOKLETS

The Agency that Transformed a Nation

A Call to Prayer

Simplicity in Preaching

Worship

PAPERBACKS

Five English Reformers

How Do You Read the Bible?

Is All Scripture Inspired?

The Power and Sympathy of Christ

Steps towards Heaven

Thoughts for Young Men

Warnings to the Churches

CLOTH-BOUND

Charges and Addresses

Christian Leaders of the Eighteenth Century

Holiness

Knots Untied

Light from Old Times

Old Paths

Practical Religion

EXPOSITORY THOUGHTS ON THE GOSPELS

7 VOLUMES

MATTHEW

MARK

LUKE (2 VOLS.)

JOHN (3 VOLS.)

If the best way to understand the Christian Faith is to read the Gospels, then the next books in order of importance have to be those which aid in the understanding of those Gospels.

Observing this need in his own parish, J. C. Ryle prepared his *Expository Thoughts on the Gospels,* which have encircled the earth for more than a century-and-a-half with undiminished popularity and usefulness.

Ryle's 'plain and pointed' words are a great stimulus to the reading of the Bible itself. While his chief aim is to help the reader to know Christ, he also has another object in view. He writes so that his commentary can be read aloud to a group. Unlike many authors, he is equally good read or heard. There are many other fuller commentaries on the Gospels, but no others make such compelling listening—whether it be in the family, in neighbourhood groups, or over the airwaves—as those of J. C. Ryle.

The Banner of Truth Trust originated in 1957 in London. The founders believed that much of the best literature of historic Christianity had been allowed to fall into oblivion and that, under God, its recovery could well lead not only to a strengthening of the church, but to true revival.

Interdenominational in vision, this publishing work is now international, and our lists include a number of contemporary authors, together with classics from the past. The translation of these books into many languages is encouraged.

A monthly magazine, *The Banner of Truth*, is also published, and further information about this, and all our other publications, may be found on our website, banneroftruth.org, or by contacting the offices below:

> *Head Office:*
> 3 Murrayfield Road
> Edinburgh
> EH12 6EL
> United Kingdom
> Email: info@banneroftruth.co.uk
>
> *North America Office:*
> PO Box 621
> Carlisle, PA 17013
> United States of America
> Email: info@banneroftruth.org

DEVIL'S ADVOCATE

TB MARKINSON
MIRANDA MACLEOD

Copyright © 2022 T. B. Markinson & Miranda MacLeod

Cover Design by Victoria Cooper

Edited by Lida Townsley

This book is copyrighted and licensed for your personal enjoyment only. All rights reserved. No part of this publication may be reproduced, stored in a retrieval system, or transmitted in any forms or by any means without the prior permission of the copyright owner. The moral rights of the authors have been asserted.

This book is a work of fiction. Names, characters, businesses, places, events, and incidents are the product of the authors' imagination or are used fictitiously. Any resemblance to actual persons, living or dead, events, or locales is entirely coincidental.

CHAPTER ONE

Ash froze at the edge of the glittering ballroom, her comfort zone disappearing faster than shots of tequila at a sorority party. At least, she assumed that was what went down at those shindigs. She'd been too busy working three jobs during the nine years it took her to complete college part-time to have any personal knowledge of such extracurricular pursuits.

Unlike the rest of the aspiring lawyers in the room, sipping their champagne and chitchatting like they'd been genetically engineered to hobnob.

The guest list for the opening reception of the McGill and Harding Mock Trial Invitational read like it had been ripped from Mrs. Astor's list of The Four Hundred. Tonight's Gilded Age mansion might have been renovated into a luxury hotel and event space, but the great-great-grandchildren of America's elite were still schmoozing within its walls like it was 1899. Ash wasn't sure whether she wanted to despise them or be them.

No, that wasn't true. She knew which she'd prefer.

But being one of them wasn't an option. That ship had sailed right along with the Mayflower, and it was *not* a coincidence that was how the ancestors of most of these folks had gotten here.

Despising them was the only sensible option.

Despite being one of the prestigious competition's finalists herself, in her bargain rack suit and discount store shoes, Ash knew full well she fit in with this elite crowd about as well as a bucket of dirty mop water. Then again, the only way one of her own forebears would've visited this place in its heyday was if they'd been hired to clean it.

Don't let that thought take root in your head, Ash commanded herself.

After all, her legal skills were kick-ass and she had the take-no-prisoners attitude to match, as long as she didn't let self-doubt creep into her head. She was better than any of them, and she couldn't afford to forget it. Her entire future depended on snagging the summer associate position that was the prize for first place. While most of the other contestants probably had hundreds of connections to help secure a job at a top law firm, this was Ash's only chance to get her foot in the door.

You'd better not blow it, she thought.

"Let me guess." Coming from behind, a feminine voice, silky smooth and delectably low, sent a shot of searing heat through Ash's core. "You're the latest woman who thinks she can ruin my life."

Clutching the delicate stem of her wineglass with more force than was wise, Ash pivoted ever so slowly, completely focused on maintaining the icy veneer she'd worked so hard to erect in preparation for the evening. In this setting, emotional detachment was more useful than a full-body shield. But as she came face to beautiful face with the voice's source, Ash struggled to maintain her composure.

Hot. Damn.

Considering the deep timbre of the stranger's voice, her small stature came as a shock—but not half as much as her pleasing face and generous curves. The woman's blush-pink cashmere suit set off her smooth blonde hair and sparkling sapphire eyes to perfection. The outfit easily cost more than all the items in Ash's closet combined.

Typical Ivy Leaguer.

This woman could've been Lawyer Barbie brought to life, except Ash was pretty sure the popular children's doll was supposed to be a hell of a lot taller than five-foot-nothin'. As the silence stretched, the stranger's glossy pink lips quirked in an amused half-smile, anticipating Ash's response to her less than orthodox conversation starter.

Don't lose your steely nerve now, Ash begged herself silently. After coming so far, she couldn't let this pretty lady be her undoing.

"Excuse me?" Ash flicked one brow upward, a practiced gesture she'd spent years perfecting. It never failed to give her an edge. "Do women often make a habit of ruining your life?"

"Aside from my ex—who did her best to elevate ruining my life to an Olympic sport—most women are smart enough not to try. I'm Caitlyn, by the way." When the woman extended a hand, the hint of hunger in her eyes unleashed a pulse of energy inside Ash. The heat shot all the way to her toes before zipping back to her center with the dangerous power of a riptide.

Oh fuck. Were Ash's ears falling victim to an auditory hallucination brought on by desperate wishful thinking, or had this diminutive vision of sexiness just referred to her ex with a feminine pronoun?

You've got to keep it together, Ash urged herself, primarily directing her command at her libido, though she was open to help from any and all parts willing to pitch in to fight for the greater good.

Engage porcupine mode!

"And *I* must be stupid. Otherwise, why would you think I would risk ruining your life when so many other women know better?" Each word was a spikey quill, Ash's sole focus being to force this overly confident woman onto her back foot. Whether inside the courtroom or out, the best defense was a good offense.

It wasn't necessary to go to Harvard to know that.

There was a flash in Caitlyn's eyes of respect with a dash of something spicier, the prospect of which threatened to unleash a host of fantasies best not entertained in polite company. Not that Caitlyn and *polite* seemed to belong in the same sentence. Beneath the pampered Persian cat exterior, Ash suspected this woman was completely feral.

Which was fine. Exciting, even. Ash relished the triumph of holding her own against this tiny but undoubtedly formidable foe. And vanquishing her in the end. That would be the sweetest part. So much better than sex. At least, that was what she would keep telling herself as often as necessary to start believing it.

Caitlyn's eyes darted around to take in the crowd of future lawyers with their expensive suits, shiny shoes, and flawless hair, looking for all the world like they'd been mass produced from the same prep school assembly line. The canny expression on Caitlyn's face after a single appraising sweep of Ash's plain black suit and neat but unpretentious hair was an excellent reminder of the need for Ash to keep her guard up.

"Sixteen contestants in the McGill and Harding Invitational this year, and I've been competing against every single one since freshman year of college. A few since high school. Except for you. It's like you floated out of the water on the back of a clamshell. So, who are you?" Caitlyn's mix of sweetness and interrogation came across as almost... flirtatious.

No, that couldn't be right. This was a competitor, and a much younger one at that. Rich. Cocky. Admittedly of the sapphic persuasion...

But no. No way would this captain of the pep squad be flirting. Not here, and not with Ash. Even so, Ash's flesh came alive with interest. A clamshell... was that a Botticelli reference? Maybe she *had* been flirting.

Like an animal emerging from hibernation, Ash slowly became aware of how foolish she must appear. If she stood still any longer, one of the catering staff was likely to pick her up and add her to the display of ice sculptures on the buffet table.

Ash blinked. Her brain refused to reboot.

She repeated the action slowly, once and then twice

more, hoping to radiate a deliberate and mysterious air. In reality, she needed to stall for time as she absorbed the woman's moxie, which was simultaneously impressive, extremely intimidating, and more than a little irritating.

Not to mention the type of sexy that had Ash's nipples pebbling against the soft silk of her blouse.

Exactly how long had it been since she'd felt a woman's body pressed against her own? Too long to remember. When did she ever have the time?

No time like the present, whispered the voice of temptation.

Under other, less important circumstances, getting Caitlyn into her bed before the night was done would've been an interesting challenge.

But not tonight.

Caitlyn was right. There were sixteen contestants in the McGill and Harding Mock Trial Invitational, and exactly one coveted summer associate position up for grabs. It was winner take all, with no points for second place. Getting groovy in the sheets was tempting as hell, but her future was far more important than getting laid.

Ash had come here to win, not to lose control of herself. She had to keep playing things cool, no matter how hot to trot she might be.

"If you were half as good as you think you are, shouldn't you know who I am?" Ash savored a sip of wine, keeping the glass at her lips longer than necessary as she devoured every nuance of emotion that crossed Caitlyn's face, all without tipping her own hand. The last thing Ash needed was for her competition to figure out exactly what effect each little movement had on certain parts of her anatomy. If she couldn't make the woman squirm from pleasure in bed, this tiny thrill would have to do.

"Ooh... I like that. Already trying to get into my head." Caitlyn was indeed squirming, but not from any type of discomfort. More like with the anticipation of a child who desperately wanted to go on a roller coaster she might not be tall enough to ride. An intriguing response, to say the least. "As a matter of fact, I do know your name. Ashley Tanner. Ash to your friends, though I'm not sure how many of those you have."

"Hey!" Ash's eyebrows skyrocketed at the unexpected insult.

"I'm not judging," Caitlyn rushed to assure her, a slightly embarrassed expression stealing across her features, as if she'd been so excited to share what she'd learned that she hadn't realized how it might sound outside her own head. "In this profession, friendship can be a liability. You never know when you'll find yourself on opposite sides of the table. There's no room for personal feelings to impede sweet victory."

Ash couldn't have said it better herself. Didn't it just figure that the one woman she absolutely couldn't pursue would end up being a perfect match?

Caitlyn leaned against the gleaming mahogany bar that ran along one full wall of the room, her eyes taking in the other law students as they mingled together with all the congeniality of sharks converging on a seal. It was apparent to Ash that Caitlyn knew them well but didn't care for them much. Or maybe she was bored of their predictability. They'd only just met, but already Ash could tell this was a woman who loved the type of challenge these cookie cutter trust fund kids couldn't provide.

"That guy to your left—the one in the tan pants and blue blazer—he's probably a lock for the Supreme Court in thirty years." Caitlyn shook her head like it pained her to say it. "He's distantly related to Roger Taney."

"The Chief Justice who delivered the majority opinion in the 1857 Dred Scott case?" Ash sized the man up with a swift glance, her upper lip curling slightly. "The one who said people of African descent couldn't ever be American citizens."

"The very one." Caitlyn's tone crackled with contempt, a fact that raised Ash's opinion of the woman by a notch or two.

"Is he as racist as his ancestor?" Ash couldn't help but ask. She stiffened slightly, unsure how Caitlyn would respond—these were, after all, her people, even if she didn't like them. But the woman's whole mouth and cheeks quivered from her barely contained laughter.

"I've never asked. Should I?" Caitlyn took a cheeky step forward.

"Go for it," Ash teased.

The woman came to a halt, shooting Ash a withering look. "You know, you're not supposed to let a friend do something like that."

"I agree. As you said yourself, in our line of work, friendship is a liability." Once again, Ash lifted her glass to her mouth to block Caitlyn from seeing a smile appear.

"Ah, but we could be friends, don't you think?"

Caitlyn winked, and Ash's tummy responded by turning a cartwheel.

"I don't need friends," Ash replied stiffly, though at that precise moment, she would've been willing to think whatever Caitlyn told her to think. Which was exactly the type of nonsense that would lose her this competition.

"You don't hold back, that's for sure."

"Hold back?" Ash scoffed, channeling every bit of disdain she could muster to cover up how close she was to drooling all over Caitlyn's undoubtedly designer shoes. No way could she let this woman, a competitor she would need to best in the courtroom in a mere handful of hours, see how bad she had it for her. "I don't see any point in playing nice, Elle Woods."

"A Legally Blonde joke. How very original." Caitlyn rolled her eyes, though she didn't do a convincing job of looking offended.

"I could've gone for Sophocles, but I wanted to ensure you got the reference."

The ghost of a smile pulled at the corners of Caitlyn's mouth, hinting she was as amused by this banter as Ash found herself to be.

Is she as turned on by it, too? Ash swallowed, her throat suddenly dry.

"I applaud your originality. As a short, blonde female lawyer, I've never had anyone make the comparison to Elle Woods before." Caitlyn narrowed her eyes, studying Ash with an unsettling intensity. "Just so you know, I'm picturing you as Colonel Jessup in A Few Good Men."

Ash did her best to ignore the fresh onslaught of bodily sensations ignited by the woman's careful scrutiny. "Please don't tell me I look like Jack Nicholson in this suit."

"I wouldn't dare." Caitlyn probed Ash's face for three searing heartbeats before adding, "You can't handle the truth."

Ash let out a hearty laugh. "I should probably feel insulted, but that was good."

"I have to be honest." Caitlyn's tone was like a spoonful of warm honey. "I was dreading this year's mock trial, but it's really looking up."

"Why were you dreading it?" Ash couldn't help asking, apparently forgetting all those reasons they shouldn't get too friendly.

"These prep school robots bore the fuck out of me." Caitlyn looked Ash up and down, her eyes showing she appreciated the view, then pointed discreetly to one guy across the room. "Josh over there always tries to go for his big Hollywood courtroom moment. It's the reason he loses so often."

"From what I've heard, grandstanding will get you nowhere with the judges from McGill and Harding. The firm prefers subtle brilliance and dedication."

"I see you've done some homework of your own."

"Naturally."

Their eyes met in a moment of mutual admiration, neither of them making a move to break the contact, and Ash couldn't help but notice the depth of blue, like a kettle pond beckoning her to dive in headfirst on a summer day.

If only that wouldn't be such a terrible mistake. It wasn't just Ash's future at stake. She had her family to think about too. With all her willpower, Ash struggled to keep the conversation on neutral ground.

"Do all your prep school buddies"—Ash flicked her hand, encompassing the entire room—"know how you feel about them?"

"I'm sure they feel the same way." Even so, something about Caitlyn's demeanor hinted at her ability to network like a professional, to turn on the charm like a faucet of liquid sunshine. Ash wondered how many were taken in by the act, mistaking it for friendship. She made a mental note not to add herself to their ranks, no matter how much her insides were beginning to glow from the woman's nearness. This could all be a ploy, a way to gain an advantage, and nothing more.

"What else do you know about me?" Ash pressed. She needed something, anything, to distract her from the way Caitlyn's pink tongue was swiping her lower lip. If conversation didn't work, she might resort to reciting multiplication tables in her head. "So far, all you've told me was my name. You could've gotten that much by glancing at my name tag at registration."

"You're a second-year law student at UMass, though you've been enrolled... a bit longer."

Ash's cheeks pricked with heat. At thirty-two, she was by far the oldest contestant in the room. The unfairness of it rankled. "Not everyone has a trust fund to cover their tuition."

Caitlyn's gaze faltered. It had been a shot in the dark, but all things considered, it wasn't hard to assume this woman belonged to the one percent.

"I believe in earning my own way," Caitlyn challenged.

Yeah, right, Ash thought. No doubt she'd had everything handed to her on a silver platter, while Ash had struggled each step of the way. She refused to let herself feel bad for pointing out the facts, no matter how uncomfortable Caitlyn's look of pained embarrassment was making Ash feel.

"I watched a clip of your opening and closing statements for the Lavender Law online competition," Caitlyn said, her attempt to change the subject as transparent as the crystals on the chandeliers above them. "You're good. Maybe even great."

The silent sentiment *but I'm better* hung in the air, as did the realization that Caitlyn's reference to Lavender Law, the largest LGBTQ+ law conference in the country, meant the woman knew a lot more about Ash than she'd counted on. It also meant Caitlyn would be anything but oblivious to the mad attraction building like molten lava beneath Ash's calm exterior.

The knowledge of this new familiarity made Ash wince inwardly, but perhaps it was time to turn a weakness into a strength. Address the elephant in the room. It was the last thing Caitlyn would expect, a tactic that frequently worked in the courtroom and just might do the trick in real life as well. Although, by now, Ash had completely lost track of what she was trying to accomplish with this woman. What would even count as a victory? Short of a night of wild debauchery, that was.

"Is that why you think I'll ruin your life?" Ash circled back to the beginning, desperately needing to stay focused on the facts instead of the way Caitlyn's curves filled her expertly tailored jacket and slim skirt. "Have I guessed your strategy?"

"What strategy is that?" Caitlyn's expression clouded with wariness, which made Ash's heart pump harder. Was she onto something?

"You planned to seduce me, to throw me off my game." Though Ash said it teasingly, a rebellious corner of her psyche hoped it was true. "But now that you've met me in person, you're not sure you can resist my charm."

After a momentary pause, Caitlyn burst into laughter, ending with a loud snort so at odds with her ladylike appearance, Ash almost couldn't believe she'd been the source. It was completely adorable. "Yes, you caught me. Well done. I've beaten everyone else here with my cunning legal mind, but now I'm helpless under your sapphic spell."

Despite being on the receiving end of some top-level sarcasm, Ash struggled not to break into a grin. Beneath the snark, it was just possible there was a kernel of truth, as it seemed the lady protested too much.

"I'll try to go easy on you," Ash promised.

"That would be a shame. There's no denying the McGill and Harding Invitational is the crème de la crème of competitions. Most of us have been competing for years to reach this level, yet here you are out of the blue. You must have something up your sleeve." Caitlyn clinked her wine glass against Ash's, arching one brow. "Care to share?"

"You expect me to reveal my secrets at the first waggle of an eyebrow?"

"No." Caitlyn took a tiny step forward, almost imperceptible but enough to send Ash's heart rate skyrocketing. "I expect you to twist me around your finger, doing what you want with me. Or to try, anyway."

Ash swallowed hard at the deluge of possibilities that flooded her mind. Lord help her, those glossy pink lips, that silky hair...

Escape was the only sane option. She had to do it now, while she still had enough resolve to walk away.

The summer associate position, she reminded herself. It would pay her more in three months than she could earn in a year, enough to finally finish law school. Get a high paying job at a top firm. Give her mom and siblings the life they'd been denied for too long. And finally, just maybe, have the resources she needed to go after the types of bastards that had stolen it all from them.

"It's getting late," she managed to choke through lips that would rather be doing so many other things.

"Indeed." Caitlyn reached around Ash to place her glass on the bar, brushing her hand in the process. "Which room are you in?"

"422, wherever that is," Ash replied, some of her earlier insecurity returning as she recalled the vastness of this place, with so many hallways that seemed to lead everywhere and nowhere at once. "This old house is so big I don't think I can find my way from one end to the other without a map and a sherpa."

"I'm in 425. Lucky for you, I know exactly where your room is and would be delighted to take you there. What happens next is up to you." A naughty smile spread across Caitlyn's face, sending Ash's stomach whirling like a rollercoaster loop. She opened her mouth to reply but couldn't make a sound. It was just as well. Ash didn't have a clue what she would've said if she could have spoken.

CHAPTER TWO

What happens next is up to you? That was *not* what Caitlyn had intended to say. *Good night* would've been the safest choice, or maybe *good luck*. She might have added *sweet dreams* and a seductive wink if she'd wanted to get daring.

Who was she kidding? Given how hot Ashley Tanner had turned out to be, she totally would've risked that much just for the satisfaction of seeing the woman blush. But basically propositioning a total stranger—and competitor—on the first night of the biggest mock trial of her career? That crossed way too many lines to count.

And yet the invitation had tumbled past her lips with all the subtlety of a bowling ball, her words now skittering down the lane so erratically it was impossible to guess if they'd score a strike or end in the gutter.

Along with your dirty mind, Caitlyn reprimanded herself.

Ash raised an eyebrow but did not immediately shoot down the suggestion, as she had every right to do. She seemed dazed. But maybe tempted? Finally, she bit her lip. "What are you, some sort of tour guide? I didn't realize you were an expert on this place."

So she'd chosen to pretend the invitation had never happened? An interesting choice. It was a wise move, perhaps, but a little disappointing. Caitlyn would've died if Ash had taken her up on the offer, but now that she hadn't, it sorta stung. But the suggestion that Caitlyn knew too much about the Harding mansion raised a whole new set of issues.

"I mean, I've been here a *few* times." Caitlyn's heart raced as she forced a carefree laugh. It was the truth, but not the whole truth.

"Of course you have." Ash's eyes swept the ballroom with its twinkling crystal sconces and frescoed walls that would've been just as much at home in the palace of Versailles. "Why wouldn't you be intimately familiar with one of the most exclusive spas in the Northeast? You probably have a standing appointment."

"What can I say? I like a good facial." Caitlyn's laugh was overly jocular, making it hard not to wish herself instantly mute, or maybe dead. If she wanted to succeed as a lawyer, she was going to have to get better at keeping her nerves in check.

Especially when there was subterfuge at play.

That she enjoyed the occasional spa treatment was not a lie, but it wasn't the reason Caitlyn knew her way around this particular hotel. Prior to the death of the former owner Ethel Harding—at which point her brother, Cuthbert, developed the property into a resort—this seaside mansion had been a private residence. And Ethel Harding had been Caitlyn's grandmother. That made

Cuthbert Harding—Bertie to his family, and founding partner of McGill and Harding to the legal world—Caitlyn's great-uncle.

This was one of Caitlyn's most closely guarded secrets.

She hadn't been lying in saying she believed in earning her way. Becoming an attorney on her own merit while belonging to a family like the Hardings made this almost impossible for anyone to believe. Fortunately, the connection was on her mother's side—the mother who had died giving birth to her—while Caitlyn bore her father's last name.

No one who had ever met Richard Brewster—notorious playboy and general waste of fake tanning spray, a man who'd had almost as many wives as he had pairs of shoes—would ever accuse him of being involved with a business as successful and respectable as McGill and Harding. A Ponzi scheme was more his speed. But nothing that required actual work.

And while Caitlyn knew she could have a position at her uncle's firm upon graduation if she asked, that was the last thing she intended to do. She wanted the job all right. That was the whole reason for competing in the mock trial, where the prize was a summer associate position nearly guaranteed to turn into an offer of full-time employment after graduation. She just wanted to earn it fair and square.

Caitlyn wanted that almost as much as she wanted to escort her drop-dead gorgeous competitor back to her hotel room, strip her naked, and have her wicked way with her. At most, only one of those things was likely to happen tonight, and probably not one of the fun options. Best to get on with it so she could go back to her own room, alone, and check if she'd remembered to pack fresh batteries for her vibrator.

"Clock's ticking, Tanner." Caitlyn gave the imaginary watch on her wrist an exaggerated tap. "Do you want my guide services or not?"

"As long as that's *all* you're offering." Ash tilted her head, giving Caitlyn a loaded look.

Caitlyn pressed a hand to her chest. "What else could I possibly have in mind?"

"I think you know."

Yeah. Caitlyn knew.

She also had a pretty good feeling from the starved look on Ash's face that if something more did happen to be on offer, the woman wouldn't say no. Not with a tiny push in the right direction, anyway.

The question was, should Caitlyn push?

Caitlyn's only goal when she'd first approached Ash at the reception had been to get inside the woman's head. Sow enough doubt and confusion to obliterate the only competitor who, in her best estimation, might have a snowball's chance in hell of stealing the big win from her.

But within a minute of meeting her rival, Caitlyn had realized she was in trouble. It wasn't just the woman's stunning good looks, like the long chestnut waves that made Caitlyn's fingers itch with the desire to tangle and stroke, or the way her dark eyes shimmered with golden specks when the light from the chandelier hit them just right. It was the woman's sharp wit and biting humor that truly did her in. But while Ash's intellect was her most attractive quality, her head was far from the only place Caitlyn now hoped to get inside.

Too bad that was the one thing Caitlyn could never let happen.

"Your virtue is entirely safe with me." Caitlyn drew a cross over her heart, cursing her high moral standards, the ones that kept her from taking unfair advantage of this prime opportunity. God only knew where they'd come from. Certainly not her father.

Actually, Caitlyn did know. Every summer she'd spent at this very house while her father sailed the world on his yacht, Grandma Harding had made it her mission to raise Caitlyn to be a good person.

Damn inconvenient at a time like this.

Her grandmother had valued integrity and hard work, even if her father had cared more about ditching his only daughter as often as possible for the first fourteen years of her life. Then one of his wives—Caitlyn had lost track of exactly which number he'd been on by that time—gave birth to her baby sister, Sadie. After that, her father's mission had been to ditch them both. It was the one thing in his life he'd proven to be great at.

"Fine. Lead the way." Ash's shoulders relaxed, but in a way that hinted at disappointment. At least, Caitlyn hoped that was what she was feeling. The woman was going to be missing out on some top-notch booty.

Ash followed Caitlyn out of the ballroom and down a long corridor, then into the grand entryway with the sweeping staircase Caitlyn had come racing down as a kid, riding on a massive silver serving tray Grandma

Harding's butler, Willis, had given her to use as a sled. She smiled to herself at the memory as she opened the front door, standing to one side to allow Ash to pass through first.

Her grandmother may have taught her morals, but it had been Willis who'd helped her hone her good manners.

Ash paused when they made it into the fresh night air, her mouth turning downward as her brow creased. "Why are we outside?"

"Because all the rooms in the four-hundreds are in the annex building."

"Annex?" Ash's eyes widened. "That sounds like a place you take your competition to murder them and hide the body."

"That idea never even occurred to me," Caitlyn admitted with a laugh. It was ridiculous how amused she was, especially considering her beautiful companion had all but confessed to being a wannabe ax murderer. "I'm not sure which of us should be more scared at this point, you or me."

Caitlyn had intended it to be a joke, but all of a sudden, Ash really did look scared.

"This is a bad idea," Ash stammered. "Thanks for your help, but I think I can manage from here."

As the woman pivoted to her left, raising her chin with a look of determination, Caitlyn was awash in panic. The thought of losing Ash's company left her feeling bereft. Way more than she had realized, she'd been counting on another five minutes together. To miss out felt like she was being cheated.

"You're going to want to go to the right," Caitlyn blurted, anything to keep Ash from leaving. Only after she'd said it did she realize her mistake. No number of appointments at the day spa would explain how she knew the path Ash was about to take skirted a marsh which at this time of year would destroy the sturdiest of footwear. Was it too much to hope the other woman was so out of sorts she wouldn't find that suspicious?

"And this path on the left goes where, exactly?"

Apparently it *was* too much to hope.

"Uh… I can't remember."

There was no way Ash bought that. Thanks to Grandma Harding's total insistence on the truth, Caitlyn was a terrible liar. Although she did know how to jitterbug like a champ, so at least she'd learned a few useful life skills from the old lady.

"If it's okay with you," Ash said, a hint of ice in her tone, "I think I'll take my chances going left."

Desperation tore through Caitlyn. It wasn't even about the attraction, not anymore. She'd never met anyone quite like Ash making her way in this world without any of the privileges Caitlyn took for granted. She had a sudden burning need to discover what made this fascinating woman tick, and she was about to lose her chance.

"I really wouldn't go that way if I were you."

"Now I'm even more determined to do it my way."

Ash turned on a heel. Caitlyn should have let her go, but she couldn't. Come sun up, they would be gladiators fighting each other to the death. Hardly conducive to friendly chitchat. It was now or never.

"You're not getting rid of me that easily." Caitlyn reached for Ash's arm, her fingers closing around it, determined not to let her walk away. But why? "You'll ruin your shoes."

It had absolutely nothing to do with the woman's shoes.

"These?" Ash darted a glance at her feet, letting out a laugh. "They're hardly Italian leather, although that would just make my suit look even cheaper by comparison."

Caitlyn's eyes followed to a pair of chunky shoes a bit too casual to be worn with business attire. All at once, the pieces fell into place. In an atmosphere like this one, Ash turned her sharp wit against herself so no one else could beat her to the punch. No doubt Caitlyn's fellow prep school chums—and if she were brutally honest, she would have to count herself among them—had gotten in enough hits to have driven that lesson home.

"There's a lot more to being a successful lawyer than wearing a nice suit," Caitlyn said in a gentle tone. Her heart beat faster as she realized she still had a hold of Ash's forearm. She should let go, but doing so would only call more attention to the fact.

"Says the woman in a Chanel suit." No doubt Ash had meant it as a dig, but she too seemed to have become aware of the forearm holding situation, and the words had come out less of a challenge and more of a choke.

Letting go of Ash's arm, Caitlyn made a show of smoothing the fuzzy pink wool of her skirt. "You know why I dress like this?"

"Because you have your daddy's credit card?" Ash quipped.

"Because it gives me an advantage," Caitlyn countered, not sure why she was letting an almost total stranger in on her secret, but not wanting to stop. She started to walk again, talking as they went. "Those idiots back in the ballroom have been competing against me for years. Long enough to know I can wipe the floor with them. But I show up in a cutesy outfit, my blonde hair in bouncy curls, and they're taken in. They forget who they're dealing with, at least long enough for me to strike."

"They underestimate you," Ash said with understanding.

"And they'll do the same to you," Caitlyn said bluntly. "So use it."

Ash pressed her lips together, hesitating. The pain in her eyes was so raw, Caitlyn nearly looked away. "And how do I get a top firm like McGill and Harding to see past my background and give me a chance?"

"You buy a better suit." In a different tone, Caitlyn's answer might have come across as flippant, but it was the sad, simple truth, and she spoke it from the heart. "Why do you even want to work for a firm like McGill and Harding?"

"Because they're the best," Ash stated without a moment's pause.

A crack of laughter burst from somewhere deep down in Caitlyn's belly. "No, that's why *I* want to work there. Because I'm a hypercompetitive crazy person who would rather win than have people like me."

"And you think I'm not like you? That you all are better than me?" A smoldering anger poured off Ash, not necessarily aimed at Caitlyn herself, but at all the injustice this competition represented. "I worked three part-time jobs to pay my way through school and keep a roof over my mom and siblings' heads after my dad died. I've had to work my ass off just to make it to this one competition. What did you do to earn your spot?"

"I…" Caitlyn wanted to declare that she'd worked hard, too, but as her eyes traveled from the big house and then over the field to the smaller building they were heading to, she felt no larger than a blade of grass below her feet. As firmly as she wanted to believe she'd earned her way to where she was, the evidence of her privilege was impossible to shake. "I know you've worked harder than me, okay? And maybe you're better, too. And maybe I'm wrong, because I don't really know you, but you seem like you're someone who wants to be more than a cog in the machinery of corporate law. To do more."

Ash's lower lip trembled. "To do anything, I have to be more than I am right now. That means working for a big firm. That's why I'm here. That's why I have to win."

"If you don't"—Caitlyn softened her question with a light brush of her hand along Ash's elbow—"what's your game plan then?"

"It doesn't matter. I don't plan on losing this competition." Ash crossed her arms, pulling in on herself like she had nothing else in the world.

Caitlyn had to fight the crazy urge to wrap her arms around the woman and crush her into a hug to chase the loneliness away. "You've made that clear, but surely you're hedging your bets."

Ash swallowed, the cracks in her armor widening, allowing her vulnerability to shine through. "I guess I'll just have to figure it out the way I've done everything else. On my own."

"I know how that is." Nothing Caitlyn had ever said had been truer. Instead of judging or shutting her down with a snappy comeback, Ash's expression urged her to continue. "I may have grown up with money, but there are a lot of things money can't buy."

"Like what?" Ash's words came out at half volume, like her throat had closed around them to keep them from escaping.

"Like a father who gives a shit. I could win every goddamn thing in the universe and it wouldn't make him care." Caitlyn drew a sharp breath as she realized what she'd said. "I'm sorry. I know that's nothing compared to having a father who's dead."

Ash shook her head quickly, as if urging Caitlyn to put the thought out of her mind. "Either way it hurts."

"It does."

As they reached the annex building, the moon poked its way from behind a cloud, bathing them in a soft glow. Their eyes met with understanding, and a pang of longing hit Caitlyn in the ribs. A look echoing her emotions flitted across Ash's face. It was the look of someone who was tired of facing everything alone.

How Caitlyn could relate.

Coming to a stop in front of Room 422, Caitlyn cleared her throat. "We made it to our rooms, just like I promised. Totally unscathed. Not a single murder between us."

"There were a few close calls," Ash teased, a softness around her eyes saying she'd gotten fond enough of Caitlyn's company that she'd nearly forgotten any desire to murder her. "But no. No homicides."

"I almost think we should celebrate." Caitlyn touched her tongue to her lips, noting how Ash's eyes were glued to the motion. Would it really be the worst thing if she gave into temptation, let loose for once, and had some fun?

She waited for the voice in her head to chime in with all the reasons not to, but for once, that voice had gone mute. Caitlyn's body drifted toward Ash. She waited for the woman to move away, but it didn't happen.

"How?" Ash's voice cracked with uncertainty. "How would we celebrate?"

"I don't know." Caitlyn's attention became riveted on Ash's mouth, knowing what she wanted but not certain if she dared. But didn't they both need this? Neither of them wanted to be alone. "I mean, maybe we could—"

The soft landing of Caitlyn's lips on Ash's mouth completed the unfinished sentence like punctuation. It was meant to be quick and flirty, the kiss equivalent of a period, or maybe an ellipsis, but from the moment they came together, it was nothing less than an exclamation point. Or three. Or like being a teenager again, writing in her diary, putting big puffy hearts beneath a whole row of exclamation points instead of the standard dots. In purple glitter pen that smelled like grape.

Yeah, it was that kind of kiss.

Ash's lips parted, opening, inviting. Caitlyn shuddered with longing, her chest burning in anticipation as the deepening kiss pulled her entirely into the woman's orbit. Tongues tangled, exploring and claiming.

Even if she had wanted to stop, she couldn't. No force on earth would have been strong enough to pull her away.

Caitlyn wrapped an arm around Ash, her fingers trailing along the woman's back. Snaking beneath her jacket, under the hem of her blouse, and up her bare flesh.

Heavenly, like raw silk with tiny raised goosebumps dotting Ash's skin.

Caitlyn's nostrils filled with the clean scent of soap and a hint of citrus and mint as she teased a stray lock of Ash's hair with her other hand. Ash's hands answered by gripping Caitlyn's bouncy curls with a raw desire she couldn't remember anyone showing toward her before. A similar urgency burned in her core. She wanted everything. Now.

"Should we go inside?" Caitlyn asked in a breathy whisper.

Ash instantly froze. The unexpected chilliness snapped Caitlyn back to reality and she pulled away. What had they been thinking? They were opponents! This was the last thing Caitlyn should have allowed to happen.

Allowed? Hell, she was the one who had started it.

"I'm so sorry!" Caitlyn declared. "I don't know what came over me."

"I can't believe you." Ash clasped a hand to her mouth. "This was your plan all along?"

"What plan?" Caitlyn's body trembled, overwhelmed by confusion. They'd seemed to be on the same page before, and now Caitlyn wasn't sure they were even in the same book. "What are you talking about?"

"To get me alone to… get into my head." Ash's breath came in gulps, her eyes flashing with an almost irrational anger, directed as much at herself as at Caitlyn.

"No! That wasn't it," Caitlyn insisted, her tone pleading. Ash had to believe her. But by now, the woman was in a total panic, melting down like a nuclear reactor before Caitlyn's eyes.

"Oh God, what was I doing? I don't know how I could have let this happen!" Ash's words were so fast and high that soon only chipmunks would be able to understand her. As if realizing this, her voice dropped an entire register as she added, "I don't know what mind games you're playing, but they're not going to work."

"It wasn't a game," Caitlyn said, her chest tightening as sobs threatened to escape. "I thought we were… friends."

"Friends?" A wildness flashed in Ash's eyes. "You said yourself, we don't have friends. They're a liability, right? They ruin your life."

"That was women in general," Caitlyn interjected. Unfortunately, the sentiment felt too true at that moment to lighten the mood.

"I'm not sure about ruining your life, but I promise you this." Ash paused, drawing a breath and squaring her shoulders like she was preparing to ride into battle. "If I get the chance, I will destroy you. I can't afford to lose. My whole life is at stake."

With that, Ash wrenched open the door to her room and disappeared inside.

Utterly deflated, Caitlyn slumped against the wall beside her own door, her heart racing. She should have been furious, smarting from rejection, but instead her thoughts were a jumble and her emotions a confusing whirl. In their short time together, she'd caught a glimpse deep into Ash's soul. The woman was the most formidable opponent Caitlyn had ever encountered, both awe-inspiring and heartbreaking. Perhaps even life changing.

For the first time in her life, Caitlyn had no idea what she should do.

CHAPTER THREE

The lights weren't on yet as Ash made the familiar trek from the elevator to her tiny office on the third floor of a chic converted warehouse on the Boston waterfront. This wasn't a surprise. The only other occupants at this time of the morning were the mice Ash couldn't see but knew were there as they scurried inside the brick wall behind her desk. They didn't bother her. She liked to think of them as her dedicated coworkers, industrious little fighters, like Ash herself.

No building along the waterfront was rodent free. There was a lesson to be learned there. All the Ivy League lawyers and Scandinavian minimalist furnishings in the world didn't make one iota of difference. Behind the fancy façade, there was little to separate a high-end law office downtown from the two-bedroom apartment in Brockton where Ash's mom had struggled to raise three kids after their dad had died. From public housing to the halls of government, everybody dealt with mice.

A bitter laugh bubbled in her throat, breaking the silence, but Ash didn't have time to dwell on the root cause. A stack of work taller than her computer monitor waited on her desk. It had been the same all weekend. And the previous week. And month. And year.

Hell, for the past six years, ever since Ash had started as a summer associate at McGill and Harding after capturing first place in their prestigious mock trial competition, there had been one thing she could count on in her quest to be promoted to partner.

Billable hours.

It was Ash's secret weapon, the stamina to log fifteen-hour days, seven days a week. Stamina, aided in no small part by the fact that, outside the office, she had absolutely no life. No girlfriend. No pets. Hell, she didn't even waste time on a houseplant. The closest she came to any of that was the aforementioned mice. The best part about them was they fended for themselves.

Ash was a loner through and through.

As if to prove her wrong on this assertion, Ash's phone lit up with an update from the Tanner family WhatsApp group. It was a photo her mother had taken the day before of her two little nephews in her mom's backyard wading pool. Their father, Ash's brother Mike, was manning the grill. Somehow, he managed to beam with pride even though Ash could see that every burger and dog was burned to a crisp. Behind him, Ash's sister, Breanna, stuck out her tongue for the camera. They wore the carefree expressions of two people who'd been spared the harshest realities of life's struggles.

Precisely as Ash had intended. Why else would she have worked so damn hard all this time?

The photo was accompanied by a *wish you were here* message from her mother. The sentiment was genuine, not laced with guilt. Ash's mom was a realist, a fact for which Ash thanked the stars every day. She couldn't have dealt with one of those sitcom moms, the kind who always tell their daughters that they're nearing forty and if they don't land a spouse and pop out a kid or two, they'll end up sad and alone, like Aunt Marge.

Only Ash didn't have an Aunt Marge, meaning she was probably at the top of the list for becoming the cautionary spinster tale of the Tanner family.

Ash scanned the message thread again and sighed. Despite the sincerity of her mother's words, guilt squeezed her chest. Another family cookout missed. That made four in a row. If she didn't get an invitation to the next one, she'd have no one to blame but herself.

Tuck it down, Ash, she chided herself, refusing to give in to regret.

This wasn't the time to wallow in self-pity. Not when the partner announcements were four months away. Ash had one job until then, to keep her butt in her seat and keep working. She'd come too far to slow down now. That wasn't in her nature.

It had taken her nine years to finish college, while flipping burgers, bartending, and cleaning houses the whole time to pay tuition and make sure her siblings always had money for field trips and after-school clubs. No small feat. When she'd landed a temp job after graduation at a law firm in her hometown and a kind paralegal had suggested enrolling in law school, Ash had risen to the challenge. She'd worked full time while going to school at night. Five years later, she'd started at McGill and Harding, the only first-year associate who hadn't graduated from Harvard or Yale.

Ash hadn't stopped for breath once. She couldn't afford to. In fact, in all that time, she'd only wavered from her purpose once. On a moonlit night on the grounds of a Gilded Age mansion, the temptation had been so very hard to fight. But she'd done it. She'd overcome her desires and put her feet firmly back on the path to success, a path she'd been walking tirelessly ever since. She'd learned to play the game, to blend in. She did it so well, sometimes she could barely remember who she was.

But she couldn't let that worry her. Even now, her family depended on her ability to keep doing what she was doing, and do it well. Mom would be retiring soon, and how much longer before Breanna decided to get married? Weddings were expensive. Her nephews might need braces. There was always something.

The motion-sensing light flickered on as Ash shuffled to her chair, turning sideways to pass through the narrow space between the filing cabinet and the desk. While all attorneys at the firm, whether associates or partners, had their own offices, they were not created equally. In addition to the long-term career stability and generous income bump, what Ash really looked forward to with a promotion was having an office where she could open the bottom file drawer and stretch out both of her legs at the same time.

Until then, Ash would continue to bury her nose in her work, making the surroundings fade into irrelevance.

"Please tell me you didn't sleep here last night."

"What?" Ash glanced up, her body still hunched over the open case file. Jenna, one of the paralegals, stood in the open doorway.

"You were sitting in exactly the same position when I left here on Friday." Jenna perched on the lip of Ash's desk, crossing her arms. "I've been here three years, and it's always the same. You're the first in the office and the last to leave."

"How do you know I'm the last to leave?"

"If you want to know the truth, the paralegals have a weekly pool going."

Ash straightened her back and slanted her head. "Tell me more."

"Every Monday, we bet on which associate logged the most hours and which was the biggest slacker. Becky in payroll checks it against the key card swipes."

"Should you have access to that?" Ash's eyes narrowed. "Wait a minute. How am I doing? And who's the slacker? It's gotta be Zach. He thinks he can skate to partner on charm alone."

"Wouldn't you like to know?" Jenna boosted her brows, laughing as Ash let out a frustrated grunt. "You're in first place when it comes to hours. No contest. Actually, we've started betting on second place because it's just no fun anymore."

Ash gave a derisive snort, though she couldn't help the flames of pride that flared inside her at hearing she was number one. "Sorry I ruined your fun with all my hard work."

"Just wait. I have a feeling the competition will be heating up."

Ash frowned. "Why's that?"

"Didn't you hear about the new hire?"

"What the—?" Ash stopped short of saying fuck. Even though Jenna was the closest thing Ash had to a friend in the office, a mentor had once told Ash that swearing at work was unprofessional and made her sound unrefined. She'd broken the habit years ago, but still kept a diligent watch in case she regressed. "I thought the firm was freezing hiring due to the harsh—"

"Economic environment," Jenna finished the sentence in her best imitation of founding partner Cuthbert Harding. "He uses that gem to justify everything under the sun. Did you know they've replaced the Starbucks coffee in the break room with that generic shit from Costco?"

"A travesty." The corners of Ash's lips twitched. Jenna had no problem swearing in the office, one of the many reasons Ash liked the paralegal. They'd come from similar backgrounds and Ash found Jenna's rough edges comfortingly familiar when surrounded by so many pretentious, rich assholes—a category that included clients and colleagues alike. "Good thing I drink tea."

"And not even the good kind." Jenna made a face, not that Ash cared. Lipton was perfectly fine, no matter what anyone said. "But all things considered, that makes bringing in someone new very curious, doncha think?"

Ash shrugged. "It's a little premature, given the bar exam results won't be released for over a month, but—"

"No, it's not a first year."

"Then what is it?" Ash massaged her right eye to temper an annoying twitch. "I mean, who are they?"

"Another fifth year, like you."

Ash bolted upright in her chair. "What the fuck?"

"I thought that might get your attention."

"I don't understand." Ash's heart raced as her head rushed to recalculate the odds of making partner with this new wrench thrown into the works. There were too many variables, which only made Ash's panic boil. "They haven't held interviews. I haven't heard a goddamn thing about this bullshit."

Ash's no swearing in the office rule had officially gone out the window, or would have if her tiny office actually had one.

"It's someone who's just moved here from the New York office. Between you and me—" Jenna glanced over her shoulder, edging closer to the desk. "I hear they're some sort of legacy."

"You mean legend?" Ash fought back the urge to be sick. Just what she needed, a hotshot with a New York attitude to swoop in and try to steal her promotion.

"No, legacy," Jenna repeated. "Like, related to somebody important or something. I don't know. You know how little we have to do with that office, so little overlap with cases. No one here knew the four-one-one for sure, but that was what I heard."

"Naturally." Ash would've rolled her eyes at this revelation, but the twitch had worsened to the point she feared her eyeball might become dislodged and roll across the floor if she tried. "It's how half these assholes get into college. Might as well be how they get their jobs too."

"I looked up her record," Jenna offered. "She brought in several new clients last year. Some real whales."

Translation: clients with deep pockets.

Ash's spirits took a nosedive at the revelation the newcomer was both female and competent. Two things she definitely was not looking for in a competitor. "Shit."

Ash didn't even notice she'd said that out loud, but based on Jenna's grim nodding, the paralegal was in complete agreement.

Once Jenna headed to her cubicle, Ash returned to work with a heavy heart and troubled head. The pace that had been smooth and steady at the start of the morning became painful and plodding as Ash's brain picked at this latest threat to her plans.

How did this always happen?

It seemed every time Ash was on the verge of getting ahead, something snatched the victory away. Her dad's injury on the construction site where he'd worked when she was twelve had only been the beginning. The pain medication he'd been prescribed had seemed like a miracle until it snarled him in addiction and eventually robbed him of his life. She'd forfeited a college scholarship because her family couldn't afford for her to leave home, spending years at community college instead.

Winning the mock trial competition six years ago, along with the coveted summer associate position that entailed, had felt like a turning point, but maybe it would end up as another disappointment in a string of them. What good was a position at a prestigious firm like

McGill and Harding if Ash would always be passed over for someone with a better pedigree? At thirty-eight, she was running out of time to move to another firm before age discrimination reared its ugly head. She'd never expected to work in corporate law for so long—certain she'd be doing more to right the world's wrongs by now—but with a partnership so close she could feel it brushing her fingertips, Ash couldn't picture going anywhere else.

"Ash." Jenna was back in Ash's doorway, her harsh whisper brimming with urgency. "It's time."

"What?" Ash wasn't sure how long it had been since Jenna had left, but it was definitely long enough to have no idea what the woman was talking about.

"What's-her-name. You know, the new girl. We need to go right now." Jenna didn't bother with formalities, yanking Ash out of the chair and force-marching her to the break room, where they had a clear but unobtrusive view of the elevator.

They arrived just in time for the ding.

Lawrence Cooper, an equity partner who had emerged from his mother's womb already middle aged and lacking even a trace of humor, stepped from the compartment first. His face was bright red and a sound that in any other person might be described as laughter burbled out of him as if he was having some kind of fit.

Ash's eyes darted to the defibrillator mounted beside the first aid kit on the break room wall. This had all the makings of a medical emergency. Would restarting Coop's ticker give her a leg up in the partner race? It was worth a shot.

Just as the elevator doors started to slide shut, a petite woman with blonde hair stepped out. Though her face was obscured by a potted palm, Ash could plainly see she was wearing black stilettos at the ends of her shockingly bare legs, which stuck out from a shiny red cocktail dress with a slit on the side all the way up to god-knows-where. Ash blinked, but the spectacle remained unchanged.

"I thought you said the new girl was coming." Ash cringed at how much like a middle schooler she sounded, but she couldn't stop herself from asking, just as she couldn't seem to stop gaping at a fifty-something year old man guffawing like a possessed lunatic while grasping the arm of a woman half his age.

"Get a load of that," Jenna whispered out of one side of her mouth. "Mr. Cooper brought a hooker to the office."

"I don't think that's a prostitute." To be fair, Ash wasn't certain of this, but she'd noticed the woman in the red dress was clutching a briefcase much too feminine to belong to Lawrence. Plus, there was something about her neat but no-nonsense manicure that gave off business-woman vibes. "I think that's the new girl."

"In a cocktail dress? She looks like she's doing the walk of shame." Jenna shook her head, jaw slack. "Maybe I should transfer to the New York office if this is their way of life. Clubbing until work starts."

"Sounds like my idea of hell. The less any of us have to do with New York, the better."

Jenna hefted her shoulders, clearly not in agreement

but not wanting to argue. "I'm sorry I ruined your morning by getting you all worked up for nothing."

"What do you mean?" Ash's head swiveled so as not to miss Coop and Cocktail Dress as they whisked by, still yukking it up.

Jenna hooked a thumb over her shoulder. "You clearly have nothing to worry about when it comes to Caitlyn Brewster."

Ash drew in a breath so sharp it nearly sliced a hole in her esophagus. "Who did you just say?"

"Caitlyn Brewster," Jenna repeated, making the edges of Ash's vision go black. "That's the new girl's name. I just remembered."

The air seeped out of Ash's lungs. What were the odds the world contained more than one short, blonde Elle Woods lookalike who went by that name? A woman so conniving she would use any dirty trick to get ahead. Even seduction, as Ash herself could attest, and judging by what she'd just witnessed outside the elevator, little had changed in six years.

Ash could only sum it up one way. "Fuck. My. Life."

CHAPTER FOUR

"I can't believe what a good sport you're being." Larry Cooper raised his arm, but before his hand could hit Caitlyn's shoulder, he dropped his appendage, a hint of concern crossing his ruddy face. "Are you sure you don't want me to go out there and explain the situation?"

"Explain it how?" Caitlyn shook her head at the man who was technically her boss but whom she'd known since she was a child. "You doused some poor woman from the DA's office with a full cup of coffee in the lobby as she was rushing to court, and I just happened to be the same size as her and willing to loan her my suit to score some points?"

"We don't want to get on the DA's bad side," Larry said, still chuckling. "I would've offered her my suit, but that was not going to help."

Caitlyn raised an eyebrow at the lawyer's unfashionable tan suit and made a face. Larry was a brilliant divorce attorney, but he lacked a single shred of style. "It's lucky for all of us I'd just picked up Sadie's homecoming dress from the tailor on my way to work. Imagine how much more of a stir it would've made if I'd arrived at the office on my first day wearing nothing but your trench coat."

"I still can't get over little Sadie being old enough to go to a homecoming dance." Larry wore that wistful expression older people tended to get when they realized a child they'd known was all grown up. At the age of thirty, it was a feeling Caitlyn was just starting to become familiar with, especially where her baby sister was concerned.

"She may technically be old enough to attend, but not in this getup. My father might not care if she goes to the dance looking like she's being paid by the hour, but I do."

"She might be ready to move back into the dorms after a couple weeks of living under your rules," Larry joked.

"Thanks again for agreeing to bring me on board here on such short notice. I know it wasn't easy." Caitlyn smoothed the wrinkles from her sister's dress as she lowered herself into a chair across from Larry's desk, trying to be mindful of the indecently high slit. "I had no idea Sadie's anxiety had gotten so bad until Moorehead Academy called and said she wouldn't be able to live on campus again unless she got it under control."

"Your father's still out of the country?" The man couldn't entirely disguise the disgust on his face.

Caitlyn nodded, sharing his disdain. "And her mother

got remarried to some oil tycoon billionaire who hates kids. They've shuffled her from one boarding school to another for years. Poor kid. She's only sixteen."

He shook his head. "She's lucky to have a sister like you who would drop everything and move home so she could continue to attend school."

Yeah, lucky, Caitlyn thought. Of course, it would've been a lot luckier if they'd both had a father who gave enough of a shit about his kids to cut his sailing time short and come home to take care of things himself. But that's not how it worked in the Brewster household.

"I couldn't have done it if the firm hadn't been so flexible about offering me a transfer."

"Well, your uncle—"

Caitlyn held up her hand. "Do you think we could keep that connection strictly between us?"

"Your uncle?"

Caitlyn nodded. "I went through all the standard hiring procedures when I first started, and in the five years I worked in New York, no one managed to figure out I was Bertie's niece. I'd rather keep it that way."

"Yes, of course." Larry's expression lacked understanding, making it obvious if he'd been related to someone like Cuthbert Harding, he'd have shouted it from the rooftops. "Now, about your unorthodox entrance this morning. How should we handle it?"

"I vote for letting it be." Caitlyn plucked at her unfortunate attire with her index finger and thumb. "I've always found with office gossip, once you let it loose, you can never rein it in. If you try to explain what really happened, they'll twist the story into us having a threesome with the DA in the parking garage. Next thing you know, squirrels will appear, and probably clowns, and unicycles. I don't know about you, but I do *not* need that headache on my first day."

Larry slapped his knee, looking like he hadn't laughed so hard in ages. Caitlyn knew she was laying it on a little thick, but making people laugh could be a secret weapon. Between her over the top humor and her small size, most people underestimated her. That gave her a tremendous advantage. Let the entire office think she was a ditz. It would make it that much easier for her to run rings around them.

Out of the corner of her eye, Caitlyn caught a streak of brown passing quickly by the glass wall of Larry's office. It was a nutty shade of chestnut that teased Caitlyn's memory, like a comb working out a tangle, slowly and painfully.

Who was that?

There was something she was missing and shouldn't be, like a word on the tip of her tongue. Her mind filled with foreboding, but her body simultaneously lit up with a sweet anticipation, the type she hadn't felt in ages. Not since swearing off romance in favor of getting ahead in her career. One thing was certain. The bald man standing in front of her had not caused the sudden tingling in her clit.

So, who the hell had?

Caitlyn turned her head to see if she could get a better look at the woman who'd gone speeding past, but she was long gone.

Settling into his chair, Larry plastered on his serious face, the one that signaled it was time to get down to business. "Caitlyn, we're glad to have you here, but I'm sure you've been made aware this isn't the firm's best year. The economic climate—" He cleared his throat, suddenly uneasy. Caitlyn had noticed a superstition surrounding the word recession, like the way people avoided saying Macbeth in a theater. "Bottom line, by bringing you on board, we're limiting the number of partnerships we offer this year."

Caitlyn wasn't surprised. She'd heard the Boston office was struggling. Under any other circumstances, she never would have made the move, but there wasn't much choice. Still, she had to ask, "Limiting by how much?"

"The truth? It's not public knowledge quite yet, but we're only offering one. There are eight fifth-year associates vying for the promotion."

"Eight?" Caitlyn swallowed. It was worse than she'd thought. Eight lawyers fighting for one partnership slot would be a bloodbath. Thank goodness becoming a permanent installation at the Boston office wasn't on her radar.

Larry offered an encouraging smile. "It's not as bad as it sounds. Between you and me, you only have one true competitor."

"Me?" Caitlyn's eyes widened. "No. I have no interest in a partnership in Boston. As soon as I'm able, I'll be heading back to New York."

"Are you sure?" It was possible Larry had never heard a young lawyer say they weren't interested in a promotion before.

"Positive." Caitlyn was going to leave it there, but curiosity got the better of her. "Okay. Tell me more about this one true competitor."

"I knew you'd change your mind."

"I still don't have an interest in being made partner unless it's back in New York," Caitlyn admitted, "but I've never backed down from a challenge. I might want to have some fun while I'm here, so tell me who I have to beat."

"Her billable hours are legendary. Unless you're truly a superhero, you won't one-up her on that front."

Inwardly, Caitlyn smiled, appreciating that even someone who'd known her as long as Larry was quick to underestimate her. Hopefully, Miss Legendary Billable Hours would do the same. Caitlyn had never lost at anything in her life.

Well, there had been the one time, six years ago. But that was different.

"You have something she doesn't have, though."

"What's that?" Caitlyn had to wonder, if Cuthbert Harding wasn't her great-uncle, would Larry be telling her these inside tips?

"Your connections. We're always on the hunt for whales."

And to answer her own question, he was telling her all this precisely because of who she was, and who her family was. That was the very reason she'd chosen New York to start her career, to earn her own reputation outside the shadow of her family. Yes, she'd ultimately gone to work for the family firm, but she'd done it on her own merits. Unease seized her gut as she wondered how much longer she would be able to make that claim.

"I thought whale hunting was Uncle Bertie's domain." Larry's eyes darted around the office in an odd display of nervousness. He leaned closer to his desk, lowering his voice. "This can't get out, but your uncle has taken a step back recently. From the day-to-day operations."

"Retiring?" Caitlyn frowned. Not a hint of this rumor had reached the legal circles in New York, or competitors would be circling the firm like sharks smelling blood.

"No, no." Larry shook his head with a little too much force, grimacing as something seemed to pop in his neck. "Just a well-deserved uh... slowing down, let's say. Temporarily."

"A slowing down that has left a lot of potential business from connections I might have on the table?" Caitlyn was pretty sure she already had the answer to that.

Larry offered a smile that was half grin and half smirk. "Reel them in and you'll be a shoo-in for partner."

"I told you. I have no plans to stay. But even so, I do like to win." Caitlyn was already running through the mental contact list of potential clients she could pursue. "I guess I should find my office and settle in. I've got to get started on smoking my competition."

As Caitlyn rose, Larry did the same.

"I admire your determination," he said. "But you haven't even asked the name of your illustrious opponent."

Caitlyn gave her head a tilt. "And ruin the fun? Give me a week and I bet I can guess."

"Knowledge is power," he countered.

"So everyone tells me." Stepping out of Larry's office, Caitlyn shrugged. "Okay, go ahead and point her out so I know who I need to send my assassins after."

"That's her over there." Larry pointed across the office to where a woman with long, dark brown hair stood with her back to them. Her well-tailored suit was a deep, rich navy blue, fitted to perfection in a way that enhanced every curve. Not that the woman's curves seemed in need of much improvement. Even without seeing her face, Caitlyn felt that same niggling of memory she'd experienced earlier, along with a physical jolt that almost stole the breath from her lungs.

I know her, Caitlyn thought. *I'm sure of it.* The wheels in her brain spun but failed to produce a result.

"She's tall," was the best response Caitlyn could manage. "And a snappy dresser."

She didn't used to be.

Caitlyn sucked in a breath as the gears finally clicked.

It was her. The only person in all of Caitlyn's life who'd ever gone up against her and won.

"Ashley Tanner." It was Larry who said the name out loud, but it was already echoing through Caitlyn's head before he'd uttered it.

Ashley Tanner.

It was the name that danced through Caitlyn's head late at night when she was exhausted and let her walls down. The one that haunted her and wouldn't let go. The memory of their one brief but sizzling kiss would traipse through her mind at three in the morning when her brain decided to torment her by second-guessing every decision she'd ever made. Every pleasure she'd given up.

How had Caitlyn not anticipated Ash would be here? McGill and Harding had offices in multiple states, but Ash was a Boston girl. It should have been obvious she would choose to stick close to home. And yet with all the craziness surrounding her last-minute move, Caitlyn hadn't registered the possibility until she was standing in the middle of the office.

In a red satin party dress that barely covered her... assets.

Dear God.

Had Ash seen her dressed like this? Of course she had. How could she have missed it?

Mortification swept through Caitlyn like a category three hurricane. It quickly amped up to category five as Ash turned and stared right at her from across the sea of cubicles.

Caitlyn clenched her fists, wanting desperately to bolt, to hide under one of the desks until Ash had gone home, or at least until someone could bring Caitlyn a change of clothes.

But it was too late. They'd already made eye contact.

All Caitlyn could do was lift her head and face the situation with the confidence of a woman who didn't know the meaning of the word humiliation.

In other words, lie.

Luckily, she'd gotten a lot better at that since the last time she and Ash had clashed.

Caitlyn raised her chin and channeled the most cool,

calm, and collected person she could think of. Which, somewhat annoyingly, happened to be Ashley Tanner. Whether or not it worked, Caitlyn couldn't tell. Ash's gaze was already off her, drifting far away. And for all the nights Caitlyn had obsessed over this woman and what might have been, there wasn't so much as a hint of recognition on her face.

CHAPTER FIVE

"You haven't gone to the break room yet?" Jenna set a heaping plate of food on top of a pile of folders on Ash's desk. "You're missing out."

"Traitor!" Ash hissed. She eyed the offering as if the paralegal had tossed a bag of garbage at her. "I can't believe you went to the welcome reception for my nemesis."

"Look, Ash. We're friends and all, but I have two words for you. Free food." Jenna snatched a cracker from Ash's untouched plate and popped it into her mouth. "I loaded up another one just like this back at my desk. That's lunch for the rest of the week. You might be the only person in the office who hates free food. And it's good free food too. See that cheese? It's gouda. None of that white cheddar shit. This is from Europe."

"Cheddar's from Europe too. Well, the UK, anyway." Ash ran a hand through her hair, giving it a slight yank to stop herself from launching into an explanation of why the UK wasn't part of Europe anymore. Jenna didn't care about geopolitics. She was too obsessed with free cheese. "I thought management was cutting back. They can't buy you Starbucks anymore, but there's money to throw a party for some princess from New York?"

Jenna glared at Ash and grabbed a red grape. "This is fucking delicious. Why do you have to ruin it?"

With a sigh, Ash reached for a cube of cheese, but Jenna slapped her hand away. "Get your own!"

Ash's brow furrowed. "I thought this was for me."

"Yeah, well, I changed my mind." Jenna scooped up the plate in both hands. "If you want a snack, you're going to have to go in there like everyone else and make nice with the new girl."

Ash shifted her gaze from the plate, focusing instead on a spot in the corner of her office and wishing she had the power to shoot lasers from her eyes. How many times in her life would that have come in handy? Like if she'd fired eye lasers at Caitlyn Brewster six years ago, before they'd had a chance to kiss, imagine how much better the world would be. She and Jenna wouldn't even be having this conversation. Nobody bought party platters for a pile of cinders on the sidewalk.

"I guess I'll have to buy my own cheese. The last thing I want to do is make friends with the one person in the office I have to destroy."

Jenna started to laugh, but it came out as more of a crumb-filled snort. "You've already reached *that* stage, I see."

A memory flashed through Ash's mind of Caitlyn's lips on hers, lush, velvety, and inviting.

Shit.

Her throat had gone dry and the hair on the back of her neck stood on end. Now that she'd opened the door to remembering that night, there would be no shutting it off. It wasn't only Jenna who was the problem. Ash's own brain was being just as traitorous.

"What stage?" Ash stared at the red Swingline stapler on her desk and fought the urge to staple her hand to the desktop as punishment.

"Destruction," Jenna replied. As if reading Ash's mind, the paralegal shifted the stapler out of Ash's reach. "You do this exact thing every time there's a new hire in the office."

"I never tried to destroy you when you started working here," Ash argued. She was pretty certain it was true.

"I'm not a threat," Jenna explained with a tone like she was talking to a child. "You don't destroy paralegals. You bribe us."

"I'm supposed to bribe you?" Ash was taken aback.

"Yes, and I'm glad you finally asked about it, because it was getting super awkward. Ralph supplies me with my morning donuts. James brings me a daily medium regular from Dunks—"

"Every day?" Ash squeaked. She could almost visualize the dollars adding up. How much was this going to cost her?

"Of course every day." Jenna stroked her chin, deep in thought. "By my calculation, you owe me 643 whiskey shooters to go with my afternoon coffee."

Ash grabbed a pencil and a scrap of paper. "You've been working here three years, so I think your number is off by… let's see, there are 260 work days in a calendar year, so that's a grand total of 780."

"You work every day. I want—what's 365 times three?"

"One thousand and ninety-five."

Jenna tapped her fingertips to her lips with a look of pure glee. "It's going to be a banner year."

Did Jenna have to be touching her lips? Try as she might, Ash couldn't get her mind off those stupid things. Not Jenna's lips. The *other* woman's. Ash slammed her hand onto her stapler to make the thoughts go away.

"Geez." Jenna eyed the stapler. "I'm only kidding about the whiskey shooters."

"You mean Ralph and James don't really bribe you?" Ash picked up the stapler, opening it to check if it was full. It was.

"They do," Jenna admitted with a shrug, "but that's because I don't like them, and they know it. For some insane reason, I do like you, even without being bribed."

"I have that effect on people," Ash deadpanned. She closed the stapler and set it back down, not sure why she kept fiddling with the thing except that it gave her something to do with her hands other than wring them, an impulse she'd barely been able to control since Caitlyn Brewster had walked through the elevator door.

"Oh, honey." Jenna burst into a fit of laughter. "I think I might be the only person in this office who doesn't mind hanging out with you."

"Harsh!" Ash swiped a cookie from Jenna's plate in retaliation, even though she knew it was most likely true. "Do you really think no one likes me?"

"The equity partners love you," Jenna assured her. "No one else can deliver on those sweet, sweet billable hours the way you do. But as for the others... Let's just say if I'm not the one bringing you the plate of food, I'd caution you not to eat it."

"Maybe this is why I'm not as big a fan of the break room food fests as you are," Ash grumbled. Though she did nothing to endear herself to her colleagues and couldn't name anyone besides Jenna she actually cared much for anyway, it still kind of stung to have it implied most of the people she shared an office with would be just as happy to poison her with a celebratory cupcake.

It wasn't that Ash was incapable of making friends. She simply didn't see the point.

"By the way"—Jenna licked crumbs from her fingers —"in case you're wondering, she's still wearing the cocktail dress."

"Who is?" Ash rested her hand on top of her stapler again. She knew exactly who Jenna meant and the image of the fabulous body snug in said dress was seared into her mind forever.

Jenna took a step back, taking the plate with her while keeping a wary eye on the stapler. "The woman you want to destroy. What's her name again?"

"Caitlyn Brewster."

"That's right. Wait... how do you know that? You weren't there when she was introduced."

"You told me, remember?" Ash lifted her hand from the Swingline to tap the side of her head. "Memory like a steel trap."

As if to prove her point, her memory treated her to a

graphic play-by-play of the feel of Caitlyn's arm pulling her close as they kissed under the light of the full moon.

Ash smashed her fist onto the stapler, sending a tiny, twisted piece of metal flying into the air.

Jenna handed over the plate. "You know what? Keep this. You're getting hangry."

Ash glared at her as she put one hand on the plate and pulled it closer. "How last-minute was this hiring, by the way? Usually we know days ahead of time before any free food is going to be on offer. The boys—excuse me, *men*—in the office like to train their stomachs like they're Joey Chestnut."

"Who's that?"

"Are you pulling my leg?" Ash gave Jenna a look of genuine surprise. "You don't know who he is?"

The paralegal shook her head.

Ash tossed her hands in the air, hardly able to believe she possessed a piece of pop culture trivia someone else didn't already know. "He's the world hot dog eating champion. Everyone knows that."

"Trust me when I say this. That is not the case." Jenna was looking at her like she'd sprouted an extra head. "Who the hell watches eating contests?"

"Plenty of people. I saw it on ESPN," Ash said defensively. Jenna was always telling her she needed to do more "normal person" things, and yet as soon as she did, all she got for her efforts was grief. "That's a channel *normal people* watch, right?"

"They had hot dog eating on ESPN?" Jenna's tone was incredulous.

"It might have been ESPN2. It was late at night," Ash

admitted as she watched her tally of "normal person" points tick lower with every word. "I couldn't sleep."

"So you tuned in to a sports channel to watch hot dog eating. I thought you hated sports."

"I like some sports," Ash grumbled. Why was she friends with Jenna again? Oh right. Because everyone else in the office hated her for being too competitive and wanted to see her dead.

Yay.

Jenna eyed Ash like she didn't know what to make of the turn their conversation had taken. "You've never once joined the office Super Bowl squares."

Football? Ash's nose wrinkled, showing her true thoughts on the matter before she could stop herself. "I'm not into teams."

"Shocker."

"I prefer individual sports." Ash placed three grapes in her mouth and bit down. She would never admit it, but they tasted amazing. Damn Jenna and her traitorous free food.

"Look, you don't have to indulge in public snack munching, but if you know what's best for you, I suggest marching your bee-hind into the conference room and playing nice with the new arrival. If you don't, people will notice. You might not like teams, but you do need to be a team player if you want to get ahead."

"I was already planning on it." Ash took a deep breath, hoping to strengthen herself for the task ahead. "I'm not that much of a moron."

Jenna tossed an extremely doubtful look in her direction, though a hint of teasing shone through. "You didn't know that bribing your paralegal was a thing. Just sayin'." With that, Jenna swanned back to her desk, probably dreaming of all the whiskey shooters in her future.

Ash contemplated her poor abused stapler, her mind stuck in the past. Six years ago, everything had been on the line. The mock trial competition had been her one shot at making the big time. That summer associate position paid more than Ash could earn in a year of fast food jobs and housekeeping gigs, enough to finally go to school full time. Not to mention it was the only way to get herself on the radar of a top firm like McGill and Harding.

Caitlyn Brewster and her trickery had nearly ruined it all. The more Ash had thought about it over the years—which was way more than she would admit to a living soul—the more she was convinced that was exactly what it had been. Caitlyn hadn't been into her. She'd been playing games, doing anything to win. She'd been a helluva competitor too. In the end, only a rookie mistake in the woman's closing argument had allowed Ash to clinch the victory. And now she was back just in time to take away the partnership Ash had worked so hard for.

This time, Ash was well aware of the woman's ploys. Caitlyn was the type who would do anything to get what she wanted. Like kissing an opponent just to throw her off her game. Or showing up on her first day of work dressed like a stripper in an office where seventy-five percent of the equity partners were male.

The woman had no scruples.

Ash hoisted herself out of her chair, wishing she had a plausible excuse that would prevent her from walking all the way down the hall to the conference room. Maybe a broken leg. No one would expect a woman on crutches to hobble all that way for a meet and greet. Not even people who didn't like her, which apparently was everyone in the office.

Lacking crutches and not thinking she could pull off a good fake limp on short notice, Ash forced herself to make the trek toward the conference room. The space was nearly empty, the free food vultures having already descended, leaving only a few broken crackers and sad-looking baby carrots behind.

"There you are." The space was not as empty as Ash had hoped, as evidenced by Frank Lamont, another of the equity partners, flagging her down the instant she'd crossed the threshold. "Come over and meet Caitlyn Brewster."

He steered Ash by the shoulder, depositing her in front of the last woman on earth she wanted to talk to, and then disappeared into the hallway before she could utter a single word. So much for hoping Frank might carry the bulk of the conversation weight.

"It's nice to see you again," Caitlyn said, offering what anyone else no doubt would mistake for a genuine smile. She was taller than Ash remembered, probably because of the four-inch heels. Shinier, too.

Red really was an excellent color on her.

Ash narrowed her eyes, wishing there was a stapler nearby to which she could give a good whack. "Have we met before?"

A flash of disappointment stabbed at the corners of

Caitlyn's eyes before she relaxed her facial muscles. "My mistake. I could have sworn we had."

Score one point for me! Ash thought. And here Jenna had claimed Ash didn't like sports. Although, Ash had always assumed there would be more sweetness to a victory against her old nemesis. Instead, it tasted a little flat, like a can of soda left open in the refrigerator overnight. Regret for lashing out in such an immature way made her stomach turn sour. Maybe she shouldn't have acted so cold. It couldn't be fun being the new person in an office of strangers, after all.

Caitlyn studied Ash's face in a way that brought goosebumps to her skin, reminding her of all the reasons she'd been taken in by the woman's charms six years before. "I know what it is. You remind me of one of my nannies."

Charms? Ha!

And the score was tied one to one.

Had this conniving weasel managed to call Ash old and also insult her social class with one sentence? The dig landed like a physical blow. It was a much-needed reminder of exactly what Ash was up against. Even so, if Caitlyn hadn't been gunning for the same promotion, Ash might have admired her skill at putting a competitor in her place.

Before Ash had a chance to respond, Caitlyn left the room. A hundred scorching zingers raced through Ash's head, all the things she could've said in reply to really chastise the new associate, and there was no one to say them to. What a tease.

Since the conference room was empty and no one

could see her do it, Ash paused to pick through the pathetic carrots to find a few decent ones. She grabbed those and the last two chunks of cheese to tide her over till dinner. It was shaping up to be another late night, during which she doubted she'd have time to order any food.

Just as it had been when they'd faced off six years before, only one of them would remain standing when the partner announcement rolled around. Ash would work twenty-four hours a day if she had to, but that promotion was hers.

CHAPTER SIX

Caitlyn glanced at the clock on the bottom of her laptop screen. A quarter to five on Friday afternoon. Somewhere in the world there were probably people looking at the time and thinking about ducking home early to start the weekend, but Caitlyn wasn't one of them.

What she *was*, though, was running late.

She was in no danger of missing the meeting, which didn't start until five on the dot, but given that it was her first week, she needed to grab the best seat at the table to establish dominance in the office pecking order. Caitlyn lived by three rules: show up early, stay late, and never end up in the standing room only section for a company meeting.

Any idiot could set an alarm for fifteen minutes before they had to be somewhere. That was why Caitlyn usually went for seventeen minutes, to give herself an extra edge. She hadn't meant to blow past her deadline, but she'd been waiting on a contract from a new client. It had arrived, which was excellent news. Even so, she hoped no one else at the office was as diligent at arriving early for meetings as she was. So far, Caitlyn could only think of one person who would be.

Ashley Tanner.

In the five days since Caitlyn had started this job, she had done as much digging as she could into the woman. Topping her list of discoveries was that Ash hated Caitlyn with the fury of a thousand suns. Nobody had told Caitlyn this. They didn't have to. Ash made it obvious with every breath, from the way she pretended not to remember who Caitlyn was to the way she found so many tiny but annoying ways to get under Caitlyn's skin.

In short, Ash was playing mind games, and Caitlyn was here for it.

Mind games, it seemed, were Ash's specialty. As were the same long hours and insane work ethic Caitlyn prided herself on. But unlike Caitlyn, who had perfected the art of getting on everyone's good side, even the complete morons—and there were way more of those working in law offices than people might think—Ash wasn't winning any popularity contests. Not a single associate in the office had a good thing to say about her.

Caitlyn had no trouble understanding that. The woman was meaner than a rabid dog.

To think she'd once felt bad for Ash, concerned the woman's humble beginnings would keep her from the greatness she seemed to deserve. Caitlyn had felt it so keenly that she'd—

No. Caitlyn had promised herself she wouldn't think about that anymore. It was in the past. What was done was done. Suffice to say, if Ash expected Caitlyn to roll over this time and let her sail into a partnership promotion without breaking a sweat, she was in for a rude awakening. Caitlyn didn't even want the job, but that didn't matter. It was the principle of the matter.

She didn't want Ash to get something she didn't win fair and square. Not again. Not if Caitlyn could do something about it.

She might be small in stature, but when it came to getting what she wanted, Caitlyn was a gladiator.

A gladiator who, when she entered the conference room at 4:46, found she was not the first to arrive as she had hoped. Ash had beaten her to it and was sitting in the best spot at the conference table.

"Do you need something?" Ash didn't bother to look up, as if eye contact were beneath her.

"You're in my seat." Caitlyn should have kept her complaint to herself, but the woman was too annoying. It just slipped out.

Ash made a full-scale Broadway production of checking the chair, leaning over to the left side and then the right. "Is your name on it? I'm not seeing it."

This over the top display was like a scratchy tag along the back of Caitlyn's neck, small on its own but capable of ruining the entire day. "Maybe you need your reading glasses."

"An age joke. I've never heard one of those before, Elle Woods."

A Legally Blonde reference? Caitlyn's core temperature reached a boiling point. The woman had made the exact same joke six years ago, yet continued to maintain she had no recollection of it. The nerve!

"That is where I always sit for company meetings." Caitlyn sounded like an angry bear, and an irrational one at that, but she was beyond caring.

"This is your first one," Ash pointed out. "You've been here a week."

Caitlyn balled her fists, itching for a fight. While she wasn't a violent person, Ash rubbed her the wrong way.

Instantly, several graphic suggestions of how Ash might rub her the right way zipped through her head, leaving Caitlyn off-balance and even more irate. No other woman had ever had this effect on her, not even her evil college ex. Caitlyn's self-control was legendary. So why couldn't her willpower wrestle her libido to the ground and subdue it once and for all?

"I meant back in New York." Caitlyn burned with the urge to stomp over to the chair and upend it just to watch Ash slide to the floor on her ass. The upheaval of the past couple weeks must've taken more out of her than she'd thought. "That's where I sit. Always."

"Maybe you should go back to New York, then. I'm sure your chair and booster seat miss you." The iciness in Ash's tone rang loudly in Caitlyn's head. It was clear Ash didn't want Caitlyn in the same room, or even the same city.

Wait. Had she made a crack about a booster seat? Caitlyn's blood got that much closer to boiling.

Why did Ash have to be so caustic? It went beyond the race for partner, or so it seemed to Caitlyn. There was something personal in Ash's petty attacks, something deeper than a work rivalry. But why? It wasn't like they had a history, aside from one measly little kiss.

A kiss that had meant absolutely nothing.

This thought provoked only the slightest twinge of unease, proving her ability to lie had improved considerably over the past six years. Even—or especially—to herself. But if she *had* attached any meaning to the kiss—which she hadn't, as she had just established—she wouldn't any longer. Not when it had obviously meant so little to the other party involved.

Clenching her jaw, Caitlyn seated herself in the chair directly across from Ash. It was the second-best spot in the conference room, allowing her to keep an eye on her rival's every move. Like a lioness waiting for the kill.

Over the next several minutes, the conference room filled to capacity, the stragglers lining up along the walls as Caitlyn had anticipated. At precisely five o'clock, Larry Cooper strutted in. Though Caitlyn was fond of him because of their history, even she could admit he wasn't overly formidable. His lack of hair and overall shabbiness undercut his image. Like Caitlyn, people were prone to underestimate Larry. They usually came to regret the error. He was a genius at divorce settlements, if little else.

Everyone in the room sat up straighter when Larry arrived, proving to Caitlyn that her new colleagues weren't stupid. A senior equity partner, no matter how unassuming in appearance, was to be respected and feared. "Welcome, everyone, and thanks for making the time on a Friday afternoon."

As if we had a choice. Caitlyn pressed her lips together

firmly so as not to laugh out loud. Scheduling a mandatory meeting for the end of the day on a Friday was a move that could've come straight out of *Power Plays 101*.

Obviously pleased with himself, Larry took his seat at the head of the table. He rested his chin on steepled fingers in a practiced way that made Caitlyn think he'd been watching law shows on television while practicing the actors' gestures in a mirror.

"Mr. Harding has asked me to address an important issue with you all regarding partnership offers." Larry motioned to the Polycom device in the center of the table, suggesting Mr. Harding was present on the other side, but Caitlyn knew this to be false. She'd been in the room long enough to know no one had set up a call, and besides, she knew her great-uncle had a standing appointment at the nineteenth hole of the country club on Friday afternoons.

It appeared, however, Caitlyn was the only one who knew this, as there were murmurs all around the room the moment the man's name was mentioned, growing more urgent when the topic of partnerships was raised.

No, she was not the only one after all. From the way Ash was pinching her lips together to ward off a smirk, she knew the Polycom ruse was bullshit too.

Larry waved for them to simmer down. "Due to the difficult economic environment, the number of offers we can make will be limited. Furthermore, we will be looking especially closely at the ability to bring in new business, in addition to billable hours."

Caitlyn glanced around the table, taking in the people whispering behind their hands, trying to determine who among them thought they had a chance, and which ones had already started sending out their resumes. From what Caitlyn had observed already, Ralph and James were too lazy to go the extra mile. Hopefully they were getting their affairs in order. Bruce was efficient and conscientious. At any other firm, he'd be a contender, but his billable hours paled in comparison to Ash's.

Zach, a talented if overly obsequious fourth-year associate she'd met at the start of the week, gave off an air of relaxed amusement. He had another year before his own partnership panic kicked in. If there'd been plenty of partnerships to go around, he might have had a chance.

Caitlyn would've felt guilty that her presence had made the competition harder, but it was the nature of the business, and if they hadn't used her paycheck as an excuse, they would've found something else. So anyway, better luck to Zach next year. Regardless, Caitlyn pegged him as a useful ally and made a note to get to know him better. One never knew when having an eager brownnoser on one's side would come in handy.

"I don't need to explain what you need to do to impress us." Again, Larry motioned to the Polycom where the phantom Mr. Harding sat in silent judgment. "Billable hours and signing clients."

Caitlyn sat on her hands to keep herself from palm slapping Larry. Had no one ever taught him that if you tell people you don't need to say something, the last thing you should do is proceed to spell it out? It was a good thing he never had to go in front of a jury. They would eat him alive. He was a good lawyer in his own sphere, but a thought began to worry away at the back of her consciousness. Without Uncle Bertie's firm hand guiding them on a daily basis, what exactly was going on in the Boston office?

Also, how long was this meeting going to last, anyway? Caitlyn stared at Ash, silently seething as she realized her rival had a view of the clock while she did not.

"It's no secret Ashley Tanner is killing everyone in the billable hours department," Larry announced, basically pinning a target on the woman's back if there wasn't already one there. "You can try to catch up, but by my calculation, you'd have to work every minute for the rest of the year to have a chance."

As nervous laughter broke out around the room, several people made eye contact with their confidants, and Caitlyn did her best to make mental pictures, to map out the jostling alliances in the office. Meanwhile, Ash looked at no one, but bit down on her bottom lip so hard it turned white. Any harder and she would draw blood.

Caitlyn wanted to tell her to stop, that a lip that lush didn't deserve to be punished. It would be a ridiculous thing to say. Caitlyn shouldn't even be thinking it. She couldn't decide if Ash disliked being the subject of laughter, or if it was a pathetic attempt to rein in her gloating.

"On that note," Larry said when the laughter died down, "does anyone have new clients they'd like to announce?"

No one spoke up. Caitlyn waited while the others shifted nervously in their seats. Finally, she lifted her hand and addressed the group. "It's not exactly a whale, but I received a signed retainer from Moorehead Academy about half an hour ago."

"Moorehead Academy?" Larry was nearly salivating as he swept his eyes around the conference room. "Most of you probably know that as the prep school you applied to but didn't get in. Although, as I recall from her résumé, Caitlyn here did."

"Class of 2013. Go Badgers." Noticing Ash was staring daggers at her, Caitlyn winked, then held back a chuckle when Ash's cheeks went up in flames.

"What's the case?" Larry asked.

"A senior on the rowing team was expelled last fall after an altercation with the coach that violated the Code of Conduct," Caitlyn explained. "The parents are alleging breach of contract based on the student's previously identified learning disability. Frankly, it sounds like a nuisance lawsuit. These types of cases are almost always dismissed."

"Even so, they'll appreciate having good legal representation. And I don't think I need to explain how Moorehead can open up more business connections." As Larry paused, Caitlyn counted the seconds until he added, "Parents. Legacies. Former presidents. Heads of Fortune 500 companies." He didn't need to explain, but he seemed compelled to do it anyway. He concluded with, "And she brought this in on her fifth day on the job, folks."

And now there was a target pinned on Caitlyn's back too.

Caitlyn's eyes flicked to Ash's and she nearly wilted. The teeth gnashing was now directed solely at Caitlyn, and if she was being honest with herself, it was fucking terrifying. Also exhilarating, if in a frightening way. There was no question Ash saw this as a two-horse race. A fight to the death.

Was Caitlyn the only one who had a sudden vision of the two of them stripping down and oiling up to wrestle for the partnership like Greek Olympians?

"Great job," Larry said to her, but Caitlyn barely heard him. Sweat beaded on her brow as though she'd been hit with a wall of flames, unable to tear her eyes away from Ash, who would certainly notice the bizarre and lust-filled expression almost certainly plastered on her face. She wouldn't last another second in this meeting if she didn't get that imagination of hers under control.

"Uh, thanks," Caitlyn muttered, forcing herself to turn her head toward Larry. "I thought I'd go over on Monday to sit down with them and get a fuller picture of the case before I draw up a motion to dismiss."

Larry stroked his chin. "Actually, why don't you take another associate with you?"

"Okay, let's see." Caitlyn's eyes panned the room, stopping on Zach. "How about I take—"

"Ashley," Larry supplied. He nodded, looking pleased with himself.

Caitlyn nearly choked. "Someone more junior, surely. This case sounds about as routine as they come."

"Nevertheless, I think we want to put our best foot forward on this one," Larry argued, his mind clearly made up. "We want Moorehead to know we consider them an important client, no matter the size of this first case. I think the two of you will make an impressive team."

She and Ash a team?

If Caitlyn had been praying for a cold shower moments before, Larry's words were like a barrel of ice over her head. It was one thing to work in the same office as a woman who was hellbent on destroying her, and quite another to be forced to work with her so intimately.

No! Not intimate. That wasn't the right word at all.

She'd meant... Caitlyn had no idea what she'd meant. Apparently the word *intimate* when applied to Ashley Tanner was enough to start her body buzzing and turn her brain into melted goo. For the first time since arriving in Boston, Caitlyn doubted her ability to come out on top.

CHAPTER SEVEN

"Breanna, quick!" Mike barked through the open sliding patio door as Ash stepped through the gate into her mother's backyard. "Grab the boys and their go bags!"

With a look of alarm, Ash's younger sister set her beer down on the wicker table. "What's wrong?"

"Look who's here on a Saturday." Mike extended a freckled finger at Ash. "It must be the end of the world."

"Smart ass." Ash let out a pained sigh as she marched up to her brother and hip checked him. "Always lovely to see my family."

"We're related?" Breanna shot Mike a conspiratorial look. "Is she a distant cousin or something?"

Sensing the arrival of someone he didn't know, the scrappy little dog next door raised the alarm, with another mutt a few houses over taking up the battle cry. The silly creatures were as intent on giving her shit as Ash's siblings were. She'd known every single one of them since they were pups.

"What's the ruckus out here?" Ash's mom stepped through the sliding door and onto the patio. "The boys are leaving the neighbor's dog alone, aren't they? You know how he feels about anyone teasing his poodle."

"No one has bothered the poodle—or the neighbor's noodle—in years, Mom." Mike held out his fist for Breanna to bump, absurdly pleased over his juvenile joke.

"I'm serious, son," Ash's mom scolded. "Where are those boys of yours?"

"Playing with their trucks by the tree. See?" Mike pointed to where Ash's nephews were crashing toy trucks into rock piles, completely oblivious to the barking dogs or their aunt's arrival.

Ash was beginning to wonder if her mom was conspiring with her siblings. She hadn't smiled or even acknowledged her eldest daughter's presence. Ash was just about to clear her throat when her mom turned, yelping at nearly the same frequency as the dog next door.

"Heavens, Ashley!" Her mom affixed her glasses, which had slid down her nose as she jumped backward in surprise. "I didn't even see you there. Have a seat. Make yourself at home. Mike, grab your sister a beer."

"Are her legs broken?" Mike grumbled.

"No, but yours will be if you don't get moving, buster!" Her mom shook a fist playfully at her son before settling onto one of the wicker loveseats. She patted the dark blue cushion for Ash to join her.

"Okay, okay." Mike held his hands in the air. "We wouldn't want the princess having to serve herself. Hey Bree, maybe you can start peeling the skin off some grapes in case our sister needs a snack. Should I grab a palm leaf to fan you with?"

"Maybe you should." Ash's tone was sharper than she'd intended, but her brother's teasing irrationally annoyed her, considering how much she'd sacrificed over the years for him to enjoy a relatively cushy life. "I don't remember you turning me down when I signed the check for the boys' summer camp earlier this year."

"Hey, relax." Mike's cheeks were bright red as he turned toward the cooler full of ice-cold brews. As a police officer, it wasn't like her brother didn't work his butt off. He just didn't get paid anywhere near what Ash did. Clearly it wounded his pride to have it pointed out, and Ash felt somewhat bad about bringing up the issue when she'd been the one to insist on paying in the first place. Still, would it kill him to acknowledge how hard she worked for the family?

"Why aren't you at the office?" Breanna demanded. She took a seat across from Ash, fixing her with an intense stare that suddenly made the afternoon feel more like an inquisition than a friendly get-together.

"It's Saturday," their mom chided. "Her office isn't open on weekends, Bree."

"Like that matters," Breanna countered. "Did the building catch fire or something?"

Ash snatched the can of beer her brother held out for her, tilting it toward him in salute before taking a swig. "The servers are down this weekend for maintenance. Some sort of system migration. They told us not to come in."

"Don't you have a laptop?" Mike asked.

"It's like you don't want me here or something," Ash snapped, perturbed by the barrage of questions and how central her perpetual absence from family gatherings was to their line of inquiry.

"Of course we do," her mother interjected in the voice that always ended sibling bickering.

"Where's Felicia?" Ash asked, determined to keep things pleasant. It was the first day she'd had off in months, and despite what she liked to tell herself, she really had missed spending time with these idiots.

"Home, resting." Mike sat in the chair next to Breanna, looking over his shoulder to keep a vigilant eye on his boys, who were now driving their trucks through the wading pool, dirty wheels and all.

"Everything okay with the baby?" Ash sipped the beer, the tension easing from her shoulders in a way she hadn't experienced in forever. And this was only the first day off. She had another one coming tomorrow. After two days in a row of not working, she might be nothing but a quivering mound of Jell-O when she got back to the office on Monday.

"It's just too hot for her right now. Swollen ankles and those Braxton Hicks contractions. The last trimester is a bitch." He winced as if he were the one in physical pain.

"Wow. Yeah. It must be terrible for you," Ash quipped, making Breanna titter. Ash raised a hand in the air for her sister to give a pretend high-five, even though a table separated them.

Mike rolled his eyes at their antics, downing a huge gulp of his beer and looking wounded.

"Looks like you're still part of the family after all," Breanna said. Just then, Breanna's phone buzzed, and she jumped off the chair. "Jose's here. I gotta run."

"What do you mean, run?" Ash demanded. "What about family time?"

"She has a date with her new beau," their mother replied. "Breanna, you bring him out here to meet your sister before you go."

"Mom..." Bree whined.

"My house, my rules, young lady." Ash's mom spoke in a stern tone. "You don't like it, you can always find an apartment of your own."

Breanna let out a growl. "Fine! But everyone be on your best behavior."

"No way, Jose," Mike taunted.

"I swear to God, Mike. I'll kill you." Breanna wagged a threatening finger at him.

"Do I have to remind you I'm a cop?" he replied. "I'll arrest you for murder."

"You'll be dead, ya moron!" Breanna called over her shoulder as she retreated inside the house.

"She has a point," Ash informed Mike. "I'm not sure I've ever encountered a murder victim collaring their own perp. So, who's this Jose she's willing to commit a felony over?"

"New boyfriend." He slammed his beer down on the arm of the chair, lunging in the general direction of a loud splash accompanied by a shriek. "Oy! Dylan, Grant, don't make me come over and knock some sense into you."

Ash couldn't help but chuckle. It sounded exactly the

way their dad had scolded them, back in the days before his addiction had taken hold. Mike and Bree had been so young. Ash wondered how much they remembered of the good old days.

"Your sister really likes this one," Ash's mom said in her serious mom tone. "You two better behave, you got me?"

Breanna reappeared on the patio a few minutes later with a young man trailing behind her. He was clean shaven with no visible tattoos despite wearing a short-sleeve shirt. He also wore the expression of a man being led to a firing squad. All three facts earned him points as far as Ash was concerned.

"Jose, this is my sister." Bree pointed to Ash. "Ash, this is Jose. Okay. We're outta here."

"Hold on," Ash called out before Bree could get more than halfway through the sliding door. "Jose, it's nice to meet you. Before you go, I have a few questions."

"Okay, uh…" Jose swallowed hard, his Adam's apple bobbing in his throat.

"What do you do for a living?" Ash asked in her best courtroom voice.

"I… I work at a biotech company in Cambridge," he stuttered.

"A division of Parker Pharmaceuticals," Bree added, glowing with pride as she looped an arm through her boyfriend's. "He's the youngest lead researcher in his department."

"Pharmaceuticals, huh?" Ash's mood soured. "The evil empire."

No matter how many years passed, Ash would never

forget her father would still be alive if it hadn't been for greedy pharmaceutical companies pushing addictive pills over patient safety. There'd been a time when she'd been certain she would spend her career going after bastards like that. Life had taken her in a different direction, often working on behalf of corporations instead of the little guys, but she still hadn't entirely given up on the dream.

"They make cancer drugs. They're the good guys." There was a hint of warning underlying Bree's words, reminding Ash she'd promised to be polite.

Technically, she hadn't promised. She'd been ordered to behave. Even so, Ash supposed now was not the time to indulge in a long diatribe on her feelings about the drug industry and how it had killed her father. There were so many other topics to discuss. Ones even more likely to make Bree squirm.

"Tell me, what are your intentions toward my baby sister?" Ash held back a grin as all the color drained from Jose's face.

"Mom!" Bree screeched.

"Ashley Rachel Tanner!" Ash's mom scolded, and Ash knew she'd stepped in it. She hadn't gotten the full name treatment since high school.

"What?" Ash schooled her features to come across as innocent as she could manage under the circumstances. "It's a valid question. Mike? Back me up here, buddy."

Mike shook his head, holding his hands up. "No way. You come around a few times a year. I have to deal with her every week."

Ash exhaled loudly. "Fine. Go. Have a good time."

As soon as Bree and Jose were gone, Ash started to

laugh. Mike joined in. Their mother, on the other hand, looked like she wished her two offspring were still little enough for a spanking.

"You two are terrible. No wonder your sister didn't want to introduce you. How would you feel if the rest of us acted like that when you introduced someone you were dating?"

"To be fair, they pretty much did that when I first brought Felicia over," Mike said. "Boys! Stop eating the sand!"

Ash pressed her hand to her mouth as her brother rushed off to stop his children from poisoning themselves, or whatever would happen if they ate the contents of their sandbox.

"Ash, you should be nicer to your sister," her mom insisted. "Someday, you'll bring a girlfriend over—"

"Mom, since when have I ever brought a girlfriend over?" Even Ash wasn't sure of the answer. When was the last time she'd had a relationship that qualified for that title? She'd had some crushes, a few flings, but the truth was she'd never gone to the effort to pursue anyone seriously. If she ever did, common sense dictated keeping the woman as far away from this motley crew as possible.

"Listen to me, my darling daughter. You have to make time for the things that are important."

"I came over today, didn't I?" Ash folded her arms across her chest, knowing it was a weak argument. She'd literally had to be told not to come into the office today, or she would be working just as she did every weekend. Even so, she couldn't help feeling a sense of betrayal. Her mom was usually so cool and understanding when it came to her career. What was up with the sudden lecture? "I'll be better about it. After the partnership offers are made in January."

That was always Ash's promise, only this time it served as a reminder that the competition for the promotion she'd been working towards all these years had shifted significantly in the past week. For her faults—and there were too many to count—Caitlyn Brewster was a machine when it came to working long hours. Which would have been fine. Ash was used to other associates in the office burning the midnight oil sometimes. It was just that none of them had ever been so goddamn distracting while doing it.

That blonde hair that defied all natural laws of gravity and humidity, staying bouncy and shiny even after an eighteen-hour workday. Those legs that had no business looking so good on someone so short. The way the top button on her blouse would—

"You look troubled." Ash's mom was never slow to pick up shifts in her children's moods. It was one of her most annoying talents. "Is there a problem at work?"

"Not a problem, exactly. Just… a new woman I have to deal with." Ash's body slumped against the loveseat cushion. "I'm being forced to team up with her on the new Moorehead Academy account."

"That's good, though." Her mom smiled warmly. "You must have impressed your bosses if they want you to mentor someone new."

"Trust me, Mom. The last thing Caitlyn Brewster needs is me mentoring her."

Her mom sat bolt upright. "Did you say Caitlyn Brewster?"

"What?" Ash squeaked, her heart pounding hard enough she could hear it in her ears. "Why are you acting like you've heard of her before?"

"Because I have. Remember? You talked about her nonstop for at least six months after the mock trial competition a few years back."

"I did not!" If this had been a courtroom, Ash would've yelled *I object* at the top of her lungs. Her body tensed as if waiting for the judge's gavel to come cracking down, with a solid *sustained* accompanying it, naturally.

"Oh, you most certainly did," her mom insisted. "Caitlyn did this and Caitlyn did that. You always got this faraway look about you."

"Now that's just—"

What was it, hearsay? Leading the witness? No, Ash knew neither of those were right, but her brain had suddenly shut down like a computer rebooting. Maybe she'd spent so much time at the office she'd actually merged with the computers there and this sudden brain malfunction was a symbiotic response to the office system being shut down. That could happen, right?

"Was there ever anything between the two of you?" Her mother's expression was innocent, her tone neutral, but Ash nearly jumped from the loveseat like she'd been accused of a crime.

"That's ridiculous!" When Ash blinked, she could almost see Caitlyn's face in the moonlight, her lips getting closer and closer... "If I talked about her at all, it was only because she was so irritating."

"Yes, I picked up on that too," her mom agreed, chuckling. "That's part of why I thought you might've had a crush on her."

"That makes no sense," Ash spluttered. "Clearly, I can't stand the woman. She's smug. And sarcastic. And so damned competitive."

"Qualities you tend to admire," her mom pointed out, most unhelpfully. "Not to mention traits you're pretty full of yourself."

"I'm nothing like Caitlyn Brewster." Ash slapped her palm against her thigh, wincing at the sting. "She's a total floozy. I think she only got the job because she's sleeping with one of the equity partners. You should have seen her in the office on her first day, swanning around in a red satin cocktail dress like the Devil herself."

Only, even as Ash said it, she knew she was being unfair. For one thing, red dress aside, Caitlyn hadn't acted inappropriately even once since her arrival. If anything, she'd been obnoxiously professional and competent. Ash should know. She'd been keeping an eagle eye on the woman, eager to spot any infraction.

As for showing up in the dress, Ash had heard from a contact in the DA's office that Caitlyn had loaned her suit to one of their attorneys after an unfortunate coffee mishap in the lobby of McGill and Harding. It was almost too crazy a story not to be true. And if that was what had happened, it meant the newcomer might actually be... *nice*.

Ash shuddered. She didn't need to tell her mom any of this.

Ash's mom sighed, the disappointment hard to miss.

"In that case, I guess I was wrong about you having feelings for the woman. Forget I said anything."

Forget?

Ash prayed it would be that easy, but anxiety from her mother's words burned a trail straight to her heart, causing it to stutter and quake. Why had her mom put the thought in her head that she might have a crush on Caitlyn Brewster?

It was impossible!

And yet, Ash had a terrible suspicion that, rather like a spilled jar of syrup with an army of ants marching toward it, there would be no forgetting about it. Not without seriously unpleasant consequences. Now that the possibility had been raised, Ash wasn't going to be able to rest until it was good and exterminated.

CHAPTER EIGHT

The eight o'clock bells had just finished tolling from a tall white steeple as Caitlyn settled into a heavy wrought iron chair outside a local coffee shop on the main road of the quintessential New England town that was home to Moorehead Academy. She set two tall disposable cups on the small bistro table, their contents still too hot to drink.

Most days she would be in a rush to reach the highway after dropping Sadie off in time for class, but today she had a reprieve. She wasn't expected to meet Ashley on the front steps of the administrative building until a few minutes before their eight-thirty appointment with the Head of School.

That gave her at least fifteen minutes with nothing pressing to do. It was almost enough to make her believe in miracles. Caitlyn's eyes closed as she enjoyed the gentle autumn breeze on her cheeks.

"Are you having a stroke?"

Caitlyn cracked one eye open, already knowing whom

she would see. Was this interruption a manifestation of Ash's pathological need to arrive everywhere early or had the woman done it on purpose just to rob Caitlyn of her few minutes of solitude?

"If I were having a stroke, would you call an ambulance or stand there and watch me die?"

"Are you kidding? Of course I'd call for help. My one goal in life is never to get sued," Ash added dryly. "So much paperwork."

"Spoken like a true lawyer." Despite still being irked by the woman's premature arrival, Caitlyn couldn't help but laugh.

"Should I be concerned about an addiction?" Ash gestured to the two cups emblazoned with the coffee shop's logo.

"Against my better judgment, I got one for you." Although, come to think of it, maybe addiction was the right word. What else would explain Caitlyn's bizarre compulsion to do nice things for a woman who was incapable of showing the slightest hint of appreciation?

Ash wrinkled her nose, regarding the hot drink. "I prefer tea."

Case in point, Caitlyn thought as she handed off the one closest to her left hand. "Black tea. No sugar."

"That was… thoughtful of you." Confusion appeared in Ash's eyes, as if trying to decipher a darker hidden meaning in Caitlyn's friendly gesture.

"It's not poisoned, if that's what you're thinking."

Ash frowned at the cup. "I wasn't until you mentioned it."

Not wanting their exchange of social pleasantries to

become any more awkward than it already was, Caitlyn rose, grasping her own coffee with cream and two sugars. "Might as well head to the campus. Have you been there before?"

"To Moorehead Academy?" Ash snorted. "Pretty sure they charge a toll just to look at their sign when you drive by."

"Yes, the gawker fee," Caitlyn replied with mock seriousness. "Don't worry. They waive it as long as you're accompanied by an alum."

"How lucky for me." Ash's snooty tone rivaled that of any prep schooler. Much to her dismay, Caitlyn again found herself amused by Ash's antics. Had she learned nothing?

"Follow me." Instead of heading left toward the main entrance, Caitlyn started off to the right, which would lead them to the path along the river. It was a longer walk but worth it for the view and they had the spare minutes.

"Why are we going this way?" Ash demanded. "I thought the school was over there."

"If you must know, it's easier to dump a body in the river this time of morning without witnesses. I've put a sedative in your tea. If I've timed it correctly, you'll fall asleep the moment we're halfway across the stone bridge. You'll topple right into the water and I'll be rid of you once and for all."

"You've put a lot of thought into this." Ash sounded more impressed than dismayed at the news of her impending demise.

"Not really. I came up with all of that on the spot. Too bad it isn't true."

"It's a solid plan."

"Imagine if I put real effort into it. I could totally plot the perfect murder." Caitlyn cast a sidelong glance at her companion, who instead of looking horrified was nodding thoughtfully.

"I like to do that when I can't sleep at night," Ash confessed. Was it bad that Caitlyn found this endearing?

"You probably have a hit list, like all the fifth-year associates vying for partnership."

"If only it weren't so obvious," Ash said with a sigh. "I'd be the prime suspect."

A breeze whipped up around them as they reached the river path, rustling the red and yellow speckled leaves on the fading grass. Caitlyn may have imagined it, but Ash seemed to relax somewhat as she slowed her gait and inhaled the fresh fall scent.

"This is my favorite time of year," Ash said, perhaps wishing to steer the conversation to safer ground.

"Anything that stamps out the humidity is a blessing." If she hadn't been concentrating so hard on keeping pace with Ash's freakishly long limbs, Caitlyn would have loved to stop a moment to enjoy the playful gurgle of the water as it danced over the rocks along the river bank.

Ash pressed a hand to her chest. "Do we actually agree on something?"

"It's possible," Caitlyn said with a laugh. Spying one lone tree ablaze with red leaves in a sea of mostly green, she extended a finger in its direction. "Every year, that tree right there is the first to change color, weeks before any of the others."

"A free thinker," Ash said with approval. "Dangerous."

"I'm glad to see it hasn't bowed to peer pressure." Before Caitlyn could add to her thought, a barrage of shouting, peppered with occasional obscenities, floated their way from the direction of the boathouse.

"What the hell is that?" Ash stiffened, her once-relaxed expression shifting to distress.

"One of the rowing coaches." Caitlyn sipped her coffee, not giving the matter much thought. In the six years she'd served as a coxswain on the Moorehead rowing team, she'd heard it all and then some.

"Did he just say what I think he said?" If Ash had been wearing pearls, Caitlyn was certain she would've been clutching them.

Caitlyn raised an eyebrow. "I take it you didn't participate in varsity sports."

"No." The disdain in the woman's voice was enough to make Caitlyn's toes curl. "I assume you did?"

"Rowing, actually. I was the coxswain."

"The cock—" Ash nearly choked before dissolving into laughter. "I'm not sure that's something you should go bragging about in public."

Caitlyn's jaw tightened. "The coxswain is the person in charge of steering and telling the rowers what to do."

"A know-it-all who bosses everyone around?" An uncharitable glint in Ash's eyes accompanied this statement, a quick reminder that despite the slight thaw in their relations, Ash was not Caitlyn's friend. "I'll give you credit for choosing the perfect sport for your personality.

And the perfect school. I've heard the locals call this place the More Brats Academy."

Caitlyn folded her arms across her chest, regarding Ash with a tilt of her head. "You might as well get all of this out of your system before we meet with our clients, whom you clearly detest almost as much as you do me."

"I have nothing against our clients," Ash responded. "And detest is a strong word."

"Strong, but not completely off base?" Caitlyn pressed, not missing the fact Ash had specified she didn't detest their clients, but had not extended Caitlyn the same courtesy.

"It must have been nice to go to a place like this. That's all." Ash's tone suggested that wasn't all, but it was enough. "I went to a cramped school in the city with no air conditioning and thirty-five kids in a room. They never turned on the heat before December first. We didn't have a rowing team, or a lacrosse field, and whatever else you all took for granted. But I'll tell you one thing. If we shouted words like that coach is using, we'd have landed ourselves in detention."

"You can't fault a coach for being passionate. It's how they motivate people." Caitlyn shot Ash a loaded look, not appreciating having the woman's public school experience tossed in her face like somehow she was personally responsible. "You should try it."

"Being vulgar?"

"Motivating people. Look, I may be new, but it's not a secret you're hardly Miss Popularity back in the office. Didn't anyone ever tell you it's easier to attract bees with honey instead of vinegar?"

"I'm allergic to bees. And as I mentioned earlier, I'm not much of a team player."

"You've made that abundantly clear." Caitlyn stopped walking. The imposing brick façade of the administrative building was within sight and it was time to make a few things crystal clear to this partner who'd been foisted on her. "Here's the thing. Like it or not, we're working on this case together. Take the class warfare hostility down a notch or ten."

"I have no idea what you mean." Ash, too, had come to a stop, but she seemed poised to bolt at the slightest provocation, like a cat watching an approaching toddler with sticky fingers. She seemed uncharacteristically uncertain of herself. "I may be competitive but I'm not hostile."

"Bullshit." Caitlyn hopped to the next step up so she could look Ash in the eyes without having to crane her neck. "You work with some of the best lawyers around, but you act like we're all inferior because you had to work so hard to get where you are. Newsflash, sister. We *all* worked hard. I sure as hell did, anyway. And I managed to climb to where I am without kicking everyone out of my way."

"You expect me to believe you got to where you are without using any special connections?" The incredulity of Ash's tone made Caitlyn's blood turn red hot. But as much as she wanted to deny the accusation, she couldn't.

Not anymore.

For the first time in her life, Caitlyn had knowingly used her family connections to get transferred to the Boston office despite a hiring freeze. And even though she'd had little choice, she hated herself for it. And she hated Ash for the reminder.

"Stop with the grass-is-greener shit, okay?" Caitlyn spat. "Yeah, I went to boarding school. My mom also died when I was born and my father blamed me for it and left me to be raised by a butler and a housekeeper. Everyone has their own hardships."

Much to Caitlyn's surprise, Ash's demeanor changed, hostility softening as a look of embarrassment came over her. "I'm sorry about your mom. I don't know if I ever said, but I lost my dad when I was young. I know that's hard."

"You did mention it once, yeah. What happened?" Caitlyn found herself asking, even though she should have let it rest. They had only a few minutes left before they needed to report for their meeting, making this the worst time to start a personal conversation.

"My dad worked construction. He hurt his back and—well, you don't show up, you don't get a paycheck. He went to the doctor and got this new miracle drug. Totally nonaddictive, the doctor swore. Turned out he was prescribed Oxycontin." Ash shrugged, leaving it for Caitlyn to fill in the devastating blanks.

Caitlyn did just that, her heart squeezing in sympathy for the terrible loss. "I'm sorry."

Ash shrugged a second time, after which the petulance drained out of her and was replaced by an almost eerie calm. "It's almost time for our meeting. Just so we're clear, once I'm through those doors, I'm a hundred percent focused on our client. None of the rest of this matters. Not what school I went to, socioeconomic issues, or anything else."

"I'm glad to hear it."

Caitlyn believed it. From what she had seen, Ash had no trouble turning off her own personality. When it came to getting the job done, the woman was a fucking machine. Whether it was wise for Caitlyn to continue trying to scratch beneath Ash's robotic exterior, especially given their history of mutual attraction, was a very different question.

With a simple answer: No.

"Thank you for coming in this morning." Mary Welling, the academy's Head of School, sat up straight in the chair behind her desk wearing a pinched expression Caitlyn had noticed was common among clients when meeting for the first time. She tried not to take it personally. Meeting with a lawyer was almost never good news.

"It's our pleasure." Had it not been for Ash's presence, Caitlyn might've made a crack about being glad this meeting wasn't about Sadie. However, she'd already decided it was in her best interest to say as little about her family life as possible. The less said about Sadie, or Caitlyn's abrupt return to Massachusetts, the better.

Ms. Welling opened a folder and sifted through the contents. "I have Alex Foster's academic records for you as requested. My assistant is preparing a copy of the transcript from the disciplinary board hearing."

"Great, thank you. Before we go further"—Caitlyn gestured toward Ash—"would you mind recapping what happened with Mr. Foster for my colleague's benefit?"

"Certainly." The Head of School cleared her throat. "Alex transferred to Moorehead Academy as a Second Form student, or what would be known at most schools as an eighth grader. He had been in a special education class at his previous school but his parents believed a mainstream classroom would be better for his college potential."

"He'd been diagnosed with a learning disability?" Ash asked, tapping the tip of her pen against her lip as she looked up from the open notebook in front of her.

"That's right," Ms. Welling confirmed. "He had a mild language processing disorder which, combined with moderate attention deficit hyperactivity disorder, was more than his public school could accommodate in a regular classroom setting."

"But you felt Alex would do all right handling the classes at Moorehead?" Caitlyn asked. Ash's mouth had opened at the same moment as hers and it was clear from the woman's half smile that she'd intended to ask the same thing.

"We have an average class size of nine pupils," Ms. Welling explained, unable to conceal a hint of pride. "It's not at all uncommon for students who struggle in traditional learning environments to thrive here at Moorehead."

"Would you say Mr. Foster did that? Thrived?" Ash asked. She tapped the pen again and this time Caitlyn struggled to pull her eyes away from lips that were shiny and red from a fresh application of lipstick.

"I..." Ms. Welling shifted in her chair, hesitating. Caitlyn leaned forward, curious about the pause and not wanting to miss anything important because she was inappropriately distracted by her coworker's mouth. "Alex's grades improved significantly, as did his scores on standardized tests. But he continued to experience disciplinary issues throughout his time here. I'm not certain I would describe that as thriving."

"Could you explain what led to Mr. Foster's expulsion?" Caitlyn prompted, wanting to get to the crux of the matter and be on her way back to the office before Ash drew any more unnecessary attention to those full, lush lips.

"It was last fall, at the start of Alex's senior year," Ms. Welling said. "He'd been made a co-captain of the varsity boy's crew team and was putting in a lot of extra practice hours leading up to the Head of the Charles Regatta. During one of these evening practices, Alex took issue with the directions Coach Dryden was giving. It was at that time he used an obscene word toward the coach that is a direct violation of the Code of Conduct in the student handbook. The issue was raised with the disciplinary board, and in light of previous infractions, they had no choice but to expel him."

"This obscenity the student used," Ash began. "Was it racially motivated, or perhaps a slur against the coach's religion, national origin, sexual orientation, or gender identity?"

Caitlyn instantly recognized the categories Ash had

chosen as being protected characteristics under Massachusetts law. If Alex Foster had targeted the coach for any of these reasons, it might constitute a hate crime. This meant two important things. One, Moorehead Academy could potentially countersue the Fosters. And two, Ashley Tanner was one smart cookie.

Unfortunately, the Head of School shook her head. After consulting her files, she replied, "Coach Dryden reported that Alex told him to, and I quote, *go fuck yourself*."

What sounded like a coughing fit erupted from Caitlyn's partner, but she knew better. Ash wasn't choking. She was laughing.

"I'm so sorry," Caitlyn said quickly, "but do you have some water? I'm afraid Ms. Tanner must have swallowed wrong or something."

"Of course. I'll be right back." Ms. Welling jumped up from her desk and darted out the door, shutting it behind her.

As soon as they were alone, Caitlyn turned to glare at Ash. "What the hell are you doing?"

Ash squeezed her eyes shut, breathing deeply to regain control. "Sorry. I couldn't stop it."

"My God, woman," Caitlyn chastised. "Do you really think private schools are so prudish that hearing the Head of School use the F-word is enough to send you into giggles?"

"It's not that." Ash dabbed her eyes with the edge of her suit jacket, somehow managing not to smear her mascara in the process. "After hearing that coach out there this morning screaming every slur in the book, you're telling me this kid got expelled for a single F-bomb?"

Caitlyn pressed her lips into a thin line. Ash was right. The double standard was glaringly obvious, and undoubtedly an angle the plaintiff would seek to exploit. If this case ever made it to a jury, that could be bad news. Not that she planned for this to make it as far as a jury. The courts traditionally deferred to schools in educational matters. But it made it all the more important their motion to dismiss be backed up with as much substance as possible.

Ms. Welling returned with a cup of water, handing it to Ash, who had mostly managed to pull herself together by this time. When the Head of School was back in her seat, Caitlyn pointed to the files on the desk.

"Do those contain a detailed history of Mr. Foster's disciplinary infractions during his enrollment at the school?" she asked. If she could build a solid argument as to how the obscenity was just the final straw in a history of infractions, the judge would be that much more likely to dismiss the case.

"I don't think so," Ms. Welling answered, "but I can get a copy sent to you, if it would help."

"Yes, it would." Caitlyn snuck a glance at Ash, grateful the woman was too busy finishing her water to notice. Like her or not—and the jury was still out on that one as far as Caitlyn was concerned—Ash's keen observation may have saved the firm a great deal of embarrassment.

That didn't mean the arrogant attorney deserved to be given the chance to gloat.

CHAPTER NINE

Ash rolled her neck to the right and then the left. She'd spent all day in her office chair, barely moving. That wasn't necessarily different from how she spent any other day, but the fact it was Saturday had sparked an uncharacteristic feeling of regret in her chest.

Maybe it was time to call it a day. There was nothing pressing in her never-ending pile of work, and frankly, her attention was waning.

There was a popping sound from one of the vertebrae in Ash's neck, followed by a rush of sweet relief that brought a faint smile to her lips.

"You seem to be in a good mood." Caitlyn leaned against the doorjamb, some papers pressed to her chest. The woman's unexpected appearance shot frissons through Ash's center, making her feel like a flustered teenager.

"Looks can be deceiving. However, I've been trying for an hour to work out this kink and—" Hoping to cover for any earlier awkwardness, Ash placed one hand on the top of her head and the other on her chin, and gave her neck a twist. "Voilà! I can turn my head again."

Caitlyn's brow furrowed, a look of worry coming over her. "You really should have a chiropractor do that for you."

"Spoken like a rich person."

Caitlyn laughed, and Ash was glad. She hadn't meant it as a dig, but Ash knew her sense of humor was an acquired taste, one not many bothered to stick around long enough to develop a liking for.

"What's up?" Ash moved her head side to side, inordinately pleased with the result. "Working on the Moorehead motion?"

"What else? It needs to be filed first thing Monday and I won't lie. I'm struggling." Caitlyn held up a stack of papers almost as thick as her hand.

"Is that your motion to dismiss?" Ash stared agog at what could easily have passed for an unabridged dictionary.

"No. This is the Moorehead Student Handbook. Although at two hundred and seventeen pages, the motion is nearly as long. But something's still missing."

"Other than brevity?" Ash put up a hand to quell her colleague's inevitable retort. "Why do you think something's missing?"

"Because I'm not sold on my own argument," Caitlyn admitted with surprising candor. "And if I'm not, a judge certainly shouldn't be. The trouble is, I've gone through the disciplinary records the school provided and compared them to the rules set out in the Student Handbook. While I believe they've acted within their rights when it comes to the decision to expel—even if I'm not sure I agree with them—the justification for it is shakier than I'd like."

Ash flipped through her mental filing cabinet of case law. "I thought the educational deference doctrine meant the courts were inclined to side with schools when it comes to educational decisions."

"Yes, but only when the dismissal is based on academic reasons, such as plagiarism or cheating. According to Judge Wilson's decision in *McAllen v. Harvard*, disciplinary dismissals are an exception to educational deference."

Ash leaned forward, her earlier desire to quit for the day evaporating. "We need to establish that the disciplinary board followed the guidelines set out in the handbook down to the letter when deciding Mr. Foster's punishment."

"Exactly. And therein lies the problem. Their points system is sufficiently vague that the plaintiff can easily argue the number of demerits assigned for his offense was capricious in nature." Caitlyn's flagging energy seemed renewed, matching Ash's interest in the problem at hand. "I was wondering if maybe I could ask you to give the handbook a look and see if anything jumps out at you to counter that argument."

"Sure." Ash took the handbook from Caitlyn, all thoughts of heading home forgotten.

"Thanks." For a moment, it seemed Caitlyn was going to say something, but in the end, she remained silent as she turned to the door.

"Was there anything else?" Ash wasn't sure why she was asking, except suddenly the prospect of an empty office with no one to talk to on a Saturday seemed dull.

"No. I was just going to say, it's almost like teamwork actually, you know, works." Caitlyn wiggled her fingers in an awkward wave before beginning the trudge back to her office on the other side of the building.

A ghost of a smile remained on Ash's lips as she pulled the student handbook toward her and flipped it open to the first page. A name was scrawled across the top in purple ink. Sadie Brewster. The academic year listed was two years prior. Ash frowned as she turned the page. As far as she could remember, no school she'd ever attended had ever had this many rules.

After several minutes, Ash found a passage she thought might afford them the way out they needed. This time it was her turn to make the trip all the way down the long hallway, past dozens of darkened offices, to the only other occupied room at the far end. For some reason, it reminded her of one of those old movies where two people sit at opposite ends of a long dining table and keep having to get up to pass the salt. By the time she reached Caitlyn's office she was chuckling at the image.

"First a smile and now laughter." Caitlyn capped her highlighter. "Soon enough, you'll be skipping with glee."

"I just might, considering what I found in the handbook." Ash placed the heavy tome on Caitlyn's desk. "Open to the disciplinary system section and read the paragraph under levels of probation."

Caitlyn scanned the page, her brow furrowing. "*A second probationary offense would incur a disciplinary hearing regardless of probation level.* Okay. I've read it. What does it mean?"

"Wasn't Alex Foster issued a probationary warning for setting a fire in a trash can in the boy's bathroom?"

Caitlyn's frown deepened. "Yes, but that was shortly after he transferred into the school, almost four years before this incident. I could have sworn the handbook said the second probationary offense had to be within three years of the first."

"Probably because you were referring to the current online handbook, in which the language surrounding this rule has been modified."

Caitlyn put her hands out, palms up. "How does that help us, then? We can't very well argue a policy that's no longer in effect."

"Because the change was made during Alex Foster's senior year, but the new handbook wasn't finalized until two weeks *after* the altercation with Coach Dryden. It seems unreasonable to apply a new rule retroactively." Ash flashed a triumphant grin.

An echoing smile spread slowly across Caitlyn's face, sparking an ache deep inside Ash that had nothing to do with work. "That's brilliant. Given his prior offense, under the policy still in effect when he cussed out the coach, a disciplinary hearing could've been triggered by just about any infraction more serious than a dress code violation. Is that why you were laughing when you came in here?"

"No." Ash's cheeks tingled as she recalled her uncharacteristically jovial mood.

"What then?"

"It's silly." Ash could feel the heat spreading down her face and neck.

"Humor me," Caitlyn insisted in a beguiling tone impossible to resist.

"I was thinking of those comedy skits where two people are seated at a ridiculously long table and one of them has to get up to walk all the way to the other end for the mashed potatoes or something. Then the other has to do the same thing to get the gravy. With no one else here, I—" Ash's words were interrupted by her stomach grumbling loud enough to be heard across the office.

"I think all this talk of mashed potatoes and gravy is making you hungry," Caitlyn said with a laugh.

"Starving," Ash admitted.

"I'm afraid I can't offer more than a granola bar by way of food, but if you promise not to eat me—" Caitlyn held up a hand as Ash failed to repress a snicker. "Don't you dare. A joke that easy is beneath both our dignity."

Ash raised an eyebrow. "Are you implying you think I have dignity?"

"What I was going to say," Caitlyn continued, ignoring Ash's comment, "is I would be amenable to working in a conference room together, to save us walking back and forth."

Ash's stomach roared again. "I'm sorry, but if I don't eat soon, I may die."

"We wouldn't want that." Caitlyn's sarcasm-soaked tone was way more of a turn on than Ash would've expected it to be. Considering the effect it was having on her, now was a good time to put some distance between them.

"I think I'll head out." Ash paused, knowing she should leave it there but unable to stop herself from asking, "You thinking of doing the same?"

Caitlyn shook her head. "There's a Bruins preseason game tonight. Traffic in and out of this area is going to be a nightmare for hours."

Leave now, Ash urged herself, but her legs didn't respond.

"Good thing I live within walking distance." Why was she still talking? The whole point of making an escape was to *escape*. Instead, a spark of curiosity prompted her to ask, "Do you have a long drive?"

"Remember where Moorehead Academy is?" Caitlyn asked. "I'm another two towns to the north."

"Jesus. That's over an hour's drive on a good day."

Caitlyn shrugged, a sour expression on her face. "It's where I live."

"Yeah, but there are hundreds of great apartments within fifteen minutes of here. People only move out of Boston when they have…" She'd been about to say kids, but as she remembered the name inside the school handbook, Ash went cold. "Who's Sadie?"

Caitlyn's eyes widened. "What?"

Though mostly known as a college preparatory school, Moorehead Academy began boarding children as young as eleven. If Caitlyn was thirty now, that would mean… Ash did the math in her head, her brain stopping on its axis when she came to the answer. Nineteen. It was young, but certainly possible Caitlyn had become a mother at that age.

Caitlyn burst into laughter. "Do you know how ridiculous you look right now?"

"Me?" Ash scrambled to recover her composure, praying she didn't look as thrown off as she felt.

"Sadie's my baby sister, you dolt. She's a sophomore at Moorehead but was having some issues adjusting to dormitory life this year. She was desperate to live at home, only our father is… away. So…"

"So you moved from New York?" Ash regarded the woman with an increased measure of respect as she nodded in response. "You uprooted your life completely—"

"She's my sister." Caitlyn sounded defensive, as if she'd been told more than once that she'd made a mistake. "She needed someone to take care of her and that someone is me."

"I didn't mean it that way…" Ash tripped over her words, suddenly uncertain how to behave as her entire view of the younger lawyer shifted in an instant. "It's just, that's really responsible of you."

It had been easy to dislike Caitlyn when she was a spoiled brat, but now… If there was one thing Ash respected, it was duty to family. There was no stopping the way this revelation warmed her, threatening to thaw every bit of ice that had remained around her heart. And then where would Ash be?

"A smile, laughter, and now an actual compliment? Weird," Caitlyn teased as her cheeks turned pink. "Careful, Ashley Tanner, or you might end up making a friend."

A friend? That was something new. Ash hadn't bothered much with friendship, not since she'd moved in high school and had to leave all her old friends behind after her father's death. New ones had been hard to find, and she hadn't had the time. Or the heart. What use were friends when they disappeared the moment you needed them most? Jenna was the closest thing to a friend in her adult life, but even there, the workplace boundaries were firmly engaged.

And yet, when Caitlyn said it, the word *friend* suddenly held an indescribable appeal. Or maybe it was the way she'd said Ash's name. While she'd never admit it to another soul, Ash was fairly convinced she could listen to Caitlyn saying *Ashley Tanner* all day. Or just reading from an instruction manual for installing a dishwasher.

That realization should have sent up a major red flag, but Ash's stomach let out a deafening rumble of protest, distracting her from all other matters save one.

"I may live within walking distance, but I don't have any food in my apartment," Ash admitted. Her heart skipped a beat as a reckless idea took hold of her. "You're stuck in the city until traffic dies down. What if we take some of our work to a restaurant in the North End?"

Caitlyn tilted her head. "Isn't that the Paul Revere area, with all the Italian restaurants? I thought it was for tourists."

"Trust me," Ash urged, even as she wished her mouth would stop talking on its own because with every word she uttered, she was probably digging her own grave. "I know all the authentic places where tourists never step foot."

"I remember hearing they have really good cannoli at—"

"Don't say it!" Ash's hands flew to her ears, even as she laughed at herself for the over-the-top reaction. "Don't even utter that name. The line is always a mile long, and they're far from the top of the list."

"A cannoli snob?" Caitlyn snorted, obviously amused.

"Why settle for adequate when you can have the best?" Ash argued. Her lips twitched with the need to express some of the sudden giddiness she felt, like a kid about to ditch school to go to an amusement park.

Caitlyn's laugh was hearty, clear and sweet like a bell. "Here you busted my chops about attending a private school, but you and I aren't so different after all."

"Are you going to sit there mocking me?" Ash put her hands on her hips, pretending to scowl even as her pulse quickened with anticipation. Oh God. She was really doing this. "Or would you care to join me for the best meal of your life?"

CHAPTER TEN

"The best meal of my life," Caitlyn said as they stepped into the elevator. She hit the button for the lobby and the doors slid closed. "Are you sure you can live up to that promise?"

"I never make a promise I can't keep," Ash replied.

"How awkward. I seem to recall six years ago you promised to destroy me." Caitlyn held Ash's gaze, daring her to say something snappy.

Instead the woman simply laughed, tickling Caitlyn's ears like a symphony. "I meant as an opponent in the mock trial. Not in general."

Jolted by surprise, Caitlyn made a mental note that, for the first time, Ash had admitted to remembering her from before. "You should laugh more."

"Why's that?" Despite it being the type of thing a guy would call out to a woman on the street if he wanted to get his teeth kicked in, Ash seemed more amused by Caitlyn than annoyed. There was another first.

"Because you have a lovely laugh. That's all." It

wasn't all, and Caitlyn was pretty sure Ash knew it. Caitlyn's insides had gone gooey, and it wasn't just the laughter that had brought it on. Something had shifted between them today. From the moment Caitlyn had mentioned Sadie, there'd been a thaw in Ash's frosty demeanor, along with a corresponding warming of desires Caitlyn had no business entertaining.

Not tonight. Not tomorrow. Not ever.

Ash clutched the strap of the canvas bag that had taken the place of her usual briefcase. Since it was a Saturday, both women were dressed more casually than on a regular workday. Caitlyn noted Ash's dark jeans, gray cashmere sweater, and silk scarf that added a dash of both color and elegance. It was a far cry from the utilitarian clothing she'd worn when they first met. While Caitlyn got the impression Ash didn't spend her money frivolously, it was clear when it came to fitting in with a firm full of Ivy League lawyers, she'd learned to dress the part.

The look suited her, way too much for Caitlyn's comfort.

Despite her usual poise, Ash seemed nervous. It came as a relief to Caitlyn, considering her own insides had started feeling like a cage full of hummingbirds the moment she'd found herself alone with Ash in an enclosed space. It was a small elevator, too, hardly big enough for them both, though the occupancy certificate claimed it could hold seven. Caitlyn knew this because she was focusing all her attention on the rectangular plaque bearing the information. It was either that or start dwelling on the sweet vanilla notes of Ash's perfume, which filled the compartment and threatened to overwhelm her senses.

"Did you know there's a National Talk in the Elevator Day?" Caitlyn heard herself ask in what had to be the world's most pathetic attempt at breaking a silence in an actual elevator.

"Is it today?" Ash's fist tightened around the canvas strap on her shoulder.

"No. July." Which made it an even stupider thing to have brought up.

The corners of Ash's mouth twitched. "I didn't know you had a thing for elevators."

"I have a thing for many things." Running that statement through her head, Caitlyn wished she could die. *A thing for many things?* Was English actually her native language? Her blonde hair and small frame often had people mistaking her for an airhead, but tonight she seemed determined to live up to the reputation.

The elevator doors slid open. Instead of making a dash for her freedom and leaving Caitlyn in the dust as any sane person would've been tempted to do, Ash stepped out and waited, chuckling in a thick, throaty way that made every inch of Caitlyn's body catch fire.

"You really do have a nice laugh." Caitlyn had no pride left to salvage, so why bother pretending? But it did seem in her best interest to change the subject. "I can't believe how decadent it feels to leave the office before sunset. I may even order a glass of chianti with dinner."

It was no more than a ten-minute walk from the offices of McGill and Harding to the start of the neighborhood known as the North End. A faint scent of the sea hung in the air with Boston Harbor only a street away. Here and there the sweet smell of roasted nuts tickled Caitlyn's nose from street vendors set up near the carousel at the Rose Kennedy Greenway.

They walked mostly in silence, often single file because of the thick crowds of tourists in town for the beginning of fall foliage season. But a few blocks before Hanover Street, which Caitlyn knew was the main attraction of the area, Ash made a sharp turn onto a narrow alley that seemed too crowded to allow for cars.

"Is this it?" Caitlyn asked, surveying the crumbling brick walls and old gas-lit street lamps typical of this old section of the city. "Is this where you kill me and dump my body?"

"You really need to lay off the true crime shows, Brewster," Ash teased. "Your obsession with where to murder people and dump bodies is becoming creepy."

"Tell me this doesn't look like the setting of a Jack the Ripper movie," Caitlyn countered.

"I think it's quaint. I thought you'd like it." Ash almost sounded hurt.

"Honestly, I do," Caitlyn was quick to say, not wanting to wound Ash further. Plus, it was true. Despite her maudlin imagination, the old buildings with their mazes of iron balconies and ladders were endearing. "This may be the first time since coming back that I'm realizing all the things I missed about Boston."

"So many places to commit the perfect murder?" Ash's lips twisted to hold back a grin.

"So much history," Caitlyn corrected. "There's a scrappiness about Boston that I admire, and the way the old is maintained alongside the new. As much as I love New York, its modern look and huge size have stripped away some of the old-world charm."

"If you like history, I should point out Paul Revere's house up ahead." Ash gestured toward a squat, dark wooden abode at least a century older than the taller brick buildings flanking it.

"Rachel Revere Square." Caitlyn read out loud the inscription carved in a slab of granite. "I wonder what she did to earn her own square. I don't remember her from the one if by land, two if by sea poem."

"As if raising dozens of children and keeping the revolutionary men in line wasn't enough to earn a monument," Ash said with a sniff. "Though I've always preferred Sybil Ludington who, at the age of sixteen, rode forty miles to rally the militia after British forces set fire to Danbury."

There were three Italian restaurants in view around the square, but Ash motioned for them to continue. Caitlyn fell into step. "Ludington. That name doesn't ring a bell."

"Only because Longfellow immortalized Revere with his poem," Ash explained. "I did a report on her in elementary school."

"Here you keep trying to convince me public schools are inferior." Caitlyn bumped her shoulder into Ash, which given their height difference, hit somewhere midbicep, shockingly firm beneath the soft sweater. When did Ash have time to work out? "Seems like you got the better end of the stick."

"Are you kidding? Half my class insisted I'd made the

story up. The only reason I learned a fraction of what I did was because my father gave me a library card for my fifth birthday."

"Really? I got a pony," Caitlyn deadpanned. She burst out laughing when Ash's eyes widened. "I'm joking. I have no memory of what I got when I turned five, but I know without a doubt my father didn't pick it out. That's what nannies were for."

"I'm sorry." Ash's words seemed heartfelt.

Caitlyn shrugged, eager to put the painful childhood memory behind her. She'd meant it as a joke, a sort of gallows humor, but Ash's genuine concern was touching, and threatened to bring tears to her eyes. That wouldn't do. "I have to admit, I'm kinda surprised how thorough you've been on the Moorehead case, given your opinion on private schools."

They reached a restaurant off the beaten path that was little more than a hole in the wall, but even before Ash opened the door, Caitlyn's mouth was watering at the delectable aromas emanating from the unassuming establishment.

"Moorehead is our client," Ash said as she ushered Caitlyn toward the hostess desk. "That means they deserve the best representation I can give them. Do you let your personal opinions color your work?"

"Oh no. I always color in the lines." It was true, but Caitlyn could tell from Ash's quizzical look that her companion wasn't sure whether to take her seriously.

A woman in a simple polo shirt and dark trousers greeted them, grabbing two laminated menus from a stack before leading them to one of two empty tables. It appeared they'd arrived just before the dinner rush, which was either good luck or a sign that Ash was as much an expert on this neighborhood as she claimed to be.

Caitlyn scanned the offerings, which ranged from omelets to burgers, with surprise. "No Italian food? I thought you said you knew the best place."

"This *is* the best place," Ash said. "I never said it was Italian. Dana's Grill has been voted number one for brunch and burgers five years running."

"Impressive of them," Caitlyn said. "But tricky on your part. You know I was expecting Italian."

"I probably should've said, but I wanted it to be a surprise. Did you still want that chianti?" Ash glanced at the menu. "There's a cocktail menu too."

"I probably should pass. I'll be driving home after this."

"Right." Ash set the drinks menu to the side. "I usually stick with water myself."

Caitlyn wondered if this was just because the woman didn't know how to unwind, or if it had a deeper meaning in connection with Ash's father's addiction struggles. Luckily, she managed not to let the thought slip out. Even though their relationship had thawed, it was the last thing Caitlyn had any business asking.

"What should I get?" Caitlyn asked instead, studying the menu in earnest. "I'm torn between the ham and fig sandwich and the autumn burger."

"Either one is fantastic, but whatever you do, make sure you get the rosemary fries."

When the woman came back to take their orders, Ash waved for Caitlyn to go first.

"Autumn burger."

"I'll have the ham and fig sandwich," Ash said when it was her turn, adding to Caitlyn, "That way you can try them both."

"And for your sides?" the server asked.

"The fries," they said in unison.

"Great minds think alike," Ash said with a laugh as the server returned to the kitchen. The relaxed atmosphere, the sharing of food. If Caitlyn hadn't known better, it would've felt like a date. "May I ask you something?"

"Sure." Caitlyn's stomach tightened, whether from the prospect of an interrogation or the word *date* was anyone's guess.

"Don't worry," Ash added, as if sensing her nervousness. "It's work related. You said back at the office that you didn't necessarily agree with the school's decision to expel Alex Foster. I was wondering why."

"Oh." Caitlyn took a breath, letting it out slowly as she shifted back into work mode. "I guess I've been thinking about what you said that morning we went to the school, about the coach saying things that would have landed you in detention."

"Yes, the *motivational speech,* as you called it." Ash traced air quotes with her fingers.

"I stand by what I said about coaches always acting like that when I was in school, but I also realize times have changed." Caitlyn took another breath, steadying herself against troubling thoughts. "I do remember how it bothered me when coaches used certain words, the way they would accuse the boys of being effeminate, implying they were gay like it was the worst insult in the world."

"It kind of was." Ash lifted one shoulder in a *what can you do* way. "Especially for the guys, I'm sure."

"Yeah. And chances are, some of them *were* gay," Caitlyn continued, embarrassment pricking at her insides at how thoroughly her upbringing had conditioned her to think this behavior was normal. "In fact, I could almost have placed a bet on which ones. They were the guys who went out of their way to bully others, to turn the attention off themselves."

Ash frowned. "You think Alex Foster is gay?"

Caitlyn shook her head. "Not that. But he has a diagnosed learning disability, and the other thing coaches loved to harp on if you got something wrong was how stupid you must be. A kid who's already sensitive about his intelligence could certainly be provoked by being berated like that."

"We don't know the coach did that," Ash reminded her as the server arrived with their plates.

Caitlyn gave her a *let's be real* look as she picked up a fry and popped it into her mouth. "In front of the jury, I'll one hundred percent agree with you. Oh my God." She ended her sentence with a moan.

"Best fries ever, right?"

"You were not joking." Caitlyn spent the next minute scarfing down bites of juicy burger and crispy fries as Ash tucked into her sandwich with equal aplomb. Finally, she came up for air and said, "Anyway, you asked why I had reservations about Foster's expulsion. That's the reason.

And if I can think of it, so can Alex's lawyers. And the jury."

"Luckily the motion to dismiss you're working on will be rock solid." Surprisingly, there wasn't even a hint of sarcasm behind Ash's compliment. "I doubt this will ever get in front of a jury."

"Thanks. Now it's my turn to ask you something." Caitlyn clutched her water glass, not wanting to lose her nerve. "My first day in the office, you pretended you didn't know me. What was that about?"

Ash's face flushed. "In my defense, you were wearing a stripper costume."

Caitlyn leaned forward. "I was *not*. That was Sadie's homecoming dress."

Ash's eyebrows shot up. "Are you telling me you let your baby sister wear that dress?"

"Hell no." Caitlyn rolled her eyes, grabbing a few more fries and putting them in her mouth. "I can only assume Sadie chose that monstrosity without parental supervision—a time-honored family tradition. I realized as soon as I saw it there was no way I would let Sadie out of the house in it. But that's not the reason you pretended we'd never met."

In fairness, that might have been the reason, but Caitlyn's gut feeling told her it wasn't. She leveled her gaze at Ash, giving the same treatment she would to a hostile witness on the stand, until Ash fidgeted in her chair and showed signs of cracking as she set her half-eaten sandwich onto her plate.

"I didn't know what to think. At the mock trial, you

made it clear you'd stoop pretty low to win. I assumed the dress was just another Caitlyn Brewster mindfuck."

Caitlyn's hand tightened into a fist, capturing her fork in a death grip as she trawled her memories for any clue of what this accusation could be referring to and coming up empty. "What the hell is that supposed to mean?"

"Just... look, we have different lines we will and won't cross. That's all." It appeared that Ash was trying to soften whatever it was she'd been implying, but Caitlyn was still at a loss.

"I have no idea what you're talking about."

"I understand that making partner is a big deal. I want it too." Ash's jaw tightened. "And I intend to get it. But I won't use my feminine wiles to win it."

"Wait... You think..." Caitlyn's brain short-circuited as she tried to make sense of Ash's accusation.

"The dress. The..." Ash swallowed, clearing her throat. "The kiss."

Caitlyn sucked in her breath as understanding hit. "You honestly believe I kissed you six years ago to throw you off your game, to gain an advantage, so I could win the mock trial competition?"

"Well..." Ash swallowed again. "Didn't you?"

Caitlyn massaged her temples with ice cold fingers. "You think I did that, and that I showed up to my first day of work dressed like a prostitute to somehow get the upper hand in the race for a partnership at my new office?"

"I mean..." A light sweat appeared to have broken out on Ash's forehead. "Didn't you?"

"Are you fucking kidding me?" Caitlyn made a sound

between a laugh and a sob. "The only reason I'm even here is my sister. Once she heads off to college, I'll be on the first train back to New York. I have no desire to be made a partner in Boston."

Ash narrowed her eyes. "If that's true, how did you convince the Boston office to hire you for such a short time when they're cutting back all over the place?"

"Other than promising hand jobs to all the equity partners?" Caitlyn let out a bitter laugh. There was an easy answer—her family connection to the firm's founding partner—but this was hardly the time or place to admit it, and certainly not the person. "For my brilliant legal mind, naturally."

"Come on. You don't expect me to buy that."

"I do." Despite her best efforts, tears stung Caitlyn's eyes. She was used to people thinking she was a garden variety ditz, but this was far worse, and hit all the harder coming from Ash. "Because it's the goddamn truth."

"Okay, okay." Ash put up her hands, remorse flashing in her dark eyes. "I'm sorry to have implied otherwise. That was unfair."

"Yes. It was." Caitlyn poked at her remaining fries, her appetite gone.

"Did… did you want to try a bite of my sandwich?" Ash offered.

"No." Caitlyn was still mad, but she couldn't help chuckling. "You suck at peace offerings, Tanner."

"That's a fair assessment." Ash took a sip of water, looking like she wished she'd ordered something stronger. "Going back to six years ago. Why did you—"

"Why did I kiss you?" Caitlyn held up her hand to

silence Ash. "If you're still trying to ask if it was part of my strategy, it wasn't. I had no idea you'd even think that until after I'd done it, and even then, I thought you were being hurtful on purpose to throw *me* off my game."

"I... Oh." The check arrived and Ash whipped out a credit card before Caitlyn could process what was going on. "Let me get this. To say I'm sorry, or something."

"Or something?" Caitlyn arched an eyebrow but the half smile that followed hinted her anger had mostly passed. "Thanks."

"For dinner, or for admitting I no longer think you routinely dress as a hooker for personal gain?" Ash offered a silly grin, making it clear she was the intended butt of her own joke.

Caitlyn laughed. "Both."

Surprisingly, she felt more at ease with Ash now than she had since her arrival. Whatever had passed between them at dinner seemed to have worked the weirdness between them out into the open where it could dry up and blow away like old autumn leaves. Now that their collective branches were bare, they could wait with anticipation of something fresh and new.

Like... spring?

Or something like that. Caitlyn was a lawyer, not a poet. The fact she was thinking in metaphors and similes would've come as a shock to her teachers back at Moorehead, almost as much as it did to her.

There it was again, the D word. *Date.* Caitlyn couldn't shake it off so easily this time. If she were in anyone else's company...

Outside of the restaurant, the night sky glowed with

the full moon hanging overhead. The crisp air tasted full of spice and was chilly enough that Caitlyn drew her jacket closed with one hand.

"I guess I'd better head back to where I parked," she said, looking one way and then the other to get her bearings. The abrupt ending to the evening came as a shock to her system nearly as much as the cold air, but again, this wasn't a date.

It's not, she reiterated to herself, just to make sure the point was understood.

"Let me walk with you," Ash insisted, throwing that whole not-a-date thing into utter chaos. "I want to show you something. That is, if you have time."

"As long as this isn't another ploy to lure me back into a deserted alley to murder me," Caitlyn joked, even as she repeated *not a date* to herself one more time.

Ash raised one hand. "I solemnly swear I am not a serial killer."

"Okay. I guess if you can admit you misjudged me, I can do the same." And that was all it was, Caitlyn assured herself. Letting bygones be bygones. Getting off on a better foot. She nudged Ash with her shoulder as she had earlier in the evening, just to reconfirm the friendly and totally platonic nature of things. Much to her surprise, the air between them crackled as a whole host of sensations she barely remembered were possible zinged through her body like candy pop rocks being dissolved directly in her bloodstream.

The streets were quiet as they walked back past Rachel Revere Square. The tourists had gone home, and even most of the diners at the restaurants Caitlyn had noted before seemed to have moved on. How late was it, anyway? Caitlyn had lost all track of time, immersed in good food and company. It was so out of character she was tempted to look around for a time vortex, although she wasn't sure what that would look like, exactly. Still, it was the most plausible explanation for this feeling, one that was both out of body and almost painfully in body at the same time.

She could feel her heartbeat in her teeth. That couldn't be normal.

Seemingly unaware of the bizarre physical sensations taking place in her companion's body, Ash led them down a cobblestone-paved street until they reached an open plaza with a statue in the middle of a man on horseback.

"While we're both in agreement that the Midnight Ride was overrated, I thought you'd like to see Old North Church at night." Ash made a ta-da motion as she gestured to where a tall white steeple was bathed in moonlight.

The outdoor pedestrian corridor, wide and lined with trees, was as empty as the streets had been. The city noises were muted here, the surroundings looking nothing like downtown with its tall buildings, or even the waterfront with its rows of sleekly renovated warehouse office space. Despite the cold, the air had an earthy smell, like the scent of a coming storm. Caitlyn breathed in deeply, awareness of the sheer romance of the moment washing over her.

"It's beautiful." Caitlyn placed a hand to her mouth, surprisingly overcome with emotion at the sight of the famous church. She turned toward Ash, becoming transfixed as the woman's sparkling eyes drew her in.

Caitlyn wondered what Ash was thinking. Was she, too, experiencing this moment out of time feeling? Was she also hyperaware of the pulse in her teeth?

That was a stupid question, and yet Caitlyn found herself wishing she could peek inside Ash's head, just to know. And to know if she felt the romance of this place as acutely as Caitlyn did. Was that why she'd brought her here? Was she hoping for something more, something like that night six years ago?

Seconds ticked past but neither moved.

Perhaps more importantly, was Caitlyn hoping for more?

Almost unaware, Caitlyn licked her lips.

Ash's head bent lower in response.

Electricity thrummed through Caitlyn's veins as her pulse sped up. Could what she was thinking possibly be happening?

Caitlyn fought the urge to stand on tippy-toe. After all that had passed between them, there was no way Ash would so much as consider something so reckless. They might as well light matches in a pile of dry leaves and hope nothing burned.

And yet, Ash inched closer.

A moment later, Caitlyn was swept into Ash's arms. Caitlyn's jacket buttons pushed into her chest as their bodies pressed closer. If only she could shed it, and the rest of her layers as well. God, how amazing would it feel to have nothing between them, just bare skin?

Their mouths were so close. Any minute now, Caitlyn

was certain Ash would break free and run, just as she'd been sure she would make a dash for it after that excruciating elevator ride. But she hadn't then, and she didn't now.

And finally, their lips met, sparks transforming into fireworks as every reason they shouldn't be doing what they were doing flew from Caitlyn's consciousness, replaced by one word.

More.

CHAPTER ELEVEN

The moon. The sky. The steeple. All of it had disappeared. The only thing that existed in Ash's vision was Caitlyn.

Ash grabbed a fistful of the woman's jacket, pulling her closer. All she wanted was to fill her lungs with Caitlyn's delicate scent, to twine her fingers through the woman's golden strands of hair while exploring every inch with her lips and tongue.

Caitlyn shuddered in Ash's arms, moaning against her mouth. Ash's every muscle tensed. She ran her lips down Caitlyn's neck, desire threatening to burn out of control. In the next heartbeat, Caitlyn's hands cupped Ash's face, pulling her back so their mouths could meet again, Caitlyn's lush lips devouring her.

"Get a room!" A man in a Bruins jersey, waving a childish flashlight that changed colors, shoved past them, the stink of beer and cigarettes rolling off him.

"Gotta love Boston sports fans." Ash continued to cling to Caitlyn, ready to pick up where they'd left off, but the woman instantly pulled back as if the interruption had flipped a switch inside her, returning her to her normal, rational state. The hope inside Ash shriveled like a houseplant that hadn't been watered in months, leaving her with the same sense of emptiness at her inability to manage something that seemed to come so easily to everyone else.

"I think…" The desire was still there in Caitlyn's eyes, so palpable it was difficult for Ash to register the meaning of her words. But slowly the fire sputtered, dimming to regret. Was it the kissing that made the woman have second thoughts, or the stopping?

No way would Ash be that lucky, for Caitlyn to be as irrational right now as she was willing to be. Maybe it was for the best. Someone had to be the grown-up here.

"Of course," Ash said softly, smoothing her disheveled hair. "You're right."

"About…?" Caitlyn let her voice trail off.

The response baffled Ash even more. Was this some kind of trick? Ash didn't know if she was supposed to argue why making out in front of a Boston landmark was a good thing, or bad.

Should she fight harder to continue whatever it was they were doing? As much as she wanted to, it felt wrong. Not just because Caitlyn said she needed to go home, but because now that the heat of the moment had passed, the reality of their situation was sinking in. They were coworkers in an office where rumors flew with abandon. Ash was so close to making partner she could almost taste it. The last thing she needed was to become the subject of an office scandal. It would put both their careers in jeopardy.

"We work together." Resignation pulled Ash's shoulders into a hunch. She wished she was the type who would throw caution to the wind, to see where the night could go if they took the anonymous sports fan's advice and took this somewhere more private.

Like back to Ash's apartment, a mere block and a half away.

"We do work together." Caitlyn repeating Ash's words back to her did little to add clarity to the moment. Classic lawyer tactic.

Ash sighed. As much as she hated it, she had to be mature about this. Too much was riding on that partnership, not just for herself, but for her whole family. "I'll walk you to your car."

They trudged back toward the office in silence, the wind picking up as storm clouds blotted out the moon. If only those billowing masses had arrived sooner, perhaps Ash would not have been so quick to fall under the spell of its glow.

The moon was to blame, obviously.

The kiss had been spectacular, sure. But was it the one kiss by which to measure all others for the rest of her life?

Shit. Maybe.

Actually, there was a good likelihood that no other kiss in Ash's lifetime would come close. But Ash had to keep her head in the game, and that meant putting her career first. She had people depending on her, and beyond that, she owed it to herself to succeed.

"What the fuck?"

Ash jumped, startled at the sudden outburst from her companion. Was she angry at Ash's decision not to pursue her? But it soon became clear Caitlyn's fury wasn't aimed at Ash, but at the bright yellow metal boot affixed to the wheel of the sole remaining car parked in front of their office building.

"Is this your car?" Ash asked, pointing to the hunter green classic Jaguar even though she was almost certain the answer was yes.

"I'm going to murder someone," Caitlyn growled.

"I thought we agreed earlier that homicide is off the table." Ash smiled, hoping her joke would lighten Caitlyn's mood, but it seemed to have the opposite effect. Ash withered as a tear rolled down Caitlyn's cheek.

"How am I going to get home?" Caitlyn covered her eyes with her palm.

"I would drive you," Ash said helplessly, "but I don't have a car."

"I couldn't ask you to do that anyway. It's so far." Caitlyn walked to the back of the car, popping open the trunk. "Maybe there's something in here…"

"I'm pretty sure those tool boxes they put in the car for emergencies don't include anything that can remove a wheel clamp," Ash warned. "Even whatever fancy ones probably come with Jags."

Caitlyn let out the screech of a wounded wildebeest.

"Sorry," Ash rushed to say. "I shouldn't have poked fun at you for having a nice car. That was a low blow."

"It's not my fucking car." Caitlyn's teeth were clenched as she spoke. "The stupid thing has already been to the mechanic twice in less than a month. A vehicle this impractical could only belong to my father. As do these five or six dozen unpaid parking tickets he's shoved in the trunk."

"That explains the boot." As Ash stared at the yellow device that was the source of their troubles, a sprinkling of rain pelted the top of her head.

"Shit." Caitlyn slammed the trunk shut, tears mixing with droplets of rain on her cheeks.

"I could call you an Uber," Ash offered, pulling out her phone. She opened the app and asked for Caitlyn's home address, typing it in. "Oh, man. With the rain starting and the game just letting out, it's going to be more than thirty minutes before a driver is available."

"Thirty minutes?" Caitlyn moaned. She adjusted her jacket to protect what she could of her head from the rain. "I guess I could wait inside."

"Wait. That driver dumped the ride. Now it's forty-five minutes."

Caitlyn whimpered. "Fine."

"Shit. That ride's gone. Fifty-four minutes. Does that work?"

"I don't really have many options right now."

"You do," Ash heard herself say. "Why don't you just stay at my place?"

Caitlyn blinked as if she didn't believe the words that came out of Ash's mouth. Neither could Ash. Talk about playing with fire. After the kiss they'd shared, the temptation to do more would be off the charts. Clearly, Caitlyn realized this as well. She tilted her head dubiously. "Maybe I can rent a car."

"It's after ten on a Saturday night."

"It's not that late, is it?" Caitlyn reached for Ash's wrist to check her watch, the frisson forcing both women to lock eyes.

"It is." Ash didn't bother checking the time.

"How did the time fly?"

"I don't know, but this has been one of the most enjoyable nights I've had in a very long time." Or ever. It almost made Ash willing to consider that her mom was right. Maybe, just possibly, she was sacrificing too much for her career.

"Me too." Caitlyn's breasts heaved as her breathing grew shallow. Ash's gaze homed in on the rounded mounds, which were noticeably larger than the rest of the woman's petite frame. Realizing her own breathing was growing shallow and she was in danger of not being able to blink, she tore her eyes away.

They came to rest on the booted wheel. "I'm sorry about your car."

"I'm not." Caitlyn's voice was husky. "It means our night doesn't have to end."

Ash's pulse quickened. She draped her arm around Caitlyn's shoulder, drawing her close to protect her from the rain. "Is this the time to mention my apartment's small and really messy?"

Caitlyn tilted her head back, laughing. "I doubt I'll even notice."

"It'll be impossible to miss." Ash winced, baffled why she was arguing against her own good turn of fortune.

"Do yourself and me a favor." Caitlyn's words were

firm and demanding, sending Ash's eyebrow arching. "Shut up and take me home."

"Hurry!" Caitlyn ordered, huddling beneath the inadequate overhang above Ash's front door as rain cascaded down around them. "I'm soaking."

Ash wobbled on her feet, fumbling with the key in the lock as wetness pooled between her legs. *She's talking about the rain, you idiot,* Ash chided, though little good it did her. It didn't help that she'd spent the past six years fantasizing about dozens of similar scenarios.

Hot girl with a broken-down car.

Hot girl locked out of her apartment.

Hot girl working late in the office.

Needless to say, the role of Hot Girl had frequently been played by Caitlyn Brewster.

"You okay?" Caitlyn scooted closer to the door, rain bouncing off her back.

"Yep!" *Nothing to see here but a grown woman acting like a horny teenager.* "Almost got it."

The key turned, the door opened, and they tumbled into Ash's apartment. Puddles formed on the floor as Ash kicked off her shoes. Caitlyn peeled away her jacket, sending droplets of water all over the entryway tile.

"I'll go get some towels." Ash hurried to the linen closet, grabbing a stack of mix and match options she'd gotten as cast-offs from her mom's house.

They matched the overall shabbiness of the place.

Despite the king's ransom she paid in rent each month, the interior of Ash's apartment was on par with a college dorm. Probably because most of her furnishings had been acquired for free off the side of the road from students who were leaving town after graduation.

Piles of books—some law books and some paperbacks she always said she would read in her down time and never did—sat balanced precariously on tabletops. A box of cereal sat open on the kitchen counter. It was empty save for a few crumbs but Ash had been too distracted by a brief she'd been working on that morning to throw it away.

"I told you it was messy," Ash said as she offered Caitlyn her choice of towels.

"I've seen much worse." Caitlyn took a fluffy pink one and dabbed at her dripping hair.

"No, you haven't." Ash squeezed her dark hair with a thin piece of blue terry cloth that might have once been a hand towel.

Caitlyn tilted her head, a droplet of water beading adorably on the tip of her nose. "Are you being competitive about being a slob?"

"You agree, then. It's messy." Ash tossed her used towel on the tile to sop up the extra water.

"No."

"You said I was a slob," Ash countered.

"You're reading into my words," Caitlyn accused. "And if I'm not mistaken, you're deliberately trying to pick a fight."

"I'm not!" Realizing she'd just proven Caitlyn's point, Ash started to laugh.

"Ash, it's okay." Caitlyn bit her lip with uncertainty. "I know we can't actually do... anything. I mean, the rumors would be..." Caitlyn punctuated her unfinished thought with a shrug that didn't seem to reinforce her words. Almost as if she didn't really mean them.

Ash closed her eyes, wanting badly to ignore the truth of the situation, but her lawyer-mind was struggling to let go of the facts. "This is a fine mess, isn't it?"

"Are we still talking about the state of your apartment?"

In truth, Ash was too distracted by the desire to tear off all of Caitlyn's clothes to have spared a single thought for her messy apartment, but that seemed like the wrong thing to admit, given the circumstances. "Of course. What else would we be talking about?"

There was little doubt her husky voice had betrayed her. Caitlyn greeted the question with an arched eyebrow and wicked smirk, the type of look that made every one of Ash's internal sensations intensify.

Caitlyn took a step forward. "For a hotshot lawyer, you're a terrible liar."

"You think you know me so well." Ash inched closer, anticipation like needles along her skin.

"I sincerely doubt you let anyone get to know you very well." Caitlyn's eyes flashed with a sudden burst of heat.

Ash's breath hitched. "What does that mean?"

Caitlyn put a hand on her hip, raking her eyes up and down Ash's body. "I've seen razor wire with less-sharp edges than you."

"I'm not sure what you're implying." Ash wasn't sure

of anything, except she could almost feel her skin burn along the path Caitlyn's gaze had wandered.

"I'm saying that if anyone tried to get close to you, you'd slice them to pieces." Even as she said it, Caitlyn took another step toward Ash, leaving little more than a hair's width between them.

"Is this some sort of mind game?"

"I thought we agreed I don't play games like that. I'm speaking the truth." Caitlyn's nostrils flared, her hair beginning to dry in soft curls that Ash longed to brush from her face.

"You're embellishing, then," Ash whispered. "To provoke me."

"Prove that I'm wrong." Caitlyn's breath came in shallow gasps. "Show me who you really are."

Ash's body trembled as she fought to hold on to some remnant of sanity. "You're toying with me."

"I said, prove me wrong." The force of the order—borderline aggressive, full of need, and hotter than hell—seemed to surprise even Caitlyn. Her eyes widened and her lips parted as she pulled in a breath.

Without pausing to think, Ash's mouth locked on Caitlyn's, taking it with a fevered and unrelenting passion as she struggled to unbutton Caitlyn's blouse. With determination, Ash yanked the garment from Caitlyn's arms, sending it to the floor as she took a step towards the short hallway that led to her bedroom. A trail of clothing followed them. Ash's hunger for Caitlyn was overwhelming.

When they reached the bedroom, Ash shoved a nearly naked Caitlyn on top of the rumpled comforter, climbing onto her and using her knee to separate Caitlyn's legs. Caitlyn's back arched, her hip pressing against Ash's center with a force that drove her wild, while her tongue dove deep into Ash's mouth as if delving for secrets.

A growl escaped Ash, the type that proclaimed she might die if she didn't dominate Caitlyn right this fucking minute.

"Do it," Caitlyn urged, seeming to understand Ash's wordless cry.

Ash didn't hesitate, spreading Caitlyn's legs wider while her mouth clamped down on Caitlyn's right nipple. She sucked gently at first, increasing until Caitlyn let out an excited yip. Ash rocked her pelvis against a velvety patch of pubic hair as she continued to lap at the woman's breast.

Desire built like a pressure cooker, shocking Ash at how close she was to losing control. Never had anyone made Ash feel the way Caitlyn did, challenging her in every possible way. Not in bed. Not in life. Not ever.

Ash wanted to spend the entire night exploring every inch of this woman, searching for clues to discover what made her tick. She suddenly needed to know anything and everything.

Ash moved to the other nipple, teasing it to life, the nub hardening and demanding more.

More.

That was the key word when it came to Ash. She always wanted more. A better education, a better job, a better life for the people she loved. But when it came to relationships, it was the one thing she always denied herself, sacrificing in pursuit of every other goal.

But not tonight.

As Ash's mouth worked down Caitlyn's torso, the woman's fingers, small but strong, kneaded her shoulders at the same time her toes traced lines along Ash's legs. Caitlyn could have closed her eyes and given herself over to Ash's attentions, but she seemed intent on giving pleasure too. Caitlyn's limbs and digits conducted discovery on Ash's body with the same compelling dedication she brought to tackling a new case.

Impressive.

And Ash's alone to enjoy, to marvel at. At least for now.

With a grin, Caitlyn sank further into the mattress, spreading her legs wide. Light, damp curls confirmed that she was a natural blonde. Ash wished this moment wouldn't end, even as she longed for blissful release for them both.

It was the constant state of her life. Wanting something to last and end all at once, just for the reassurance of knowing how it would turn out. Like the race to become a partner, the fear all her hard work would end up being for naught.

Caitlyn grunted as she ran her fingers through Ash's hair, giving her head a not-so-subtle push. Taking the hint, Ash continued her descent, running the tip of her tongue along the inside of Caitlyn's thigh. Teasing. Punishing the woman for making her rush.

Finally, Ash swiped her tongue along Caitlyn's wet slit, teasing apart the folds as she tasted the divine essence of the woman's arousal, the flavor coming alive in Ash's mouth.

Her tongue circled Caitlyn's clit, slow, sensuous, and determined.

So very determined.

No matter what she set her mind to, failure was not an option. Especially not in this. They might never spend another night together after this, but Ash was determined it would be one Caitlyn would never forget. There were few guarantees in life, but this was one Ash was willing to take to the bank.

Finally, as Caitlyn's desperate moans reached a fever pitch, Ash slid a finger inside her tight opening, Caitlyn's muscles tensing in response. She eased it in, slowly, waiting for Caitlyn to relax before beginning to withdraw.

Ash repeated this motion again. In and out.

Slow.

Methodical.

Finally, Ash removed her tongue from Caitlyn's clit, replacing it with the thumb of one hand while she continued to drive two fingers of her other hand in and out. She stroked Caitlyn's clit faster and faster, keeping time with the piston rhythm of her digits.

Caitlyn cried out, arching up, both hands fisting the comforter. Her legs started to spasm and Ash knew her clit must be on fire from the relentless friction. The thought of it set a ball of desire swirling deep within her.

Ash drove her fingers in deep, curling upward until she found just the right spot.

Caitlyn almost sprung off the bed, like a cat hell-bent on hanging from the ceiling.

Victory was on the horizon. Ash could practically

count down to that moment, the crest already swelling, the one that would soon fill Caitlyn completely with exuberance and peace.

"Fuck," Caitlyn breathed out, her fingers tightening their grip on the comforter. "Fuck," she repeated, seemingly unable to form any other word.

Through the flush of triumph, Ash couldn't help but wonder if the woman had ever found herself speechless before.

A second orgasm ripped through Caitlyn, causing her upper body to buck off the bed, her hands cradling Ash's head. Finally, Ash slowed, satisfied with her performance. No matter what task she set out to accomplish, Ash always liked to exceed expectations.

They lay there for some time, motionless except for trembling and panting. But as the euphoria waned, a wave of regret broke over Ash's exhausted form.

This wasn't supposed to have happened. Not with the race for partner nearly at an end. Not with everything that was at stake. And certainly not with a woman Ash wasn't convinced she could trust, and around whom she lost all control.

It was a recipe for ruin.

Caitlyn had dared her to prove she was different, to show her who Ash really was. At the crux of the moment, though, Ash found herself unwilling to step to the ledge.

"That was—" Caitlyn, still gasping and cheeks glowing pink, couldn't complete her sentence.

"A mistake." The words were out before Ash could hold them back.

Caitlyn's eyes popped open. "What every woman wants to hear."

"I didn't mean it like that." But she had, and Caitlyn had been right about one thing. Ash was a terrible liar. The truth was all over her still-flushed face.

"Don't worry." Caitlyn's expression was instantly guarded, her tone almost clinical. "It'll be a one-time thing."

"Absolutely." Even as she said it, Ash felt like she was suffocating. "Probably best we got it out of our system, right?"

But whom was Ash trying to fool? Certainly not herself. After what she had just experienced, there was no doubt in her mind that getting Caitlyn Brewster out of her system was a physical impossibility. She'd set out to give the woman a night to remember, but she'd succeeded in making it one she, too, would never forget. No matter how badly she wanted to.

CHAPTER TWELVE

After a midnight Uber home from Ash's apartment and a restless sleep, Caitlyn padded into the kitchen early Sunday morning willing to trade all her earthly possessions for something, anything, to keep her from falling asleep on her feet.

Please let there be iced coffee, she prayed silently before opening the gleaming stainless-steel door of the catering-sized refrigerator that would have been empty if it had been left up to her pathetic housekeeping abilities.

Thank God for Gilda. The woman was a saint, especially considering she was supposed to be retired now that Caitlyn was in New York, Sadie was at boarding school, and Dad was wherever it was irresponsible man-babies with more dollars than sense went to escape their familial duties with whatever flavor of the month they were banging.

Except, of course, only one of those things was true. Which was why the faithful housekeeper had come back to keep *her girls,* as she always called the Brewster sisters, from living a life of iced-coffee-deprived despair.

At least, Caitlyn hoped that was the case as she braced herself for the blast of icy air from the open fridge. If there wasn't a minimum of one bottle of Starbucks Frappuccino inside, what point would there be to living? Maybe that was a bit overly dramatic, but given her current mood, Shakespearean drama was not out of place.

Frankly, she could really go for a good old-fashioned revenge tragedy right about now. *Hamlet. Othello. King Lear.* That Shakespeare really knew how to make the wicked suffer.

And speaking of wicked...

How dare Ash Tanner claim their night together had been a mistake? To Caitlyn's face? And right after delivering not one but two earth-shattering orgasms. Talk about heartless. What easily could've been the best night of her life was completely destroyed, and she hadn't even gotten to bask in a few minutes of afterglow.

If there was any justice in the universe, Ashley Tanner would never eat pussy again.

"Woot!" Caitlyn cried out, pumping a fist in the air not out of enthusiasm for the curse she'd wished upon Ash's sex life, but because she'd just spied a fresh pack of Frappuccino bottles on the top shelf. She plucked one out, twisted off the cap, and drained half the bottle in a couple of gulps.

"I see you found the Starbucks." Gilda rounded the kitchen island, a stiffness to her gait Caitlyn didn't recall seeing before. The older woman's hair was as brilliantly crimson as ever, but it occurred to Caitlyn that beneath the dye, it must be mostly white. Other than her grandmother and Willis the butler—both of whom were now gone—Gilda had been the one constant in Caitlyn's life, the closest thing to a mother she'd ever had.

"Nothing else gets me going in the morning like one or two of these babies. Trust me. I've tried finding a replacement and nothing comes close." Caitlyn set the bottle down on the counter and rested her head on the older woman's shoulder. "I can't tell you how much it means to me that you've come back here to help."

"What else could I do? My girls needed me." Gilda patted the top of Caitlyn's head, a sly smile forming on her wrinkled lips. "I'm still taller."

"You are not!" Caitlyn straightened her spine, doing her best to add another inch but coming up short. Literally. "How is this even fair? My father's six-foot-four."

"Your mother was a tiny thing," the housekeeper said, a sorrowful expression stealing across her features. It had been thirty years since her mother's death, but Gilda still seemed saddened by the loss. It made Caitlyn sad too. By all accounts, her mom had been someone very special.

"None of Dad's supermodel bimbos have ever been under five-foot-ten. I honestly think he measures them on the first date."

"He just can't bear any reminder of your mother," Gilda said, her voice wobbly with emotion. "He knows he could never replace her, so he tries to find the exact opposite."

"And succeeds." Caitlyn stopped herself from rolling her eyes. It was tempting, but she didn't want to hurt

Gilda's feelings. The woman had always had a soft spot in her heart for Dick Brewster, even if he'd done nothing to deserve it other than be widowed young.

"If he wasn't going to stick around to raise me, he could've at least given me his height genes," Caitlyn said. "Sadie's five-foot-eight."

"You've always been so competitive, even when it comes to things you can't change." Gilda chuckled.

The word *competitive* conjured up Ash, who happened to be the most competitive person on the planet.

No. The universe.

Caitlyn's lip curled into a snarl.

Gilda narrowed her eyes. "Everything okay?"

"Fine." Caitlyn sucked in her lips to remove the evidence of her ire. "Is Sadie up yet?"

"Do you know any sixteen-year-old who wakes up before ten on a Sunday?"

"I used to."

"I think you're remembering with rose-tinted glasses." Gilda winked at Caitlyn. "Sadie does seem to be settling in here, at least. It's better for her to be home."

Guilt tapped at Caitlyn's heart, reminding her how many years her sister had been left to fend for herself while Caitlyn was in New York. Even now, Gilda bore the lion's share of the household duties because of Caitlyn's late hours at work. An older sister was a poor substitute for a real parent, but she was better than nothing. At least, she hoped Sadie would think so, if not now, maybe someday.

Caitlyn let out a puff of air. "It's got to be hard on her, with a mom who ships her back to the States because her new hubby hates kids, sending her to live with a father whose specialty is letting people down. No wonder the kid started having panic attacks at boarding school. It stresses me out just thinking about it."

Gilda clucked her tongue in a soothing way, shaking her head. "Poor dear. Not that you had it any better."

"I did, because of you." Caitlyn placed her hand on Gilda's shoulder, giving it a squeeze. "My nannies didn't give a damn, but you did."

"I'm a sucker for cute babies."

"I wish you'd been able to spend more time with Sadie before her mom whisked her off to Europe after the divorce. That woman isn't exactly warm-blooded. More like the type to eat her own young."

"Sadie has you," Gilda said with affection.

Guilt nudged her again. "Not sure that's such a great consolation prize."

"What makes you say that?" Gilda's perky nose crinkled.

"I'm not exactly—" Thoughts of how things had gone with Ash whizzed through Caitlyn's brain but she swatted them away. "I'm not sure I'm very good at close relationships."

"You've always had lots of friends," Gilda argued.

"But… have I?" Caitlyn frowned as stray concerns that had plagued her since her move all landed on her conscience at once. "I lived in New York for over four years, but not one colleague has called to check in since I left. Not even about work. And no one here has reached out even though I still have plenty of school friends in the area."

"Have you called them?"

"That's just it." Caitlyn let out a long sigh as she flipped through her mental contact list for a single true friend. She came up empty, leaving her off-balance and vulnerable. Or maybe that feeling was still left over from the number Ash had done on her confidence the night before. "I can't think of anyone I want to call. Isn't that pathetic? Is there something wrong with me?"

"Don't you ever think that," Gilda scolded. "When the school called about Sadie, you didn't hesitate. It took you less than three weeks to pack up your life and move here so she could come home. You have a big heart, Caitlyn."

Caitlyn shrugged away the compliment, swigging down the last of her Frappuccino. "I mostly have Uncle Bertie to thank for all that, taking me on board so last minute. Especially since we've never been close, and he's not even related to Sadie. He's the kindhearted one, really."

"Nonsense. Your uncle knows when he's getting a lucky break. You're an excellent lawyer. I'm sure the Boston office will be better off for having you." Gilda held out her hand for Caitlyn's empty bottle, tossing it in the recycling bin. "Have you seen your uncle since you started?"

"No, and just as well. I'd prefer to keep the family connection under wraps. It makes me laugh how the equity partners pretend my uncle's still running the show, blaming mean old Mr. Harding for all the unpopular decisions." Caitlyn shook her head. "I'm sure finding out I'm the big bad boss's niece wouldn't go over well. I'm not planning on sticking around for long, though."

"No? You might change your mind." Gilda looked out the window, the ocean waves breaking on the rocks just beyond the edge of the property. "This is your home. Maybe that's what you've been needing. To put down some roots."

Caitlyn shuddered at this prospect as she always did. The last thing she needed was to plant herself in one place like a tree, or at least that was what she'd always believed. But with as unsettled as she felt, was there an upside to belonging somewhere that she'd missed? "Sometimes I wish life came with an instruction manual."

Step one, Caitlyn thought, *don't have sex with your unobtainable and coldhearted coworker.*

"Everyone wants the secret sauce to life, but there isn't one," Gilda said. "Aside from getting out there, living it, and trying to be the best version of yourself."

Caitlyn mulled this over. Was that what she was doing? As far as she could tell, she wasn't even close.

"I'm heading to the store." Gilda grabbed her purse from a hook by the kitchen door. "Do you need anything?"

Caitlyn glanced around, struck by how clean it was, without so much as a trace of her recent move. Tears stung her eyes. "I can't believe how much you've managed to accomplish. I don't know what I would have done without you."

"My sons did a lot of the heavy lifting, literally. Oh, by the way, Billy says you need a new lawnmower."

"Oh?" Caitlyn gazed out at the pristine lawn, still green but starting to fade as the cool autumn weather settled in.

"Between you and me, he's got his eye on a zero-turn one that costs as much as a used car, but it can pick up acorns."

"We do get a lot of acorns." Caitlyn rubbed a spot on her head where one had fallen when she was a kid. Funny how she could still feel it after all these years, but maybe that was how it was when things hurt you.

"I think he's out of his mind," Gilda said, "but he made me promise to tell you."

"Tell him to get it. I'll write him a check."

"Are you sure?" A tinge of guilt colored Gilda's expression. "I shouldn't have brought it up. It's too expensive."

"What did Dad say every time he left me in your care for one of his walkabouts?"

"Not to spare any expense…" Gilda's voice trailed off, the sadness filling in the gap. "I'll let Billy know. And I won't be gone long."

When Gilda had left, Caitlyn grabbed a second Frappuccino from the refrigerator and went to the back deck. She closed her eyes, breathing in the fresh sea air that she had missed more than she'd realized over the years. It smelled like home, which was odd, considering she'd hardly ever thought of this house in those terms.

Caitlyn's phone rang with a call from Lawrence Cooper.

"Hi, Larry. Checking up on me over the weekend?" Caitlyn laughed to let the lawyer know she was joking.

"Just wanted to make sure you're all set with the motion to dismiss for Moorehead."

"I'll be ready to file first thing tomorrow morning," Caitlyn assured him.

"That's great news. How did it work out between you and Tanner?"

"Ash?" Caitlyn's stomach knotted. "Uh, she's..."

"An acquired taste," Larry finished with a laugh.

Caitlyn winced. The last thing she needed was to pair Ash and the word *taste* in the same sentence. "She was fine."

"She's a good attorney," Larry agreed. "A real go-getter. She set her eye on making partner from the day she walked through the door and hasn't wavered once."

"Yeah, I got that vibe from her," Caitlyn said. Whatever her personal feelings about the woman, there was no denying she was driven. "From what I've seen, she's the lead candidate by a long stretch."

"Unless you care to reconsider," Larry nudged.

Caitlyn took a breath of salty air, a sense of peace descending on her. It was something she rarely experienced, and it felt good. She recalled Gilda's advice to set down roots. *This is my home,* she thought. To Larry, she said, "Maybe I was a little hasty to rule it out."

"You mean it?" There was no mistaking the genuine excitement in his tone. "You keep working those Moorehead connections and you'd give Tanner a real run for her money."

"I won't say for sure, but don't count me out just yet."

A twinge of guilt twisted Caitlyn's insides as she

ended the call. Ash had worked years for a promotion and didn't have the connections Caitlyn's wealthy family afforded her. On the other hand, the woman had the emotional intelligence of a spiny lumpsucker—which happened to be a species of fish in the Pacific that may or may not have lacked compassion, but whose name had become one of Caitlyn's favorite insults. Why should Caitlyn let Ash win without a fight?

The sliding door opened and Caitlyn's thoughts were interrupted as her sister stepped out onto the deck, still in rumpled pajama bottoms and a t-shirt. "Look what the cat dragged in."

"What?" Sadie yawned, stretching her arms overhead. "Is this when you tell me you've been up for hours, working?"

"No." Caitlyn struggled to keep a straight face. "I was scheduled to give you that lecture three hours ago, but you slept through it."

Sadie rewarded Caitlyn's joke with an exaggerated roll of the eyes. "Why do adults always think they're so funny?"

"Watch it, kiddo."

Sadie took a seat on a padded chaise lounge, wrapping her arms around her knees.

"How're you feeling?" Caitlyn gave the top of her sister's hair a ruffle.

Sadie closed her eyes, gritting her teeth as she buried her head between her knees like she was building a cocoon. "Please don't do that."

"What?" Caitlyn pulled her hand back, uncertain if that had been what caused her sister to withdraw.

"Stop treating me like I'm a delicate flower."

"I'm not—" Caitlyn stopped mid-sentence as she realized that had been exactly what she'd been doing. "I... it's been so hectic and I just... I just want to make sure you're okay."

"Do you know what this house needs?" Sadie asked without looking up.

"Apparently a fancy lawnmower that picks up acorns."

"I was thinking more along the lines of a puppy." Sadie looked up, donning an irresistibly hopeful expression.

Caitlyn nearly choked. "A dog?"

Sadie batted her lashes. "I think it would help me adjust emotionally to living at home."

Caitlyn put her hands on her hips. "I thought our goal was to get you back to the dorms, and me back to New York, as quickly as possible."

Sadie looked away, but not before Caitlyn detected the pain in her sister's eyes. Her heart clenched.

"My therapist said I should get an emotional support animal."

Panic swelled inside, threatening to swallow her whole. A dog was so *permanent*. They needed to be fed, and walked, and taken to the groomer and the vet... "How about a goldfish?"

Sadie's head snapped back, meeting Caitlyn's eyes with her own. "Only you would think a goldfish would make an appropriate emotional support animal."

"I-I always wanted one." That was a lie, which her stutter was quick to prove.

"I really hope you're more persuasive in court." Sadie

gave a derisive snort, but soon her expression softened, growing melancholy. "And I'm sorry I messed up your life."

Caitlyn's throat closed, her voice thick as she said, "Sadie, I want you to listen to me very carefully. You have not messed up my life. You could never mess up my life. You're my only sister. I will always be there for you."

"I'm the only sibling you *know* about," Sadie said cheekily. "Dad's probably got a kid in every port."

"The man's a walking lawsuit." Caitlyn made a mental reminder to pay all of his stupid parking tickets Monday morning so she could get the car released. Because apparently even that was her responsibility now.

Sadie studied Caitlyn's face, growing serious once more. "Did someone die?"

"What?" This line of questioning came out of the blue, taking Caitlyn totally by surprise. "Why would you think that?"

"I heard you talking on the phone. Something about ashes."

"No. Ash." Caitlyn instantly wished she could retract the name, or at least the way she'd said it, like some pining nincompoop on a reality dating show.

"Who's Ash?" Sadie sat at attention now, hanging on every detail.

"Ashley Tanner."

"Ooh, a girl?"

"A lawyer," Caitlyn corrected, as if the two things were mutually exclusive. If only.

"Is she good?"

"Very." Especially at certain skills that had nothing to

do with the law. Caitlyn's cheeks burned as she tried not to remember them. That woman's tongue should be illegal. "She's in the running for a partnership at my new firm."

"Do you want to become a partner? Would that mean staying in Boston?" The way Sadie asked, Caitlyn sensed she was trying to play it cool, like she didn't care either way. But her eyes told the real story, with a flash of excitement almost as great as when she'd talked about that damn dog. Even if Caitlyn wasn't sold on it, Sadie seemed to relish the idea of planting herself like one of the mighty oaks that dropped acorns all over the lawn.

"I haven't decided yet," Caitlyn answered truthfully. "But if I decide I do, you better believe our competition won't end like it did last time."

Sadie frowned, looking confused but fascinated. "How did it end last time?"

"The way it was intended." That was all Caitlyn would say ever to anyone. In part because she hated to admit defeat and in part because Ash's rejection had never ceased to sting.

"You're not making sense."

"I don't have to, and before you say adults aren't funny, I have terrible news for you. You're almost an adult, so you might want to get better at pretending we're hilarious."

"I could probably get better at that if I had an emotional support animal." Sadie grinned.

Caitlyn palm slapped her forehead. "I walked right into that one."

"You did." Sadie raised a fist, victorious. "Tell me

something about this Ash girl."

Caitlyn scrunched her nose. "Like what?"

"Is she pretty?"

Caitlyn crossed her arms over her chest. "Why in the world does that matter?"

"I don't know. Your breath does something weird when you say her name."

"It does not." Caitlyn's pulse ticked faster. But only because she was mad at Ash and didn't want to talk about the spiny lumpsucker anymore. Not for any other reason.

"It does," Sadie assured her, rising. "I'm going to get a cup of coffee. Want anything?"

"No thanks." Caitlyn couldn't rein in her grumpiness.

Sadie paused at the sliding door. "You know what? Maybe your breath didn't do that weird thing, after all."

Caitlyn shot her sister a suspicious look. "You're just trying to play me so I agree to let you have a dog."

"I would never dream of playing my big sister for a fool." Sadie batted her lashes again, sticking her bottom lip out.

"Geez, kid." Caitlyn laughed as she shook her head at her sister's over-the-top display. "We need to work on that."

Sadie might not be able to play her for a fool, but Ashley Tanner seemed determined to give it her best shot. But she hardly needed to. When it came to her sister, Caitlyn knew eventually she'd give in. She always did when Sadie's happiness was concerned. The same could not be said for Ash. Whatever it took, Caitlyn was determined to get the last laugh.

CHAPTER THIRTEEN

The three-minute timer went off on Ash's phone, pulling her head out of the email she'd been writing. She pressed send before pushing herself out of her chair and heading to the break room to pour her fourth cup of tea.

It was barely half past ten.

That she'd been forbidden from keeping an electric kettle in her office was ridiculous. She was the only one who used it. But the downside to working with a bunch of lawyers was that someone was always afraid of a lawsuit. Apparently small appliances were a fire hazard, though why they would be less of one in the kitchen than in an office was anyone's guess.

As Ash approached the break room, a familiar figure darted out into the hallway. The moment they locked eyes, Caitlyn looked away, pressing herself against the wall as if trying to avoid even their shadows touching as she passed.

"Oh, hey. Good morning!" Ash tried to sound normal and failed. Miserably.

It'd been almost two weeks since *that* night. When *it* had happened. Ash doubted Caitlyn had spoken more than two words to her that weren't strictly work related. The reason remained a puzzle.

Ash had replayed the night in her head over and over, trying to pinpoint the exact moment it'd gone oh-so wrong. Each time she came up blank. Dinner had been lovely. The kiss spectacular. Their run through the rain to Ash's apartment had been romantic, and the sex that came after, superb.

Where the hell was the big issue?

They'd both agreed afterward, given the circumstances, it was better if they made it a one-time thing. A rational decision. So where was the source of friction that had led to the silent treatment?

Ash plopped a Lipton tea bag into her mug, grabbed the tea kettle, and started to pour. She squinted at the contents, which barely changed from clear to an anemic beige. Not a single tendril of steam rose from the mug. Pressing her palm to the side of the kettle, it came back colder than a witch's tit.

Speaking of witches… Ash flipped around as if expecting to find Caitlyn cackling at her from the break room doorway. There was no doubt in Ash's mind that woman was the culprit.

Clenching her teeth, Ash flipped the kettle on. This time she waited for the water to boil. She wasn't about to take the chance Caitlyn would sneak back in when she wasn't looking to exact more petty revenge for transgressions unknown.

"Morning," Jenna called out as Ash returned to her desk, frowning the moment she caught sight of Ash's grim expression. "What's wrong?"

"Nothing," Ash muttered.

"Not buying it." Jenna circled a finger in the air as if tracing Ash's face. "I haven't seen you this uptight since the Maguire case. You look ready to spit."

Ash clenched the mug handle so hard she feared it would snap off. "I think Caitlyn has it out for me."

"Why would she?" Jenna sounded genuinely taken aback. "If you said one of the guys, I might agree with you. But Caitlyn? Everyone loves her. She's the friendliest associate in the office. Besides, from what I've heard, she's only here temporarily. I can't see why she would go to the trouble of making enemies."

"In that case, why did she turn my teakettle off before the water had a chance to boil?" Ash demanded.

Jenna burst into laughter. "Wow, that's some seriously evil shit."

"I know—" Belatedly, the paralegal's sarcastic tone registered with Ash. "You don't believe me, do you?"

Jenna shook her head slowly. "Let's be real. It wouldn't be the first time you forgot to hit the button to turn the thingamajig on."

"I did, though," Ash insisted. "I even set my phone alarm so I wouldn't forget to go back to make the tea."

"I never understood why you don't wait there. It's 180 seconds. What can you possibly get done in that amount of time?"

"I responded to an email."

"Gold star!" Jenna put her thumb in the air. This time Ash caught onto the sarcasm immediately.

"Fine. What about my sandwich?" Ash crossed her arms, tilting her head expectantly.

"What about it?" The paralegal looked completely baffled.

"Everyone knows the blue container is mine. They wouldn't dare touch it. Yet yesterday, my sandwich was gone, the empty container mocking me from the dish rack."

"And you think Caitlyn ate your sandwich and then washed your container just to fuck with you?"

"Who else?" Ash's pitch was much higher than she would've liked, undermining the seriousness of her accusation. Her cheeks tingled as Jenna gave her an incredulous look.

"You know that wouldn't hold up in a court of law." Jenna wagged a finger. "Can you provide me with some concrete evidence as to why the new girl would antagonize you in such a way?"

One reason popped into Ash's head right away, but she couldn't very well confess she'd had sex with a woman who, less than a month before, had shown up for her first day of work dressed like a hooker. She'd never live it down to her dying day. Besides, inter-office romances, if not completely forbidden, were heavily frowned upon.

"I just have a gut feeling she doesn't like me," Ash grumbled. "I can't explain why."

"I'm not saying this to be mean, but almost no one in

the office likes you. You've never cared about that before." Jenna lifted a brow. "What's so special about Caitlyn?"

"Nothing at all." The words came out in a rush. If Jenna had been a judge, Ash would've been found guilty on all counts.

"You're being weirder than normal and that's saying something."

"I'm not weird!" Ash protested. Right at that moment, Caitlyn appeared in the doorway. What rotten timing. The devil's sudden smirk made Ash want to scream.

"Am I interrupting something?" Though the evil twinkle in her eyes suggested otherwise, Caitlyn's words were all sugar and spice.

Ash straightened in her chair, making a show of blowing on the contents of her mug before taking a sip. "Something I can do for you?"

The tea might have been hot, but Ash's tone was ice.

Jenna shook her head disapprovingly as she scurried from Ash's office.

"Bad news," Caitlyn said.

"Just what my morning was missing."

"Oh?" Caitlyn's innocent act was top notch. "Has anything else gone wrong?"

"Not a thing." No way would Ash give her the satisfaction of admitting otherwise. She might not have known what started this war, but that didn't mean Ash intended to lose. "Hit me with it."

"Zach just stopped by my desk with the news—"

"Zach, huh? He's kissing up to you now?" Ash bristled. Whether he liked her or not, there'd been a time Zach had followed her like a stray puppy in his eagerness to get on her good side. His loyalty was as good as a barometer of who was ahead in the partner race, and the sudden shift in attention didn't bode well for Ash's prospects.

"He's been very helpful," Caitlyn argued.

"I'm sure." Ash knotted her arms across her chest. "What's this doom and gloom you came to spread?"

"The judge denied the motion to dismiss. All counts." Caitlyn's expression was grim, but for once, Ash couldn't fault her for it.

"All seven counts are moving forward?" Ash's stomach turned sour.

That was the worst possible news for their client, and also for her. The air seeped slowly out of Ash's lungs as she processed the implications. She'd been counting down the hours to when they'd hear the lawsuit had been dismissed. It would have made it that much easier to avoid having to be around Caitlyn any more than necessary.

"This thing could drag on for months." From the daggers shooting from Caitlyn's eyes, it was clear she and Ash were on the same page. "Looks like we're stuck working together."

Ash's brain spluttered and she was unable to stop herself from saying, "Fuck me."

"No thanks. Once was plenty." Caitlyn spun on one heel, leaving before Ash could reply.

Ash's mouth hung open as she watched the woman sashay away. How could everyone else in the office have been taken in by her act? Caitlyn Brewster wasn't remotely nice, or professional. The woman was a wolf in sheep's clothing, and Ash would prove it for all to see. Or die trying.

IT WAS Ash's first time attending the Head of the Charles Regatta, and as she approached the riverbank near the DeWolfe Boathouse at the start of the course, she wasn't sure what to expect. Even though a cursory search online had revealed it was the largest event of its kind, with competitors from every age group and walk of life, she still half expected to be met with spectators wearing preppy clothing, pearl necklaces, and high heels —and probably sipping champagne too, with poodles by their sides—like a photo shoot for a Ralph Lauren catalogue.

Ash's gaze swept the trees lining the riverside, resplendent in their fall colors. It was the third week of October and the leaves were aflame, their reflections turning the sparkling water of the Charles into a sea of oranges, yellows, and reds, a stained-glass window come to life. The temperature was cool but not cold, with a gentle breeze that reminded her why New England was the best place in the world this time of year.

Despite the natural beauty of her surroundings, Ash couldn't shake a sense of foreboding. Ever since the night she'd slept with Caitlyn, nothing had gone right. The

Moorehead motion was just the latest shoe to have dropped.

It was the reason she was at the regatta today.

Caitlyn had sworn the screaming fit they'd overheard during their visit to the campus was nothing out of the ordinary. Ash remained unconvinced. With the lawsuit moving forward, she wanted to immerse herself in the rowing world to get a better sense of the case. Were all coaches as abusive as Moorehead's varsity boys rowing coach, or had he crossed a line?

Ash intended to find out. Going the extra mile to do so was how she operated, another trait that set her above her colleagues. No matter what she discovered, she would use the knowledge to build a better defense for the client.

Forewarned is forearmed, as the saying went.

The area surrounding the boathouse was crowded with a mix of spectators, rowers, and coaches. The athletes were dressed in close-fitting leggings and long-sleeve shirts topped with brightly colored tank tops featuring their team colors and insignia. It reminded Ash of what cyclists might wear. Those who were not competing were mostly dressed casually in jeans, sneakers, and windbreakers. Ash was pleasantly surprised by the lack of pretentiousness.

Strolling along the bank, snapping photos here and there as she went, Ash approached an area past the boathouse where teams were queuing for their turn to enter the water. There were coaches aplenty, all giving rousing pep talks or last-minute reminders about the course. But nothing she overheard came close to the abuse Coach Dryden had hurled at his team during practice.

Which was good for the competitors. Bad for Ash.

How weird was it Ash wasn't sure which outcome she should be cheering for? It wasn't like she wanted more children out there being bullied by adults. But if Dryden was an anomaly, it sure would make defending his actions a lot more difficult.

After she'd observed what she could along the riverbank, Ash headed to the BU Bridge for a better view of the competition. Its entire span was lined on both sides with people cheering the rowers on as they passed beneath the bridge on their way toward the finish line. Though not a fan of most sports, Ash quickly found herself immersed in the rhythmic motion of the oars on the water.

"What are *you* doing here?" A familiar voice broke through Ash's trance.

Caitlyn.

"I came to watch the regatta." A burst of adrenaline had caused Ash's heart rate to skyrocket the moment she'd realized who was speaking, but Ash kept her tone even and her expression neutral.

"Why?" So far, Caitlyn had said nothing out of the ordinary, but her questions might as well have been happening beneath the bright spotlight of an interrogation room.

"I'm not sure what business it is of yours what I decide to do on my day off," Ash said, "but given your recent vendetta against me, I'll explain. I wanted to learn more about the sport in preparation for the lawsuit."

A flash in Caitlyn's blue eyes revealed a state of pique. "What vendetta?"

Ash's jaw tensed. "Do me the courtesy of not thinking I'm a moron."

"Just saying that puts a tick in the moron column, FYI." As if to demonstrate, Caitlyn licked her fingertip, tracing a checkmark in the air.

"What's wrong with you?" Ash snapped, angered by the sudden surge of warmth that flooded her core as she recalled the velvety softness of Caitlyn's tongue. "I'm here to do my job, just like you."

"I'm here to cheer on my sister, who's competing on Moorehead's junior varsity team," Caitlyn corrected, her attitude seeming to imply her reason was superior to Ash's, even though they were both hopeless workaholics. "It's a weekend. You can do what you want."

"You can stare daggers at me all day long. I'm not going to be intimidated by you," Ash informed her. "Besides, I live here."

"On the BU Bridge?" Caitlyn smirked. "I would've put my money on you living under it with the rest of the trolls."

"I meant in this city." Ash's temper frothed, prodding her to continue this childish argument against her better judgment. "This is my territory. You're just passing through."

"I'll have you know my family's connection to Boston goes back generations." Caitlyn's face was growing red, her cheeks puffing.

"All the way back to the Mayflower, I'm sure." Ash made a show of rolling her eyes. "Big fucking deal."

Technically, they weren't in the office, which meant Ash's no swearing rule didn't apply. It had been getting harder to keep herself in check lately, with more slip-ups than she'd like. It felt fucking fantastic to tell her obnoxious coworker exactly what she thought with no holds barred.

Caitlyn opened her mouth, about to let loose with a reply that seemed guaranteed to char the hair on Ash's head, when she was interrupted by a young woman shouting her name. Both Ash and Caitlyn turned toward the sound. A teenage girl, tall and lanky, was sprinting through the crowd on the bridge. She wore rowing shorts and a blue and white Moorehead team shirt. Her cheeks were streaked with tears.

"Sadie!" Caitlyn put her arms out and the girl collapsed into them, shaking. "What's wrong?"

"Is someone chasing you?" Ash tensed, scanning the crowd in case someone was in pursuit.

Sadie shook her head as she sobbed into her sister's shoulder.

"Calm down, sweetie," Caitlyn soothed. "Is it about the race?"

Ash choked back a laugh. If this was the girl's response to losing, it was clear the drama gene ran in the family, even if the one for height had passed her sister by. But the girl shook her head again. She stood upright and took a few deep breaths, though a stiff wind would've knocked her flat.

"It's Fergus Clark." Sadie's voice broke and her breaths became short gasps. "They're saying he's dead."

"Dead?" Caitlyn's eyes widened, her face going completely white.

"Who is Fergus Clark?" Even as Ash asked, the name tugged at her subconscious, a cold lump forming in her stomach.

"He's on Moorehead's varsity team," Caitlyn said quickly before turning back to Sadie. "What happened? Did he get injured? Did he fall into the river?"

"No." Sadie struggled to speak. "He never showed up."

"Okay. How come they think he's dead?" Caitlyn's tone was measured, even as a tingling sense of dread zipped through Ash.

She knew where she'd heard that name. Fergus Clark had been on the receiving end of the coach's rant the day they'd visited the school.

"He was in bed, at the dorm." Sadie closed her eyes, swallowing hard. "They think… they said maybe there were pills… it could have been suicide."

Caitlyn clamped a hand to her mouth. Ash's brain spun in fifty different directions at once, the coach's words blaring in her head. Sadie collapsed against her sister once more, racked with grief.

Caitlyn clasped her arms around Sadie's form, a lost expression haunting her eyes. Ash's heart clenched. The woman looked overwhelmed and so very small. Despite the bad blood between them, Ash's protective nature kicked into overdrive. There was a kid involved, after all.

"Let's get you two home." Her mind raced to formulate a plan. Strategizing was Ash's superpower. "Did you drive into the city today?"

Caitlyn nodded. "My car's two blocks away, on the Cambridge side of the river."

Ash motioned for them to follow her through the crowd. Caitlyn guided the weeping teen with an arm around her shoulder as people along the bridge turned to stare. Whispers drifted toward them as word of what had happened started to spread.

"Give me the keys." Ash held out her hand when Caitlyn's Jaguar came into view. "You can sit in the back with your sister while I drive you home."

Caitlyn dug in her purse, pulling out a jangling keychain and holding it out without a single word of argument. "You okay driving a stick?"

The surge of panic in Ash's gut must've showed on her face because Caitlyn pulled her hand back, taking the keys with it. "How about I drive and you sit in the back with Sadie? If you don't mind, that is."

"I don't mind at all." Ash reached for the back door as Caitlyn hit the unlock button, ushering Sadie into the car, meek as a tired puppy. The poor kid. She needed as many people by her side as possible—and like it or not, Caitlyn did too. This was no time for Ash to hold a grudge.

CHAPTER FOURTEEN

Caitlyn worried her bottom lip with her front teeth, not sure what to say or do as she maneuvered through gridlock traffic along Alewife Brook Parkway. Every few seconds she glanced into the rearview mirror to watch Ash, who was seated beside Sadie and making a valiant effort to keep the girl's mind occupied with anything other than the day's distressing news. Despite having given her colleague every reason to hate her after a petty revenge spree the past few weeks, the woman couldn't have been any more patient and kinder with Caitlyn's little sister. It was a relief, and made Caitlyn feel like absolute shit at the same time.

In a way, it was the perfect revenge.

"I heard you're living at home this year," Ash said softly. "Do you like it better than the dorms?"

"Uh-huh," Sadie mumbled. Her head hung low and she slumped against her seat like a balloon with half the air let out.

Caitlyn gripped the wheel, wishing she knew what to say or do to make things better. Only one thing was she certain of: Gilda had been dead wrong. Caitlyn lacked the skills to take care of anyone, especially a teenager. She wasn't the nurturing type. Even Ash, a workaholic who seemingly had no life outside the office, was doing a better job of comforting the girl. Meanwhile Caitlyn was grateful to be in the front of the car, alone. What did that say about her?

"Was Fergus a friend?" Ash asked.

Caitlyn stiffened at the boy's name, sure it was the wrong thing to say, but Sadie's tense muscles loosened. She looked up for the first time since they'd gotten in the car, an expression of relief, or maybe gratitude, on her young face, like she'd been waiting to be asked.

"I didn't know him well. He was a senior. I'm only on the JV team. But he was nice." Sadie let out a tortured sigh. "We talked a few times when we were both waiting in the counselor's office at school."

"Counselor's office? Were you in trouble?" Ash asked.

Sadie shook her head. "For discipline, you'd go to the Head of School's office. This is like a mental health therapist. I had to agree to go once a week this semester because of my anxiety."

"And Fergus went to the counselor too?"

"Yeah. On his own and sometimes to the group session, I think. But I don't go to that." Sadie made a sour face. "Too many people."

Caitlyn held her breath, afraid to make a peep as her sister opened up more to this complete stranger than she had to anyone since she'd moved back home. What kind of magic was Ash working on the kid?

Ash nodded thoughtfully but refrained from asking any other questions for a while. When she finally did, she'd changed to a completely different topic. "What's the best part of living back home?"

Caitlyn wished Ash had continued to ask about the boy. Other than having seen it on the team roster, his name wasn't familiar to her. That meant he hadn't been close enough friends with Alex Foster to be considered a witness in the family's suit, and his parents weren't wealthy or powerful enough to have made Caitlyn's shortlist of prospective clients to woo. Not to be insensitive, but he hadn't been important to her as far as work was concerned.

Now he was.

Caitlyn needed to know everything about Fergus Clark, and as soon as possible. With one lawsuit against the school involving its rowing coach already in the works, it hadn't escaped her that a wrongful death suit could be on the horizon. She wanted to know exactly what Sadie had overheard at practice, whether the boy who had died had ever been spoken to harshly by Coach Dryden or anyone else on the staff.

If it had been left up to Caitlyn, she might have interrogated her little sister with an intensity that would have given a CIA operative pause. But Ash seemed to have a better sense of what the kid could handle. Caitlyn would have to trust Ash to steer the conversation while Caitlyn steered the car. The sense of relief this gave Caitlyn brought with it a crushing sense of personal failure. Was she any better at caring for her sister than her father was?

"We have a big yard," Sadie replied after giving Ash's question some thought. The return of conversation in the back seat pulled Caitlyn out of her own head. "It's perfect for a puppy."

"Do you have one?" Ash asked.

"Not yet, but we're going to get one soon."

Caitlyn swallowed the urge to remind her sister they absolutely were not getting a puppy. This wasn't the time to smash puppy dreams. Caitlyn gripped the wheel even tighter as she changed lanes to get on the highway.

"I always wanted a place I could have a dog." Ash sounded so sincere Caitlyn was taken completely off guard. Was she for real, or was this just a way to make Sadie keep talking and stop her from brooding on the day's terrible turn of events? If the latter, the strategy was working.

As they continued the drive, Sadie delved into the details of all the different types of dogs she had researched, speaking at such a clip Caitlyn couldn't keep up. The kid was really dog crazy. Caitlyn hadn't realized exactly how much until now. And she couldn't help thinking about how natural Ash made this look, and how lucky Sadie was to have someone like that with her at this difficult time. Even if it was an act.

It had to be an act, right? Because this version of Ash bore no resemblance to the woman who had so cruelly declared sleeping together a mistake.

Even so, what she was doing now for Sadie was a godsend. To think, for the past couple weeks, Caitlyn had been doing everything she could to sabotage Ash's happiness. Well, assuming hot tea, intact sandwiches, and functioning ballpoint pens brought the woman joy. Guilt pricked Caitlyn's insides, weaving through her and tying up all her emotions into a bundle she wasn't sure what to do with. Like living in a pit of bubbling magma, being grateful for a person who had made her feel like total crap was not a state of existence the human body had been designed to tolerate comfortably.

After about an hour in which clogged city streets gave way to highways and finally to leafy suburban neighborhood roads, Caitlyn guided the car down the drive to the house, her head spinning as she took in what the place must look like from Ash's eyes. No one had ever accused Dick Brewster of being subtle, and he'd bought this house for the same reason he did everything else. To impress. Earlier, Ash had accused Caitlyn of being a spoiled rich brat. After getting a load of where Caitlyn lived, that image would be burned into Ash's brain for good.

"You weren't kidding, Sadie. That sure is a yard." Ash's tone was filled with an awe that sounded genuine. It wasn't the response Caitlyn had expected and she once again wondered if that was an honest reaction or was only for Sadie's benefit. The Ash Caitlyn knew had no qualms railing against wealth and excess, nor was she prone to pulling punches.

Then again, how well did Caitlyn know Ash? Maybe not at all.

As they climbed out of the car, Sadie directed Ash around the house to the backyard, chattering the whole time about dogs they weren't ever going to get. Even so, Caitlyn appreciated Sadie's excitement. Under the sad circumstances, it was better than most of the alternatives.

When her sister and Ash had disappeared from sight, Caitlyn went through the empty house—Gilda had the weekend off—to the back deck. She took out her phone to fire off a series of texts to Larry Cooper, alerting him to what had happened at the regatta. The firm would need to get their investigator on the case immediately. There were so many ways this could blow up and it was Caitlyn's responsibility to protect Moorehead Academy from legal exposure as best as she could.

"How big does the pond have to be?" Sadie was saying as she and Ash came closer to the deck several minutes later.

Caitlyn slipped her phone into her pocket and leaned against the deck railing with a casualness she didn't feel. She was on edge, vaguely annoyed that her sister and Ash's return had interrupted her work.

World's shittiest sister, right here.

"Some of them can jump over twenty feet," Ash was saying.

"Isn't that amazing?" Sadie's eyes were huge as she hugged on Caitlyn's arm. "Can you believe it?"

"What am I supposed to be believing?" Caitlyn asked, certain her confusion was etched across every inch of her face.

"Diving dogs can jump more than twenty feet," Sadie said with a laugh, not clearing up the matter in the slightest.

"What is a diving dog?" Caitlyn asked, unable to completely tamp down her jealousy that Ash had managed to connect with Sadie in a way that continued to elude her own abilities.

"It's a competition," Sadie explained, her words coming out in a breathless rush. "The dogs run down a dock and the owner tosses a toy over the water and the dog has to leap over a pool trying to catch it."

"The one who catches the toy wins?" Caitlyn guessed, baffled by the conversation she'd stumbled into.

Sadie shook her head. "It's the length of their jumps. They get three tries. Some of them leap over twenty feet. It's amazing! I need to find out everything I can about it."

With that, Sadie marched inside the house, leaving Caitlyn feeling the same as when Sadie had tried to explain the incomprehensible string of letters and emojis that passed for language between her and her friends. Caitlyn was no stranger to abbreviations and texting, but she'd felt every year of their age difference in her bones on that one. That gap yawned even wider now, although not for Ash, it would seem. The woman, though even further from being a teenager than Caitlyn was, seemed to possess an almost magical ability to understand and connect with the kid.

Which was a real kick in the teeth considering what a total disaster Ash had been at connecting with a full-grown woman less than a minute after having her fingers inside her.

"What just happened?" Caitlyn asked as soon as her sister was out of earshot and she and Ash were alone on the deck. She shook her head to stop it from spinning.

"I think your sister has found a distraction," Ash replied, chuckling. She leaned against the railing a short distance from Caitlyn, tall and lean, and undeniably gorgeous, not to mention comforting simply in her presence as fellow human being in the midst of a stressing and terrible day, regardless of how Caitlyn felt about her. She was not so close as to be inappropriate, but not far enough away not to be distracting.

Like New Hampshire, maybe.

Caitlyn offered a weak smile. "That's good, I guess."

"Fergus Clark."

The shift in subject was so abrupt it nearly gave Caitlyn whiplash. "What about him?"

"Please tell me that wasn't the name the coach was screaming that morning at Moorehead."

Caitlyn sucked in a breath as the memory clicked. "I think it was."

"Shit." Ash tapped her foot against the bottom of the railing. "We have to get ahead of this."

"I'm already on it. I just texted Larry to give him the heads up," Caitlyn said, dread pooling in her belly.

"Good. We'll need someone to investigate the coach. How long has he been at Moorehead? What other schools has he coached for? What's his reputation? Has he been fired? Left mysteriously…?" Ash was one hundred percent in work mode. Caitlyn furiously typed notes into her phone, all the while asking herself how Ash could pull it off. Just ten seconds ago she'd been chattering about puppies like she was Sadie's age. Now she was super lawyer. Meanwhile Caitlyn had been frozen stiff, unable to comfort her own sister in a time of need.

How could Ash be so self-confident, so sure about her every action? Goodness knew the woman was far from perfect. And yet she carried herself like she was incapable of failure. Caitlyn ordered herself not to notice how very attractive this quality made her.

This was not the time for it.

"Ash?" Sadie opened the sliding door with one hand, holding her phone in the other, and stepped back outside. "What do you know about Portuguese water dogs?"

"Not a lot." Ash pressed her lips together in what Caitlyn recognized as her thinking pose. Caitlyn wondered if admitting she didn't know something had killed a piece of Ash's cocky soul.

"Can we go to Maine?" Sadie asked.

"Maine?" Caitlyn gave her head a shake as if trying to get a loose wire to reconnect. Her phone dinged with an incoming text from the office, which she hurried to check.

"Sadie," Ash said softly, "can you tell us anything else about Fergus?"

"He could be crude—you know, like all the older, popular boys tend to be," Sadie responded. "But he always said hello when we passed each other. I think he had a session with Dr. Barnes, the counselor, before me. I'd be in the waiting room and he'd always say hello and something else. Like a trademark saying. What was it?" Sadie closed her eyes but shook her head. "I'm sorry. I can't remember."

"It's okay. If it comes to you, let us know." Ash placed a hand on Sadie's shoulder. "Tell me more about this Portuguese water dog you've found in Maine."

"You've found what in Maine?" Caitlyn looked up from her phone, startled.

"Seriously?" Sadie rolled her eyes. "She doesn't listen when she's working."

"I do, and I'm not working." She tucked her phone back into a pocket, determined to do better. Especially with Ash, the very model of a perfect sister, here as a witness.

"You weren't texting the office like you normally do, day and night?"

Busted.

"You have my full attention now." Caitlyn's phone dinged again and she didn't make a move, although it took a lot more restraint than it should have, a whisper of guilt in her head for not paying more attention to Sadie from the start.

As if sensing it was family time, Ash said, "Uh, I probably should call an Uber."

"You can't stay?" Sadie turned her teary eyes to her sister, silently imploring Caitlyn to stop Ash from going.

"You're more than welcome to stay. We can chat about—" Caitlyn pulled up short, not wanting to mention Moorehead Academy again with Sadie around. Her sister would just take it as evidence she was right about work consuming the elder Brewster.

"About diving dogs." As if knowing what Caitlyn was thinking, Ash was quick to jump in with an alternative that would save her butt with Sadie yet again.

"Yes!" Sadie declared. "I really want to—Wait. Hold that thought. My friend Libby's calling me. She's on the varsity girls' team. I think she had a crush on Fergus last year. She's gonna want to talk."

Sadie disappeared inside. Caitlyn sighed after the sliding door clicked closed, the weight of everything—being a guardian to a teenager, inexplicable tragedy striking a young person, trying to keep her career on track, and this sudden pressure to get a pet—closing in. "Why are you encouraging her?"

"Who?" Ash seemed genuinely befuddled. "Sadie?"

"Yes." Caitlyn's jaw tensed as she willed herself to keep things cordial. After all, Ash had been a lifesaver today, which had earned her certain privileges, like polite conversation. And probably hot tea from now on. "With all this talk about dogs."

"You're the ones getting a dog," Ash argued. "I just mentioned the diving part."

"We're *not* getting a dog." Caitlyn took a deep breath, sensing her control slipping from her. How many more commitments would she be forced to make that she wasn't ready for? As if raising a teenager out of the blue hadn't been enough.

"Have you been listening to your sister at all?" Ash's tone wasn't reproachful, but Caitlyn couldn't help reading her own guilt into it.

"I didn't want to say no, not after the day she's had." Caitlyn slumped. "You're not helping."

"How was I supposed to know?" Ash placed a hand on her chest.

"How will I manage a dog, along with Sadie, and work?" Caitlyn could no longer keep all her worries from tumbling out, even if it meant making a fool of herself in front of the one woman who had every reason to use it to her advantage. "I can barely keep track of anything. The stress is unreal. If it wasn't for Gilda, we'd starve. She's been more of a mother to Sadie than I can ever learn to be."

"Who's Gilda?" Ash wore a pinched expression, her lips pressed thin.

"Our housekeeper." Caitlyn braced herself for the inevitable comment about their privileged lifestyle, even as she wondered if that funny look on Ash's face—which had abruptly disappeared at Caitlyn's explanation—had been brought on by jealousy at hearing the mention of another woman's name.

Ash started to speak, but stopped herself, finally settling on, "I didn't know I was causing problems for you."

The statement sounded genuine, and completely lacking the woman's usual combativeness. Caitlyn felt the fight seep out of her, along with her strength. She moved from the railing, sinking into one of the curved rattan sofas that surrounded a tall, round outdoor cocktail table. Ash followed suit, choosing the sofa next to Caitlyn.

Caitlyn chuckled quietly, recalling the earlier conversation. "Do diving dogs even exist or was that all you could come up with on the spot?"

"I'd never lie about something like that." Ash raised a hand and traced a cross over her heart. "I've watched them compete."

Caitlyn sniffed. "Where? Some magical pond in a forest that only you can see?"

"I'm telling you, it's a real thing." Ash's eyes narrowed. "Why don't you believe me? I don't have a history of lying to you."

"Only about knowing who I am," Caitlyn reminded her snappishly. It appeared not all of the fight was gone after all.

"Well, yeah. That." Ash paired the admission with a shit-eating grin and something inside Caitlyn broke wide open.

"You are so goddamn cocky," Caitlyn growled, a blind anger swirling inside her chest, forcing out all the doubt and self-loathing she'd been carrying around most of the day. Anger was an emotion she knew what to do with. She leaned into it, lashing out to finally hurt someone other than herself. "You think you can come here and be a better sister than I am, huh? Because you know everything. Nothing ever bothers you."

"I was just trying to help." Ash's eyes were wide with surprise over Caitlyn's sudden onslaught of vitriol.

"By promising her a puppy?" Caitlyn was shaking. She had no business being pissed at Ash, who'd been the one to channel Sadie towards something pleasant, instead of the death of a classmate. But it felt so fucking good she couldn't pull back. The woman just seemed to have that effect on her. "It's super easy to be the favorite with a kid when you go bribing them."

"Look, I'm not trying to undermine you with your sister—"

"I'm more concerned with how you're filling Sadie's head with hopes that will be dashed." Blood pounded in Caitlyn's ears and her breath came in gulps as the memories of every time her father had failed her mixed with every way she feared she was going to fail Sadie and mess her up for good.

"I wouldn't do that." There was an underlying ribbon of steel in Ash's tone that made Caitlyn tense. All at once it was like she was standing in the eye of her own anger tornado, getting a glimpse of the damage she was causing to everything around her.

A tear burned a salty path along Caitlyn's cheek. She let it roll, not bothering to wipe it away.

"She's fragile. Not just because of what happened today." Caitlyn's words came out in a hoarse, pleading whisper. She wasn't sure what she was begging for, except maybe absolution. The universe had tested her today, and she'd failed on every front.

"Honest, Caitlyn. I never meant to do anything like that. I just mentioned diving dogs in passing. How was I supposed to know she'd run with it?" There was an earnestness in Ash's dark eyes that managed to penetrate the wreckage of Caitlyn's psyche. Finally, a sense of calm began to settle, bringing hope that the storm had passed.

"I believe you." And deep down, Caitlyn was beginning to trust her too. The latter was an odd and unexpected feeling.

"I really am sorry about the dog thing."

"And I'm sorry about..." Caitlyn ran through all the possibilities, finally settling on, "your sandwich. And the tea. And your pens."

"That *was* you." Ash slapped her palm to her knee. "Wait. My pens?"

"You might want to get a new box from the supply

closet." Caitlyn's cheeks burned as she recalled what she'd done, and she hoped Ash wouldn't push for more of an explanation. It was too embarrassing.

Ash pressed her lips together, her expression both searching and troubled. "I don't get it. What did I do to make you so mad?"

Caitlyn nearly choked on her own tongue. "Are you serious?"

"Well..." Doubt flickered in Ash's eyes. "I mean, yeah. I thought we were on the same page about everything, and then—"

"You... you said I was a *mistake*." Caitlyn stared at the woman as understanding slowly dawned on her face, flabbergasted that she hadn't gotten it until it was spelled out. Maybe Ash didn't have all her shit together as much as she wanted people to think, after all. "Do you know how many times growing up my father made me feel like that, like having me was one big cosmic mistake? Can you imagine for one second how that might have felt, right after we'd—"

"Oh shit." Now that she got it, Ash looked horrified. "That wasn't... I was only trying to say... No. It doesn't even matter. You're right. That was a fucked up thing to say. I am so sorry, Caitlyn."

"I..." Caitlyn swallowed, her throat thick with too many emotions to name. "It's okay."

"You're sure? Can you forgive me for saying something that stupid?" Ash had slid to the edge of the cushion, and it almost seemed a single harsh word from Caitlyn would send her tumbling to the floor.

"Yeah, I'm sure. And yes. I guess I can." Oddly,

Caitlyn no longer felt even a hint of the animosity she'd harbored toward Ash the past few weeks. She wasn't sure what their status would become—simply colleagues, or maybe friends—but she was glad Ash had stayed. "Back to the diving dogs. You swear to God that's a real thing?"

"A hundred percent." Ash laughed and Caitlyn couldn't help joining in. "I've only seen them on ESPN. I'd love to see it live."

Caitlyn tilted her head to the side. "You'd love to watch dogs dive into a pool, for sport?"

"Yes." Ash's brow furrowed. "Why are you looking at me like that?"

"Like what?"

"Like I've lost my mind."

"I wonder." Caitlyn couldn't quite hold back a laugh. All things considered, she figured she had the right to a brief laugh at Ash's expense.

"I can go if you want," Ash offered softly. She was looking at Caitlyn like she was a wild animal that might bite. Instantly, Caitlyn stopped laughing and grew serious.

"No, Sadie wants you here." Caitlyn blew out a frustrated breath, unwilling to admit the truth. She wanted Ash here too. The prospect of being left alone to deal with Sadie's potential mood swings was more than she could bear. Ash's competence was about the most amazing and reassuring thing Caitlyn had ever experienced in her life. "I'm not handling things well."

"It's been a peculiar day."

"I do appreciate everything you've done." That was too mild a word for how Caitlyn actually felt, but it was the safest explanation and would have to do. Colleagues or friends were both options on the table, but nothing more than that. It was better not to say anything to put that at risk.

Sadie stuck her head out the door. "Ash, do you have a second to come inside? I'd like to show you that website for the rescue in Maine."

"What should I say?" Ash whispered, eyes filled with what could only be described as terror as she scanned Caitlyn's face.

"Say yes," Caitlyn coached, propping an elbow on the edge of the sofa and resting her head against her palm. "Looks like we're getting a puppy. In Maine."

Ash disappeared into the house, leaving Caitlyn alone with her thoughts. Considering how upsetting the day had been, she felt oddly at peace, and she was shocked to realize how much Ash's presence had brought this calming effect. Ash, who could be just as ruthless and work-obsessed as Caitlyn, had a surprising gift with young people. And with making troubles fade away, regardless of one's age, Caitlyn noted. Even if she did introduce new, canine-shaped troubles in their place. Among other complications.

But was it genuine?

Caitlyn had been fooled before, not just by Ash. Bridget had seemed too good to be true too. And then she'd stabbed Caitlyn in the back during their senior year, stealing her final project and passing it off as her own, making a fool of her in front of everyone. Since that day, any time Caitlyn's gut doubted whether to trust or not, she'd always erred on the side of caution.

Except when it came to Ash.

The caring person who'd sat with Sadie and calmed her anxiety was the polar opposite of the cold-hearted officemate who seemed ready to turn on anyone at a moment's notice.

Or sleep with a woman one minute and declare it a mistake the next. Only, the sting was gone from that memory, too, and there was nothing Caitlyn could do to bring it back.

Mistakes happen. Forgive and forget.

Maybe Ash wasn't so bad after all.

Unless that was just what Ash wanted Caitlyn to think.

CHAPTER FIFTEEN

The evening sky was turning a pinkish purple as a slight breeze off the ocean caused Ash to snuggle further under a plush throw blanket on Caitlyn's back deck. She let out a contented sigh.

"You sound relaxed." Caitlyn came out from the house where she had been checking on her sister, closing the sliding door behind her.

"I don't get many nights like this." Ash knew there were serious matters to discuss, but despite the tragic reason behind it, the time she'd spent with Caitlyn and Sadie had been so much nicer than she could have imagined. After the blowout earlier and the surprisingly satisfying resolution, Ash didn't want the pleasant camaraderie to end.

"What do you mean?" Caitlyn asked in a curious tone. "Nights like what?"

Ash's arm swept the view. "Outside in the fresh air, the sound of waves hitting the shore. I love that my apartment is close to work, but I can see how it would be worth the commute to come home to this at the end of the day."

"Sadly, I don't get much time out here." Caitlyn sat down, this time choosing the sofa Ash was on, the one facing the water. "Are you warm enough?"

"The blanket's helping," Ash assured her. Though the temperature was getting colder by the minute, she was reluctant to give up the view. She doubted she'd see anything like it again for a long time. "Unless you want to go inside."

"I'm in the same boat as you. My fresh air quotient is shockingly low." Caitlyn's mouth curved into a shy smile. "Thank you for helping with Sadie today. You're really good with her."

"She's a great kid and I know what it's like. Not fitting in."

"I wish I could help her more." The doubt and self-reproach in Caitlyn's tone broke Ash's heart. In addition to shining an uncomfortably bright light on her own failings, Caitlyn's outburst earlier had given her new insight on the demons this woman was battling, and how similar in so many ways they were to her own.

"You are helping her." Ash turned toward Caitlyn, sending every ounce of earnestness she possessed into her words, willing Caitlyn to believe her. "You moved home because she needed you. Not many people would do that, even for family. I remember what it was like when my dad died. I can count on one hand how many of my friends stayed in touch when we had to move. People show their true colors in times of crisis, and in my experience, most are very disappointing."

"Tell me about it. Our own father hasn't done shit during all of this." Caitlyn released a ragged breath full of such pain it prompted Ash to shiver. Mistaking the reaction for a chill, Caitlyn said, "Let me see if I can do something to warm us up."

Instantly, Ash's brain betrayed her with several images of possible activities—all of them extremely X-rated—that would keep them very warm indeed. She wrapped her arms tightly across her chest, less to preserve body heat as to keep her hands from acting on any of these impulses before she had a chance to stop herself. Groping the colleague she'd already made the mistake—no, Ash would never so much as think the word *mistake* again where Caitlyn was concerned. But giving into temptation and sleeping together had been an error of judgement, and one that could harm them both in their careers. Ash needed to do the right thing and keep her desires firmly at bay.

Leaning forward, Caitlyn fidgeted with something on the side of the cocktail table. A moment later, blue flames danced from what had appeared to be a centerpiece of glass stones.

"Fancy." Ash let out a low whistle as she held her cold fingertips near the fire. "You really do know how to live."

"Is that another attempt at class warfare?" Caitlyn sat back, wrapping her own blanket around herself.

"I'm sorry about that too." Ash pressed her lips together as she recalled all the occasions she had given the woman a hard time for her wealthy background. "I can be an ass sometimes."

"Only sometimes?"

Ash leaned across the empty space between them, digging her elbow into Caitlyn's side. "You give as good as you get."

Ash regretted the comment the instant the words leapt from her tongue. Perhaps it was the relaxed atmosphere they were enjoying, or the sudden lack of physical distance between them, but an odd expression landed on Caitlyn's face, her cheeks turning rosy. Ash hadn't intended what she'd said to be sexual, but it sure could have been taken that way. Maybe Ash wasn't the only one struggling to keep this interaction on strictly friendly terms. She wasn't sure if that made her feel better or worse.

"How's Sadie?" Ash quickly asked, hoping to toss cold water on whatever memories might start dancing through both their heads.

It did the trick. Caitlyn rolled her eyes playfully. "She's *vibing* with her friends online."

Ash played the unfamiliar slang over in her mind. "Is that what they call hanging out now?"

"Apparently. They're playing D&D. It's all the rage."

"Whoa, like Dungeons and Dragons?" Ash chuckled as Caitlyn nodded. "No way. I know that one, although it was firmly in the domain of geeks back in my day."

"Oh, mine too," Caitlyn assured her with a laugh.

"How about Super Mario? Did they still play that when you were a kid?" Considering they'd graduated law school contemporaneously and were on the same rung of the ladder at work, this was the first time Ash had really stopped to recall the eight-year age difference between them.

"If you mean *New* Super Mario, then totes." Caitlyn giggled at the use of the slang from her childhood.

"Dang. I played the original. It was all that and a bag of chips when I was in middle school. Pretty sure I can kick your New Super Mario butt," Ash teased, unable to resist some favorite childhood slang of her own.

"We might have to test that theory someday," Caitlyn scoffed, her eyes twinkling with mischief in the light of the fire.

For a moment, Ash could picture a world in which something like that could take place between them. Deep down, a part of her longed for that world to be real, even if the stoically rational part of her acknowledged she and Caitlyn could never *really* be friends outside a professional, work-based relationship. They were too different.

Weren't they?

How the hell would I know? Ash asked herself reprovingly. It wasn't like she was exactly the friendship expert.

Before Ash could get herself into trouble exploring the answer to her own question, she changed the subject. "Any word from the investigator on cause of death yet?"

"No, not yet." Caitlyn's expression grew serious. "Plenty of speculation among the students, though. It's all Sadie and her friends are talking about upstairs."

Ash's heart became heavy. "I can imagine."

"There were no rumors of big parties with lots of

drinking, at least not last night," Caitlyn continued. "So probably not alcohol poisoning. Best-case scenario, it was drugs."

"Fingers crossed," Ash agreed. From the perspective of the school administration, that would be least likely to lead to criminal charges or lawsuits.

"I assume we won't have the toxicology report for a few weeks," Caitlyn said.

"If we're lucky. Could take longer the way the labs get backed up, although with it being a kid…" Ash's voice trailed off as she took in exactly what she was saying. "How bad does it make us that we're rooting for a teenager to have had a drug problem right now?"

"I don't know what it says about us as people, but it makes us good lawyers." Caitlyn paused, swallowing hard in a way that made Ash think she wasn't as comfortable with that reality as she was trying to pretend. "If it turns out to be suicide, it'll be a hell of a lot of work. We'll need to dig up everything about everyone. Fergus, his teachers, friends, coaches, bullies."

"Even the campus squirrels aren't off the hook."

"Murderous squirrels? That's a novel idea." Caitlyn leaned forward to adjust the fire table, making the flames stronger. When she returned to her place, her body was so close Ash could feel the heat, and for a crazy moment she fantasized about cuddling up together beneath the blanket. "Given Fergus was on campus at the time of his death, drugs that he procured from home would be the safest outcome from a liability standpoint. But until there's an official cause of death, we'll proceed as if it's the worst-case scenario."

"Agreed."

Seemingly without realizing it, Caitlyn snuggled closer to Ash. "You sure you aren't too cold?"

Ash shook her head, afraid if she gave a longer answer or called any attention to the way their thighs were now touching, Caitlyn might pull away. If that happened, Ash might become chilled all the way to her core.

"Can I ask you a question?" Caitlyn asked.

"Does it involve how to get away with murder?"

Caitlyn chuckled. "No. Given the background of how your dad died, how did you end up working at McGill and Harding?"

"As I recall, it all started when I mopped the floor with a certain Elle Woods wannabe at a mock trial competition some six years ago."

Caitlyn nudged Ash's shoulder with hers, the entire sides of their bodies pressed close. Ash held her breath, not daring so much as to whisper. It felt so good she wanted to spin around the deck in the firelight, singing at the top of her lungs like a total lunatic.

"They're like the very definition of soul-sucking corporate law," Caitlyn went on, not seeming to be impacted by the proximity of their bodies, but also not making any attempt to put distance between them. "I'd have thought you'd want to be a social justice warrior."

Ash arched an eyebrow. "Are you saying our clients are the baddies?"

"Considering I'm praying for a dead kid to have had a raging addiction to illicit substances, I think it's safe to say we spend a lot of time lurking in the gray areas."

Ash was somewhat taken aback by the sentiment, not

least of all because it was Caitlyn expressing it, the one person who was every bit as dedicated and competitive as Ash herself. Questioning the legitimacy of their work wasn't the type of thing Ash let herself do, perhaps because she knew in the furthest reaches of her conscience that she wouldn't like the result.

"When I was in school," Ash said after a long pause, "my focus was on being the best. My first step was to prove I was good enough, that I was better than so many of the pampered students who had the benefit of the right family connections. I landed at McGill and Harding because I got my foot in the door, thanks to the mock trial win."

"That's the only reason?" Caitlyn bit into her lower lip, shifting her body in a subtle way that nonetheless reminded Ash they were still touching in a hundred different spots, like tiny prickles of heat all along her body. "What was the second step? You know, after proving you were good enough."

"I don't know," Ash confessed. "I'm still working on step one."

Caitlyn's eyes widened. "Are you serious? Ash, you're the best in the office by a mile."

"Until you showed up." Ash was half teasing, but she also knew it was true. Caitlyn was her equal in a way no one else Ash had ever encountered had been. It was inspiring, and frightening. If she wasn't the best, Ash wasn't sure she would know who she was anymore. "What's your excuse?"

Caitlyn narrowed her eyes. "For?"

Ash focused on the fire. "It doesn't seem like you're

hurting for money. Why aren't you fighting the good fight on behalf of the little people?"

"You honestly think I'm that type?" Caitlyn's head was tilted, and it was hard to tell if she was offended or amused.

"Yes." For some reason she couldn't put a finger on, Ash truly did believe Caitlyn was the type to care more for justice than money. "I don't know why, but I get the feeling you want to make the world a better place. So how did you end up at a firm you referred to not two minutes ago as the very definition of soul sucking?"

Caitlyn let out a low, mirthless laugh. "The same reason as you, in a way. I have this insane need to prove myself, and nothing else does that quite as well as corporate law. In my case it's not money or education, it's me. Miss Legally Blonde. You said it yourself."

Ash's stomach clenched. "I didn't mean—"

Caitlyn held up a hand. "It's okay. But women must be perfect to succeed. The right résumé. The right appearance. One misstep and we're ruined. Failing upward only happens to members of the boy's club. I like to win."

Ash sighed, closing her eyes against the flickering flames. Exhaustion moved through her like roots through soil, establishing itself in her very bones. "I'm tired of proving I'm better than the rest in the office."

"You are, though," Caitlyn said softly.

A warm glow tingled through Ash's middle, like a ray of sunlight on a summer's day. "I may regret this tomorrow, but you are too."

"Oh, you're definitely going to regret that," Caitlyn announced with obvious glee.

It was dark and growing truly frigid, but Ash didn't want their conversation to end. "Which movie most inspired you to become a lawyer?"

Caitlyn answered immediately. *"A Time to Kill.* You?"

"The Client." Ash's response was just as swift.

"I wonder how many lawyers have been inspired by those movies?"

Ash thought for a moment before saying, "My dad's death had a bigger impact. And you were right. When I first thought about becoming a lawyer, I wanted to right all the wrongs."

"I knew it. Social justice warrior."

"It's just…" Ash swallowed the lump that had formed in her throat. "I try to remember him the way he was before the injury. He was the type of dad who took me to see the Red Sox, always getting me the ice cream in the helmet. Before the oxy took control." Ash's voice warbled. "I'm sorry. At least I got some years with a good dad. My siblings didn't. And I guess you didn't, either, from what you've said."

"Yes and no. At least I had Gilda, plus my grandmother on my mom's side. Sadie didn't get that, and I think we're seeing how much that's impacted her."

"She has a lot of anxiety?"

"Always has. This year has been the worst, so bad she couldn't live in the dorms on campus." Caitlyn's shoulders slumped. "Maybe I should get her tickets to the Red Sox game, buy an ice cream."

"Ice cream is always the right answer," Ash said. "It can't hurt."

"It's the little things we remember," Caitlyn remarked.

The woman's melancholy tone struck a chord in Ash's soul, a deep sadness that resonated within her chest. "I worry that in ten years, I won't have any little things to remember. All I do is work."

"We aren't working now." Caitlyn waved at the fire. "We're sitting outside under the stars, listening to the ocean. Like normal people, almost."

"True." The realization of exactly how good that felt hit Ash hard, nearly knocking the wind out of her. And it struck her, too, that maybe all the work she did wasn't only for the benefit of her family. Maybe it was because it allowed her to avoid certain truths about herself, like how some part of her longed for more experiences like this. And how she was afraid she didn't deserve them, or would never be able to earn them.

Wanting was dangerous.

Take tonight, for instance. How would Ash handle it when this came to an end and everything went back to the way it had been before? Minus the cold tea, and whatever the hell this crazy woman had done to Ash's pens.

"Are you okay?" Concern etched Caitlyn's face.

Ash couldn't sit and wait for the inevitable to happen. At least if she was the one to act, she could remain in control. "I should probably get an Uber and get home."

"Don't be ridiculous," Caitlyn chastised. "You can stay the night."

Ash's heart pounded. "That didn't go so well a few weeks ago."

"I meant in a guest room." Caitlyn shot Ash a wry look. "We have six spare bedrooms. You can have your choice."

"Six?" Ash turned to look back at the house. Yeah, okay, there was definitely room for six and bonus spaces as well. "Seems excessive."

"Oh, it's completely excessive. My father doesn't do anything by half measures. Including his wine collection." Caitlyn grinned wickedly. "We can open up a bottle of chianti."

"You didn't get your chianti when we went out."

"I didn't."

"I hope that was your only disappointment," Ash said before she could stop herself.

Caitlyn's mouth twitched. "I think it was sufficiently disappointing on its own, don't you? After all, you promised me the best meal ever, which always includes a glass of chianti."

"It does?" Ash opened her eyes comically wide, thankful Caitlyn had decided to joke with her about their ill-fated night instead of becoming upset again. That had nearly torn a hole through her gut. "This is a rule I didn't know. I guess we will have to fix that by having chianti now."

"And dinner."

At the mention of food, Ash's stomach rumbled. "When did we last eat?"

"I don't think we did," Caitlyn said. "Gilda has the

weekend off, and without her, I'm useless. But I just happen to know a place that makes the best pizza and they deliver."

"How fortunate for us." Ash wondered if this was as spontaneous as it seemed. Despite the smooth delivery, something about Caitlyn's performance made Ash suspect the woman had been scheming most of the evening for ways to make her stay. Or maybe that was wishful thinking.

"Shall we get the best pizza on the planet and dive into a bottle of chianti?" Caitlyn's offer was the most tempting thing Ash had ever encountered. And even though she'd already established that temptation was bad and to be avoided, she didn't have the heart to say no. It was only one night, and she wasn't ready for it to end.

"Well," she replied slowly. "Work is about to get intense with what happened today..."

"Which is why we should enjoy this night," Caitlyn said, smooth as silk. "Make it count."

"What's for dinner?" Sadie's voice floated onto the deck.

Caitlyn and Ash turned their heads toward her in unison, cracking up.

The girl frowned. "What's so funny?"

"Nothing." Caitlyn reached for her phone. "We were just talking about getting pizza."

"From Mama Maria's?"

"Is there any other place?"

"Let me know when it arrives and we can eat out here by the fire. We don't do that enough." Sadie disappeared.

"Are you staying?" Caitlyn asked. "You've already been here most of the day. You probably have places to be. If it were just the two of us, I could understand if you said no, but Sadie will be heartbroken—"

"Yes, of course I'll stay," Ash broke in to reply. The truth was, she didn't want to be anywhere else.

CHAPTER SIXTEEN

"Is that for me?" Caitlyn eyed the disposable coffee cup in Ash's outstretched hand warily, not sure if she should trust the shift in their relationship since the weekend. There was no denying how valuable Ash's presence at the house had been after the regatta, but Caitlyn had half expected the temporary truce to end with the start of the workweek. Instead, Ash appeared to have brought a peace offering with her to the Moorehead campus Monday morning.

"I wasn't sure exactly how you take it," Ash said, handing Caitlyn the cup. "But based on the ungodly number of sweet coffee drinks I saw in your fridge, I went with extra cream and sugar."

"An excellent deduction, Sherlock." Caitlyn took a sip, letting out a sigh of contentment as they headed side by side toward the path to the school.

Piles of fallen leaves swirled like they'd been caught up in miniature tornadoes as Caitlyn and Ash approached the boathouse. Caitlyn loosened the scarf around her neck, a reaction that had nothing to do with the outside temperature and everything to do with Ash, who was standing in such close proximity it was all Caitlyn could do to keep herself from running her fingers along the soft wool of the woman's coat. It was something Caitlyn wouldn't have dreamed of doing just last week, but a lot had changed since then.

"Beautiful day," Caitlyn remarked, stunned that after the intimacy of conversing together on her back deck until after midnight only two nights before, the best topic she could come up with now was the weather.

"Soon the snow will be flying." It was hard to assess Ash's mood. Was she happy about the prospect of winter, or sad? Or maybe she felt as awkward as Caitlyn did trying to strike up a conversation with someone who until recently had been a sworn enemy.

"I'm not looking forward to snow," Caitlyn replied, seeing no reason to be diplomatic about it. If Ash was psycho enough to want slushy sidewalks and icy driveways, it was better to know now while there was still a chance to return to the status quo of hating each other.

"I don't know." Ash paused and Caitlyn's belly tightened as she anticipated having to sever all ties with the winter-loving freak. "I'm not usually a fan of the cold, but lately I've been thinking about cuddling up in front of a fireplace at night, sipping c—cognac..." After correcting herself, Ash let the statement trail off.

"Big cognac fan are you?" Caitlyn quirked an eyebrow, certain Ash had been about to say chianti but changed her mind at the last second. If that was the case, it suggested their late-night gab fest around the fire table, emptying the better part of a full bottle of chianti, had impacted Ash as much as it had Caitlyn.

Ash mumbled something unintelligible, her face much redder than what could be attributed to the wind alone. Caitlyn pulled her scarf closer to her face to disguise the smile blossoming on her lips.

"Coach Clay," Caitlyn called out when they entered the boathouse, instantly recognizing the sole occupant of the space, a young man in his mid-twenties, as the assistant varsity coach.

He looked up, startled. Caitlyn and Ash didn't have an appointment, having agreed that turning up unannounced was often the best way to get information. People tended to talk more freely when given less time to prepare a statement ahead.

"No comment." The coach tucked his head down into his blue and white hoodie with Moorehead Badgers emblazoned across the chest.

"We're not reporters," Ash jumped in to assure him.

"That's right," Caitlyn added. "We're attorneys from McGill and Harding. The school administration has hired our firm to handle the Alex Foster lawsuit."

The coach poked his head up an inch, like a turtle on the verge of venturing outside its shell. "Foster? I thought you were here about Fergus, like all the rest."

"Ah." Caitlyn nodded with understanding. "Has the press been calling?"

"Nonstop." The coach's jaw tensed. "And some vultures from the tabloids have been circling campus too."

Caitlyn tucked that nugget away, wanting to get to the

other matter at hand in as delicate a way as possible. The last thing she needed was to spook the poor guy. Once they had what they needed for the Foster case, she'd try to turn the conversation toward Fergus as gently as she could.

"Look, we're just here to fill in a few missing blanks," Caitlyn soothed, using the same tone she might employ with a startled cat hiding under a mattress. "We need to ascertain the relationship style Coach Dryden uses with the team."

"In your opinion," Ash cut in, "is Coach Dryden a bully?"

Caitlyn sucked in a groan. Apparently, Ash's interrogation methods were a lot less delicate than Caitlyn's. Rather like trying to coax the frightened kitten out by waving a broom around and shouting, "Here, kitty!"

Reacting to Ash's question by immediately stiffening up, Coach Clay removed his baseball cap and shoved loose strands of hair off his forehead. "No."

"Just no?" Ash pressed.

"Ash…" Caitlyn hissed in a whisper, but the woman ignored her.

The coach took his hat off again, twirling it slowly in one hand as he contemplated the Moorehead logo. "He's not what I might call a teddy bear, but he's not a bully, either. That's an ugly word."

Caitlyn opened her mouth but Ash beat her to it. "I heard him scream at the kids with my own ears during practice just a few weeks ago, using some very ugly language."

"I'm sure he had a reason," Coach Clay argued, still fiddling with the hat.

"I don't know. He said some words I don't ever say." As Ash said this, it struck Caitlyn that her colleague hardly ever swore.

In fact, Caitlyn could only remember hearing her do it once or twice, aside from the dirty things she'd said when they'd been in bed. A wave of heat engulfed Caitlyn at the memory and she tugged at her collar. The woman could say all sorts of deliciously raunchy things when the time and place suited her. If it hadn't been for that, Caitlyn might've thought Ash was a prude.

"Dryden can be gruff," the coach was saying as Caitlyn lassoed her attention and dragged herself back to the conversation. "But he knows what he's doing."

"And what is he doing?" Caitlyn pressed, partially to give the impression she'd been following all along instead of fondly reminiscing about having raunchy sex with her coworker.

"Motivating the boys to bring their A games and level up." The coach put his hat back on, giving the bill a firm tug.

"By calling them names?" Caitlyn crossed her arms, unconvinced.

Coach Clay shook his head. "By reaching in deep to pull out their inner demons, to exorcise them."

Caitlyn had no response but Ash appeared to mull over this answer for a moment before asking, "What was Alex Foster's inner demon? Because to hear his parents tell it, he had a learning disability and Dryden ridiculed him for it."

"Alex was no different from any of the other boys when it came to smarts," the man said. "And it wasn't like we gave out math tests before hitting the water. Coach Dryden doesn't care about that kind of thing. He's focused on the sport, the team. He cares about making the boys better athletes and better men."

"And Alex?" Caitlyn prompted.

"I think Dryden understood Alex better than anyone else here."

"What does that mean?" Ash asked.

"Dryden's had to work his way to the top. He didn't have connections."

"I know how that is," Ash said encouragingly. Caitlyn couldn't help flashing her an appreciative look. This contribution was much better than the waving a broom at a kitten approach she'd been using earlier.

"Then I bet you know," Coach Clay said. "A place like Moorehead, you can barely kick a leaf without uncovering someone who had the right father, or uncle, or what have you, to get them where they are. Students and faculty alike."

"Not Alex?"

"Alex's family had money for tuition, but he wasn't a legacy. If he hadn't struggled in mainstream classes in the public school, his family wouldn't have sent him here. Coach was an outsider, just like Alex."

"They were alike?" Ash suggested.

"Only to a point. Alex was an asshole." For a moment, Coach Clay looked like he wanted to retract that last word, but then he shrugged. "I hate to say it, and I know the kid had problems, but when all is said and done, Alex wasn't a very nice guy. I suggested to Coach more than once to remove him from the team. I thought his negativity was bringing all the guys down, but Dryden didn't want to give up on Alex."

"Because he was the best rower?" Caitlyn asked. She had taken a look at the stats and knew Alex Foster had been one of the elite members of the team the previous year.

"Nah, he wasn't, though. Not after—" The coach stopped talking mid-sentence, like his battery had run out.

"After what?"

He let out a breath. "Fergus, actually. Dryden rode his ass about it hard. And say what you like, but it worked. Fergus got himself a personal trainer two summers ago and by the time last season started, he and Alex were neck and neck."

"Which meant Coach Dryden had little to lose by taking revenge on the kid with the attitude and reporting him for a minor infraction," Caitlyn pointed out. "I'm not convinced Alex was the only asshole."

The assistant coach's eyes flashed, his mannerisms becoming more animated. "Hell, Alex should have been kicked off the team a hundred times for the shit he pulled. I mean, after what he did at the end-of-summer JV barbecue last year?"

Ash's eyebrows raced up her forehead in tandem. "What'd he do?"

Coach Clay's mouth clamped shut and he shook his head. "I've told you all I'm going to say. If you don't mind, I have some place I need to be."

With that, the young man marched out of the boathouse without looking back.

"Now what?" Ash asked Caitlyn once they were alone. "Should we rifle through his things, see if we can find some clues?"

"Are you an attorney at one of the region's top law firms or a private investigator in a bad mobster movie?" Caitlyn asked with a laugh. "No, we're not going to rummage through his locker without permission."

"You have a better idea?" Ash gave her that look that screamed *I dare you*. It was the type of look that left Caitlyn uncertain whether she wanted to prove the woman wrong or push her up against the wall and ravage her mouth with kisses.

Honestly? Probably both.

"Yes, I have a better idea," Caitlyn said smugly, settling for the safer of the two options. "Sadie."

"Your sister." Ash frowned. "Want to be more specific?"

"Alex Foster's family is arguing that he was a good kid who was bullied by an evil coach, who ultimately had him removed from school for a minor infraction out of spite—and that the administration sat back and let it happen."

"Yeah…" It was clear Ash hadn't put the pieces together yet, which increased Caitlyn's smugness by about a hundred percent.

"If we can establish Alex had a pattern of poor behavior his coach overlooked out of kindness, and that the altercation that led to the expulsion was simply the last straw, it will be hard to convince a jury Alex was being bullied or that our client failed in their duty to protect him." Caitlyn watched Ash intently to see if she was catching on, but from the look of confusion on the woman's face, the answer continued to elude her. "We need to find out what happened at the JV barbecue."

"And your sister is on the JV team," Ash said, slapping a palm to her forehead as she finally figured it out. "But what I don't get is, if it was something bad, why didn't the Head of School say anything about it when we were here before?"

"She probably didn't know." Caitlyn placed her hand lightly on Ash's back to lead her out the door and in the direction of the library where Sadie and her friends were likely to be gathered before classes started. "If you want to know the real dirt of what's going on at an elite private school, you don't talk to anyone connected with the administration."

"Should we go talk to your sister now?"

"On one condition." Caitlyn held back a smirk. "You leave the interrogations to me."

Ash pressed a hand to her chest. "What did I do wrong?"

"You just about went for the coach's jugular back there when I was trying to butter him up."

"I thought we were playing good cop, bad cop."

Caitlyn laughed. "Okay, but no bad cop with Sadie and her friends."

"I would never," Ash assured her. "I don't want your sister to hate me."

Caitlyn snuck a glance at Ash as they walked, curious why it mattered to her what Sadie thought of her. Did she truly care, or was she simply looking for an ego boost?

"Sadie!" Caitlyn called out softly, spying her sister and two other girls at a small study table near the front of the library. "Just who I was hoping to see."

Sadie smiled, her eyes lighting up with extra shine when she spotted her sister's companion. "Ash! What are you doing here?"

"We needed to ask one of the coaches some questions relating to the Alex Foster case," Caitlyn explained. "But that brought up another topic I was hoping you might be able to shed some light on. What happened at the JV barbecue last year?"

The three girls exchanged worried looks.

"No one's getting in trouble," Ash soothed, taking on the role of good cop this time. "We just want to know what happened."

"The whole team got wasted," one of the girls answered.

The color leeched from Sadie's cheeks. "It wasn't our fault, I swear. Someone spiked the punch at the party."

"Why didn't I hear about this?" Caitlyn snapped before she could stop herself. A sense of panic overtook her as she thought of all the terrible things that could have happened. "Was it alcohol, or drugs? My God, someone could have been assaulted, or worse."

"Nobody got hurt. I… I wasn't trying to keep it secret or anything," Sadie stammered, tears welling in her eyes. "I swear. It's not like Dad cared, and you were in New York."

"You're sure no one was hurt?" Caitlyn pressed. She

wished her father was home so she could give him a piece of her mind. And she wished the fact she'd chosen a life in New York just to get out from under her family legacy so she could make it on her own didn't make her feel so shitty about her priorities.

"Everybody was okay by the next day," one of the friends answered as Sadie nodded in agreement. "Hungover, but that's all."

"Did the school call your parents?" Ash asked.

The other friend bit her lip. "I don't think so. It was just the coaches chaperoning, you know? I think they just wanted to keep it from turning into a big deal if the Head of School found out."

"Nobody got written up for it?" Caitlyn asked.

All three of them shook their heads.

"Like I said, it wasn't our fault," Sadie insisted. "It was Alex who put the alcohol in the drinks. He wasn't even supposed to be at the party, but he snuck in and did it, and then stuck around to watch what we'd do."

"You're sure it was him?" Ash asked.

"Absolutely," one of the friends said. "We heard him laughing about it the next day. He flat out admitted what he'd done."

Caitlyn frowned. "He didn't get in trouble?"

"Coach Dryden was really mad when he found out," Sadie said. "He yelled at him, but he never filed a report or anything."

"Because he was the star of the varsity team," one friend added. "I remember Alex telling me he could get away with murder and the coach wouldn't lay a finger on him."

"He told me that as well," the other friend said. "Sometimes I thought he would try it. I was glad when he got expelled."

"Yeah," Sadie agreed. "Even if the reason for the expulsion was sus. I mean, swearing at the coach? Please. But I think Coach Dryden was waiting for any excuse once the Head of the Charles was over."

"Why did that matter?" Ash asked.

"It's the last big competition until spring," one of the girls explained, beating Caitlyn to the punch. "And by then, a couple other boys were narrowing in on Alex's times."

"Making Alex less vital to a winning team." A faint smile tugged at Caitlyn's lips as she realized her earlier hunch had been right. Only now that she'd heard the details, she no longer thought the coach was trying to take revenge. If anything, he'd acted way too late.

There may not have been an official paper trail detailing Alex's infractions, but considering how many students had witnessed his behavior, Caitlyn was pretty certain this case would never see the inside of a courtroom. No way would the Fosters be interested in having Alex's actions come to light. Considering he'd given alcohol to multiple minors, he could be facing criminal charges.

"These other boys," Ash began, stealing Caitlyn's attention back from her musing, "was one of them Fergus Clark?"

"Yes." Sadie and her friends grew melancholy. "It was him and two others on the varsity team."

"Do or die trying," a friend added with a loud sniff.

Sadie sucked in her breath. "Yes, that's right. That's what Fergus used to say to me in the counseling center. Do or die trying."

Caitlyn and Ash exchanged glances, and it was clear her colleague was thinking the same thing. Was this a harmless mantra, or was it evidence that supported the theory Fergus had killed himself?

Before Caitlyn could ask about it, there was a hustle and bustle around them. Kids were getting up from other tables, gathering their books and backpacks.

"We have to get to class." Sadie gave Caitlyn a one-armed hug before heading out of the library with her friends.

"And the plot thickens," Caitlyn said in her best TV crime show announcer voice when she and Ash were alone.

"It sounds like Alex was a terror," Ash commented. "Do you think his parents are aware of everything he did?"

"Parents never want to believe the bad stuff when it comes to their children." Caitlyn tapped a finger against her pant leg. "Unless you're my father. Then you just turn a blind eye."

"If it makes you feel better, my mom was the type to believe the bad things. Behind closed doors, at least. Outside of the home, she fought like hell for us."

Caitlyn's heart was heavy as she studied the spot where her sister had been sitting. "Do you think the party is one of the reasons why Sadie didn't want to be in the dorms this year?"

"Perhaps, but maybe ask her when you get a chance."

Caitlyn laughed.

Ash's cheeks colored. "I didn't mean to sound condescending."

"It's not that. This will sound stupid, but that didn't cross my mind. To simply ask Sadie the question." Caitlyn rocked onto her heels. "Do you think Alex's parents didn't ask the right questions before filing their lawsuit?"

"I don't know," Ash said, "but if they didn't, they've got a surprise coming. We need to get the investigator to put together a report. I have a feeling they'll be happy to settle quietly once they hear what we have to say."

"That's one problem solved, anyway." As they exited the library, Caitlyn caught sight of a police car rolling slowly away from one of the ivy-covered red brick dormitories and a lump formed in her throat. "Do or die trying."

Ash let out a heavy sigh, clearly on the same page. "Moorehead Academy may be in the clear with the Fosters, but they're not out of the woods."

"Not by a long shot," Caitlyn agreed.

With a star athlete dead and media sniffing all around, the school's troubles were far from over. They were in for a hellish few months, to say the least.

She cast a glance at Ash, looking away before getting caught, but not before her heart was made a little lighter. Somehow, knowing she and Ash were on the same team made the difficult tasks ahead seem a lot less impossible than if she'd been facing them on her own.

CHAPTER SEVENTEEN

Ash glanced in the rearview mirror, checking for cars, but the highway traffic was sparse. Outside the windows, the scenery was a blur of rust and brown, the past-peak remnants of a fall foliage season on its way to a close. Rain droplets splattered the windshield at intervals, offering another reason most people had stayed inside on this dreary Saturday morning instead of hitting the roads.

Sadie popped her head between the front seats. "We're getting a puppy!"

Excitement rolled off the girl in waves. Clearly she had not gotten the memo that this was a day meant for staying in bed. Not that Ash minded. If she hadn't been in the car with Caitlyn and Sadie she would be at her desk by now. She knew which one she preferred.

"Is your seatbelt buckled?" Ash demanded, earning an immediate withdrawal from Sadie, followed by the reassuring click of the belt.

"We're going to *look* at a puppy," Caitlyn corrected.

Her eyes skipped across to Ash, imploring her to corroborate. "We don't know what will happen."

But Ash shook her head as she pictured the Portuguese Water Dog and Labrador Retriever mix they were on their way to meet. "Sorry, but have you seen the photo of that little doll? I'm not convinced it's humanly possible not to take her home."

Caitlyn's shoulders slumped dramatically, making Ash chuckle to herself. The action didn't go unnoticed. Caitlyn shot daggers from the corners of her eyes, making Ash laugh even more.

"If you weren't the one driving, I'd murder you," Caitlyn declared with a huff. After a moment of sulking, she gave Ash a sheepish look. "Thanks for driving, by the way. I can't believe that hunk of junk called it quits yet again."

"Jags are built to be pretty, not practical. Lucky for you, I'd already decided to rent a car for the weekend so I could meet up with my family for trick-or-treating tomorrow." Even if that hadn't been the case, Ash had a sneaking suspicion she would have done whatever she could to make sure the kid in the backseat—who was sitting on her hands right now, presumably to stop from hurling herself between the seats in excitement once again—got a shot at the puppy she so desperately wanted.

"It's a long drive, though." There was a hint of contrition in Caitlyn's tone. "I'm sure you had better things to do with your Saturday than take a day trip to Maine."

"It beats working." This was only part of the story. The full truth was Ash had never felt a stronger sense of completion and belonging than in the short amount of time she'd spent with Caitlyn and Sadie. Not even with her own family, perhaps because her sense of duty and obligation sometimes got in the way of simple enjoyment where they were concerned. But with the Brewster sisters, Ash felt a peace she'd never dreamed was possible.

"I don't think I ever expected to hear you say that." Caitlyn shot her a sideways glance with a hint of understanding that made Ash wonder how much the woman suspected about Ash's true motivations.

"Don't let anyone at the office know," Ash said with a laugh, even as her stomach tightened at the possibility Caitlyn would guess what was going on inside her and put a stop to this time together. It would be the smart thing to do. Ash simply lacked the strength to do it. "It's true, though. It's not like I wake up every morning thinking I can't wait to dig into legal briefs."

"Then why do you work so hard? Other than to make partner," Caitlyn added before Ash could offer her standard reply. "I mean, you've got a family nearby, right? From the sound of it, they'd like to see more of you."

Ash swallowed down the guilt that always accompanied this topic. It was hard enough to accept the mixed emotions that sometimes accompanied the prospect of seeing her family, the overwhelming dread that they would need something Ash couldn't provide. Ash wasn't sure that was something she could share with anyone else. Not even Caitlyn. "They're the reason I work as hard as I do. I've been doing it ever since Dad died."

"That has to have been over twenty years ago. Your siblings must be old enough to have jobs, right?"

"My sister's a teacher and my brother's a cop." A faint smile crossed Ash's face as she considered how well her siblings had done.

"Those are respectable careers with solid incomes."

Right on schedule, the worry started to seep in. "But Mike's got two little boys and a daughter on the way. And if my mother's intuition is right, Breanna will be getting engaged any minute. Weddings, college funds, retirement—"

"Retirement? Your niece isn't even born yet," Caitlyn teased. "She won't be retiring any time soon."

"I was talking about my mom. She's sixty-three, and as much as she enjoys working in the office at the school where Bree teaches, she's no spring chicken. She's worked hard and deserves to enjoy her life." Ash tightened her stomach muscles to keep the aching under control.

"And what about you?" Caitlyn asked. "When do you get to start enjoying your life?"

Instead of answering, Ash checked the side mirror before merging into the right lane. "This is the exit. The foster family's house should be another mile."

"Are we there?" Sadie called from the backseat, popping one of her earbuds out so she could hear the answer.

"Almost," Caitlyn told her. "But I don't want you to get your hopes up too high, or to start begging the minute we arrive, got it?"

The house they were looking for was at the end of a

long dirt driveway. Ash had barely put the car into park when Sadie bounced out and ran ahead to ring the doorbell. Ash and Caitlyn followed a few steps behind.

The front door opened and a woman stepped onto the wraparound porch. A golden curly-haired puppy wriggled in her arms. Sadie let out a shriek of pure delight as the woman offered the puppy to her. "Isn't she the cutest thing you've ever seen?"

"I'm bringing home a puppy today, aren't I?" Caitlyn whispered to Ash.

"Yep," Ash said with a grin, not ashamed to be enjoying Caitlyn's dismay, which she suspected wasn't nearly as deep as the woman liked to pretend. "One with button eyes and an adorable pink tongue."

"Fuck," Caitlyn muttered, but her softening expression hinted the puppy was working its magic on her too.

"Hi, I'm Roberta." The puppy's foster mom held out a hand to shake. "Which one of you is Caitlyn?"

"That's me." Caitlyn shook the woman's hand.

"There's a fenced in patch of grass right over there where you can play with the puppy, see how you take to each other," Roberta directed.

"I'll leave that to my sister," Caitlyn said. Sadie was already at the enclosure. She set the puppy down and laughed as the little animal chased her, letting out a string of happy barks. "Is all the paperwork in order?"

The woman nodded and took a seat on the porch, letting the puppy situation take care of itself.

"You already filled in the adoption paperwork?" Ash raised an eyebrow, a smile tugging at the corners of her mouth. "Caitlyn Brewster, you're a softie deep down, aren't you?"

"Don't you dare tell a soul," Caitlyn warned.

They looked on from a distance as Sadie scooped the golden puff ball into her arms, the puppy twisting into contortions, licking Sadie's face.

"Did you leave anyone behind in New York?" Ash asked, surprising even herself as the words tumbled out. She'd been wondering, but hadn't intended to ask.

Caitlyn cocked her head to one side. "How do you mean?"

"I don't know. A girlfriend, or—"

Caitlyn's eyes grew stormy. "If there'd been anyone in New York, what happened between us wouldn't have happened. If you think I'd—"

"I didn't mean to imply anything, honest." Ash put both her hands up as if to shield herself from Caitlyn's sudden ire. Ash regretted how her question had come out and had no desire for a repeat of what she'd experienced on Caitlyn's back deck. "It's just hard to believe a woman like you isn't already taken is all I meant. And don't say it's because you work so hard."

"Why not? I assume that's the excuse you use." Caitlyn remained combative, but the storm clouds in her eyes had passed, meaning she was no longer angry, just shifting back to her argumentative self. Which Ash happened to like.

"It is, which is how I know it's a cop out," Ash countered. They were too much alike in this respect to even try to deny it. "No. There's something else."

"You know that for certain, do you?" Caitlyn crossed

her arms. "Or is that just your way of leading the witness?"

"Maybe," Ash admitted.

"If you want to know the truth, I haven't had much interest in relationships since things ended with my college girlfriend."

"The evil ex. I seem to remember you mentioning her before. What made her so evil?"

Caitlyn swallowed, and for a moment Ash wasn't sure she'd answer. But then Caitlyn drew a breath and said, "She betrayed me. That's the one thing I can't tolerate from people I let in my life."

"She cheated on you?"

Caitlyn shook her head. "Much worse than that. She used me. Do you know what it's like to go into class ready to present a project you've spent a year on, only to have someone you thought loved you give the exact same presentation first?"

"She did that?" Ash went cold all over at the thought. As betrayals went, that one was extra bad, so very personal and cruel.

"If she'd copied from an exam, or turned in a paper I'd written, I might've forgiven her." Caitlyn's jaw tensed. "But she humiliated me. That was half the reason she did it. Maybe the whole reason. Who knows?"

Ash swallowed a lump in her throat. "What happened after that?"

"I threw all her stuff out of my dorm window. I was going to set fire to it, but I didn't want arson on my record when I applied to law school."

Ash couldn't hold back a soft chuckle at the vivid

image of a young, furious Caitlyn that formed in her mind. From what Ash had witnessed, the woman hadn't changed much with age. "I meant, what happened with the project? Did you get credit for it?"

"Eventually. It was a nightmare in the meantime, trying to pull together proof that the work she'd presented was mine. It took well into the summer, and I missed walking for graduation. Not that my dad would've gone anyway, but still." Caitlyn shrugged, a dismissive gesture that frequently accompanied any mention of her father. Ash recognized it for the defense mechanism it was.

"That's terrible." Ash's heart clenched, not sure if she was angrier at the treacherous girlfriend or the father who cared so little for his own offspring.

"It taught me a lesson. I used to hate it when people underestimated me, but what Bridget did made me realize it can be more effective to fly under the radar. If people don't realize how good you are, they won't know to sabotage you until it's too late."

Ash studied the woman for a few seconds, struggling to square what she knew of Caitlyn's personality with the image she presented to the world. "That's funny, because I've heard you say that before about people underestimating you, and I can't help but wonder if they're all blind. From the moment I met you, you never had any qualms about telling me you were the best."

"You're right. I have no idea why. But even before we met in person, when I was watching the videos of you from that Lavender Law conference, I couldn't bear having you think I wasn't good enough."

Ash's heart beat a little faster as Caitlyn searched her face with an expression that seemed to beg for acceptance and recognition. "There's no way that could ever happen. As for your evil ex, I kind of hope you really did plan the perfect murder."

"If I did,"—Caitlyn offered a sly smile—"you'd never know."

As Ash laughed, her phone began to vibrate. "Hold on. I've got a call coming in."

"That's fine. I should go talk to Roberta about finalizing everything."

Ash pulled the phone from her pocket and saw her mom's avatar on the screen. "Hi, Mom."

"Hi, sweetheart." Her mom's voice sounded hoarse and she punctuated her greeting with a sneeze. "You at the office today?"

Ash glanced at Sadie, who was sitting cross-legged on the grass with the exhausted puppy in her lap. "Actually, no. Are you getting sick? Do you need me to come over?"

"Just a cold." Her mom sneezed again. "But I'm calling to make sure you're still planning to go trick-or-treating with Mike and the boys tomorrow night at that event in Portsmouth."

"Of course I am," Ash replied, annoyance that her mom would think she'd consider bailing jabbing her like a pointy stick to the ribs. Sure, she didn't come around as often as she might, but she never bailed on anything she promised to do. "I told Mike three days ago I was going. Does he think I'll back out?"

"Now, don't get testy," her mom admonished. "I'm the one wanting to make doubly sure. If this stuffiness doesn't let up, I won't be in any shape to go if you can't make it, and your sister was hoping to spend the day getting her classroom decorated for the Halloween party Monday. But if she has to fill in—"

"Tell Bree it's fine," Ash said with a weary sigh. "I'm going to be there. I've got the whole day blocked off on my calendar, and I even have the rental car already."

"You do?" Ash's mom's tone perked up considerably at this news.

"Yes. In fact, I happen to have taken it to Maine today with a friend, helping her transport a new puppy back home for her little sister."

"You have a friend?" It sounded like Ash's mom could've been knocked over by a feather at this revelation. "Is it Caitlyn Brewster?"

"What? Mom!" Ash didn't know why she was getting so defensive over her mother guessing correctly, except she didn't want the woman getting any ideas into her head that didn't belong there. Not with her mom's history of weirdly accurate intuition, not to mention her absurd theory that Ash had harbored a crush on Caitlyn since mock trial. "Look, I've gotta go. I'm losing signal."

She ended the call before her mom could protest, the screen on her phone indicating it still had every one of its bars.

Caitlyn rejoined Ash near the edge of the enclosure, clutching a folder in one hand and a leash in the other. "Okay, you two—er, three, I guess. We have a pit stop to make. Roberta tells me there's a Petco not too far from here."

"She's ours?" Sadie held the puppy closer to her chest.

"One hundred percent ours," Caitlyn confirmed with a resigned expression Ash had seen on her own mom's face when making sacrifices for her kids.

"What should we call her?" Sadie asked, nearly breathless.

"What do you think or feel when you look into her eyes?" Caitlyn asked.

"Happiness," Sadie blurted. "Can we call her Happy?"

"Happy the Diving Dog," Ash added with a wink in Caitlyn's direction. She was rewarded with a look that said *I am going to kill you*. But in a good way. At least, Ash hoped so.

"That'll be her competition name." Sadie held the dog up to look into those button eyes. "Let's get you in the car, Happy."

"Put her on the leash," Caitlyn directed, holding it out to her sister. "I don't want Happy getting loose and coming into the front seat with us at seventy miles an hour."

"Okay!" Leash attached, Sadie and Happy were off to the car in a dash.

Ash and Caitlyn tailed them at a distance, waving to Roberta as the woman went back inside the house.

"I don't think I've seen Sadie this happy, ever." Caitlyn's eyes misted.

"Remember this feeling when cleaning up after Happy in that big backyard of yours tomorrow," Ash teased, giving Caitlyn's shoulder a nudge.

"I should make you stay the night, so you can be on

clean-up duty." Caitlyn's accompanying scowl was utterly adorable, which was the whole reason Ash had said it.

"I just remembered, I need to go to the office tonight," Ash was quick to say, softening the excuse with an exaggerated wink.

"Nice try, Tanner." Caitlyn shot her a look that attempted to be annoyed but couldn't quite obscure the happiness underneath. It was stunning, the type of look Ash wished she could capture in a photo to look at again and again. "You got me into this mess, so no getting out of it now."

Reaching into the backseat as she settled behind the wheel, Ash laughed when the puppy licked her knuckles. Caitlyn needn't have worried. At that precise moment, there was no place else she'd rather be.

"Do we want this soft carrier for the car?" Ash held up the item in question so Caitlyn could see. "You're supposed to be able to buckle it in."

"Add it to the cart," Caitlyn said with a sigh. She pointed to the shopping basket, which was already filled more than halfway to the top with toys, food, bowls, and whatever else had been deemed essential puppy starter gear.

"Hey, Caitlyn?" Sadie called out from the next aisle. She was still holding Happy in her arms despite the puppy being on a leash. "Do you think Happy is more a pirate or a taco?"

"What are you talking about?" A look of panic crossed Caitlyn's face as her gaze fell on the large display of pet Halloween costumes Sadie stood in front of. "Oh no. Uh-uh. I said essentials. We are not getting a costume for the dog."

"But they're on sale," Sadie begged.

"Essentials," Caitlyn repeated sternly.

Ash's phone buzzed. She tossed the carrier into the cart and pulled the device from her pocket, a frown settling across her features. "Mom?"

"Ash, honey—" Her mom's words dissolved into a long guttural cough that made Ash wince in sympathy. "I wanted to let you know trick-or-treating is off for tomorrow."

"What? Why?" Ash held up a hand reassuringly in response to Caitlyn's worried expression.

"Felicia's gone into labor," her mom replied. "Mike's dropping off the boys with Bree and taking her to the hospital now. I'll watch them while Bree decorates the classroom tomorrow, and then she can take them around the neighborhood, but I just don't have the energy to do the drive to Portsmouth, so—"

"I can do it," Ash interjected. "I told you I was planning on it."

"Yes, but—" Her mother coughed again. "Bree still has to go to the school earlier in the day, so she couldn't leave in time, and I'm not feeling—"

"I don't need you or Bree to go with me," Ash declared, not sure where her sudden confidence was coming from, but grateful for it. "I can handle the boys on my own."

"Alone?"

"Geez. You make it sound like I volunteered to wrangle a herd of rabid alligators." Ash rolled her eyes for Caitlyn's benefit, who was staring at her with a mixture of curiosity and concern. "They're two little boys. How hard can it be?"

"Are you sure?" There was no mistaking the relief in her mom's gravelly voice.

"Completely. You get some rest, and tell Bree I'll be over to get the boys tomorrow at whatever time she needs so she can go to work."

After ending the call, Ash let out a long sigh.

Caitlyn tilted her head. "What was that all about? You lost me at rabid alligators."

"My sister-in-law just went into labor," Ash replied, brain ticking with everything she needed to do.

Caitlyn's eyes grew wide. "Right now? How exciting!"

"Yeah, but it means I'm flying solo with my nephews tomorrow for Halloween." Ash's stomach tightened. Had she ever spent that many hours with two kids so young? Certainly not without backup.

"What's the plan?"

"We're supposed to go to this neighborhood in Portsmouth that's been turned into kind of an outdoor history museum. They do trick-or-treating at all the houses, and a bonfire, and kettle corn, and—"

"No way! Kettle corn?" Caitlyn clapped her hands beneath her chin, looking almost as excited as her sister when she'd found out they were adopting Happy. "This sounds amazing. Can we come?"

"You want to spend the evening hanging out with me

and two little boys on a sugar high?" Ash shot her an incredulous look.

"You're sure there will be kettle corn?"

"Pretty sure." A smile spread across Ash's face, relief flooding her at the realization she wouldn't be facing this challenge alone. And maybe something warmer and sweeter than relief, too, at the prospect of spending another day with Caitlyn. And Sadie and Happy too. But if she was completely truthful with herself, mostly Caitlyn.

"You said it's outside." The wheels were clearly turning in Caitlyn's head, analyzing the situation from every angle. It was a trait she and Ash shared, and one of the things Ash really admired. "Do they allow dogs?"

"I think so." Ash pulled up the information on her phone, nodding as she read the rules. "As long as they're on a leash, it's a go."

"Hey, Sadie!" Caitlyn called out to her sister. "Do they have a pirate costume in puppy size?"

Sadie grinned. "You mean it?"

"Turns out we're going trick-or-treating tomorrow," Caitlyn said, trying but failing to be grumpy. "I guess that makes a costume essential."

"Are you sure?" Ash asked, praying she would say yes but wanting to give Caitlyn an out. Family obligations like this were a lot. Who knew that better than Ash? Even if doing things with Caitlyn and Sadie felt like the easiest thing in the world.

"Hell yes." Caitlyn gave Ash a nudge with her shoulder, filling her with a tingly warmth. "No way are you going to hog all the kettle corn for yourself."

CHAPTER EIGHTEEN

After helping Caitlyn and Sadie unload the bags of pet supplies and getting Happy settled in, Ash had headed home. A fire crackled in the living room fireplace and Caitlyn sipped a glass of wine, her feet propped up on an ottoman. Happy was crashed on the couch between her and Sadie, sleeping soundly the way only a puppy with no worries in the world could.

Caitlyn craned her neck to get a better look at the little curly-haired mop. "It should be illegal for anything to be this cute. How are we ever going to say no to that face?"

Happy's front paw quivered.

"She's dreaming," Sadie whispered, not that Happy showed any signs of being easily roused. A marching band could parade through the front door and the puppy would probably sleep right through it.

Caitlyn closed her eyes, soaking in the peaceful silence. Despite the unexpected pleasure of family time spent with her little sister, there was a dull ache deep down. Caitlyn suspected, if she dug deep, the cause would be Ash's absence. She decided not to dig.

"Hey, Caity?" Sadie's voice was low, not quite a whisper, but not loud enough to risk disturbing the sleeping pup. "Can I ask you something?"

"Sure thing, Sadie bug." Caitlyn smiled at the old nicknames, a flood of warmth almost, but not quite, masking that hollow feeling she refused to inspect.

"You like to win, right?"

Caitlyn choked back a laugh. "You've *met* me, right? That can't be your question."

"No. I mean, you want to win for your clients when you're in court."

"Of course." She answered without hesitation. "It's my ethical obligation to protect and pursue my clients' interests."

"How far would you go?"

"To win?" Caitlyn opened her eyes, sitting up a little straighter. She studied her sister for a moment, troubled by something in the girl's demeanor she couldn't put a finger on. "I'm prohibited from breaking the law, and I have to remain civil and respectful of the court in everything I do."

"Are there gray areas, though?" Sadie traced the outline of Happy's ear with her fingertip, not making eye contact.

"How do you mean?" Caitlyn frowned, not sure she liked where the conversation was going, and uncertain why it was heading there.

"Like, can you defend a client if you know they're guilty?"

"Hey, kiddo. If you're about to confess to a crime, I'll stop you right there so we can hire a lawyer." Caitlyn forced a laugh that came out less than believable.

"Ha ha." Sadie treated her sister to an eye roll only a teenager could do justice to. "Just because you got me a puppy doesn't mean your attempt at humor has gotten any funnier."

"Harsh." Caitlyn let out a breath, doing her best to relax her muscles so as to come across as unthreatening as possible. She'd learned from Ash's approach with her sister that the best way to coax information out of her was to do it indirectly and without rushing. "Is there something weighing on you, sweetie?"

"What? No." Sadie shook her head with a vigorousness that was mostly convincing and Caitlyn relaxed a bit more. "I'm actually just curious how it works. If your clients are guilty then you can't really win."

"There's a difference between factual guilt and legal guilt." Caitlyn noted the confusion that stole across her sister's face and added, "What a person did and what the prosecution can prove to the standard needed to convict are not the same thing. The truth is, I don't often know if a client is guilty or not. And it doesn't matter."

At least, it hadn't mattered in the past. When she'd started working in New York, the main thing that she'd cared about had been getting the job without anyone knowing she was related to the Harding family. After that, her focus had been winning the biggest cases and signing the richest clients. That was how you proved you were the best in this line of work. But lately, since moving home and especially after a few conversations with Ash, doubt had crept in. Maybe it wasn't enough to be the best. Maybe being right was just as important.

"What if a client says they did it?" Sadie asked, clearly still intrigued by the conversation. Caitlyn almost felt flattered to have held the girl's attention for so long.

"Even if a person confesses, they could be lying," Caitlyn explained. "Maybe they want to protect someone else, for instance. Or they might have done whatever the action in question is, but there's a justification for it that exonerates them of having committed the crime for which they're being charged."

"But if they tell you they did it and they want *you* to say they didn't?" Sadie's demeanor had changed from guarded to openly curious, and Caitlyn got the impression that, whatever her reasons for starting the conversation, at this point her sister was mostly interested in knowing how it all worked just for the sake of learning. Being able to explain it to her felt pretty good. She was finally earning some big sister points.

"I'd remind them that I can't break the law. Nor can I put someone on the stand if I know they're going to perjure themselves."

Sadie pondered this as she stroked Happy's head. "What if you thought your client was totally guilty. Like a real scumbag. Would you ever lose on purpose?"

"I can't do that," Caitlyn explained. "Lawyers have to zealously represent their clients. My only option if I truly felt I couldn't do that would be to *not* represent them."

Sadie wrinkled her nose. "Does it ever make you feel gross?"

Caitlyn thought of some of her most loathsome

clients and felt her own nose wrinkle in a way that was unfamiliar to her. There really had been some grade A assholes in the mix over the years.

"Sometimes," she admitted, unable to lie.

"But you've never lost a case on purpose?" Sadie pressed.

"No. Well…" Caitlyn's voice trailed off as she remembered the one exception to that rule. "It wasn't quite the same thing. I mean, it wasn't a real trial. There was a competition a long time ago. A mock trial. I made what I knew were rookie mistakes in the final round."

"You let your opponent win?" Sadie's jaw hung slack. "On purpose?"

"I guess I felt at the time that the other person needed the win more than I did." Caitlyn petted Happy's head, warm and comforting. As she replayed that decision from six years ago, knowing what she knew now about who Ash was as a person and what she'd become as a result of the opportunity she'd been given, Caitlyn stood by her choice. "What's with all the questions?"

"Nothing really." The cagey look had returned to Sadie's eyes, her words not quite ringing true. "We've been discussing ethics at school."

"Ethics, huh?"

Sadie nodded.

Caitlyn's stomach knotted in suspicion. "You're sure everything's okay?"

"Yeah, totally. It's just hypothetical. Me and some of the girls on the rowing team were debating some things for fun."

Caitlyn arched an eyebrow. A bunch of fifteen and

sixteen-year-olds having an ethics debate instead of discussing their favorite bands?

Yeah, right.

Caitlyn smoothed her face, not seeing any benefit in calling her sister out on this absurd premise, at least for the moment. She'd take a more subtle approach. "How have things been with the team lately? Since Fergus."

"Weird." Sadie shrugged, her chin falling a bit. "Sad. And... there's been a lot of pressure to perform better."

"Is the coach asking for extra practice?"

"That," Sadie said, "and some of the people are spending more time in the gym. They're obsessed."

"You know," Caitlyn chose her words carefully, not wanting to influence her sister's decisions unduly but wanting her to know she had choices, "you don't have to be on the team if you don't like it."

"I do, though," Sadie was quick to assure her. "It's mostly great. It's really just a few of the boys on the varsity team who act like jerks."

Caitlyn nodded, her tension easing once again. Teenage boys acting like jerks certainly checked out. No red flags on that front.

An instant later, Happy's head popped up with a sudden alertness that made Caitlyn wonder if someone had inserted a fresh battery.

Sadie jumped off the couch. "I think it's time for us to run in the yard one more time before it gets too dark."

Alone in the living room, Caitlyn took a long sip of wine as she stared into the fire. Her sister's giggles and the enthusiastic puppy barks that echoed through the house lessened her worries. Even so, Caitlyn wondered how parents managed it. Having a teenager in the house was a rollercoaster, and a hundred times harder when Ash wasn't around. Caitlyn made a fervent wish that the woman had stuck around for the rest of the night, and as she continued to drink her wine, she didn't even bother lying to herself by pretending to feel any differently.

HOPPING down from the cab of the pickup truck she'd borrowed from Gilda's son Billy to tide her over until the mechanic could deliver a verdict on the broken Jag, Caitlyn surveyed the parking lot with the sense of having landed on a different planet.

It was early evening and there were families everywhere. Almost everyone was dressed in Halloween costumes, even the adults. Some were pushing strollers or lugging giant diaper bags while others held onto children's hands and called out warnings to watch for cars. As a kid who'd been raised by a housekeeper and a butler, Caitlyn had never experienced anything like it in her life.

In a losing battle to cover her cleavage, Caitlyn tugged her white peasant blouse up a little higher. It was at least the fiftieth time she'd done it since donning her costume. "I still don't think I should've worn this."

"What are you talking about?" Dressed in a peasant blouse similar to Caitlyn's, with a short velvet skirt and an eye patch, Sadie came around to the driver's side of the truck. Happy scuttled around her feet. The puppy wore a costume that made it look like she had a peg leg, and a tiny pirate hat was perched on her fuzzy head. "Don't be a spoilsport. Everyone's dressed up. It's Halloween."

Caitlyn pulled at her skirt, wishing it was three inches longer. "A real pirate wouldn't have—No, Happy! Don't eat that rock."

Alerted by her sister's cry, Sadie swooped into action and stuck her fingers into Happy's mouth. "She has zero preservation. I have to watch her like a hawk."

"All part of the trials and tribulations of having a puppy," Caitlyn reminded her. "Just wait until Ash arrives and adds two little kids to the mix."

"It'll be fun!" Sadie declared.

"It'll be chaos," Caitlyn corrected, but even though she knew her assessment was spot on, she was looking forward to the evening. It hadn't even been a full day since she'd last seen Ash and already her body hummed with anticipation of seeing her again.

In a completely appropriate, *only coworkers*, kind of way, naturally. Or maybe not. But it didn't matter. They were in a public place where, regardless of how great the temptation, nothing could happen. It was freeing, almost.

Over the past weeks, it had grown more and more difficult for Caitlyn to be around Ash alone, when the desire to touch, to kiss, and so much more, threatened to overwhelm her resolve not to let things go too far. Tonight, knowing they were in a family setting where nothing could get out of hand, maybe Caitlyn could indulge—*just a little*—in a few innocent touches, like cracking the lid on a pot so it wouldn't boil over. Surely that would be enough to help her put her head back on the right way where Ash was concerned. The woman was a good friend, which was already more than Caitlyn had expected. Asking for anything further was inviting trouble.

"Is that them?" Sadie pointed to a woman with dark hair coming toward them dressed in a khaki jumpsuit with a Ghostbuster's logo on it, holding the hands of two small boys who were dressed as Spiderman and Superman.

"I can't tell." Caitlyn squinted. The woman was a dead ringer for Ash—in fact, the moment she came into view, the tingling in Caitlyn's insides kicked up several notches in that way that was becoming familiar when Ash was around—but surely it couldn't be her. Caitlyn would've put money on her by-the-book colleague being more willing to wrestle a grizzly bear than wear a costume in public.

"That's her. Did you hit your head or something and can't see?" Sadie raised her arm, giving a vigorous wave.

"Watch it, kid," Caitlyn warned, but she did it with a smile lighting up her face as Ash drew closer.

The two little boys squealed as soon as they spotted the puppy.

"A pirate!" the older one said, putting his hand out toward Happy.

"Careful, boys. You have to be gentle," Ash warned.

Sadie had already hunched down to show them how to pet the dog the right way. "What are your names?" she asked.

"I'm Dylan," the taller boy, who was dressed as Spiderman, said.

"Grant," said the younger one, who was dressed as Superman and pronounced the R in his name like it was a W.

"All of you look adorable," Caitlyn said, her heart about to burst from all the cuteness. And yes, she was including Ash in that. Ashley Tanner in a Halloween costume? It was more than she could've hoped for, even if the outfit did cover every inch of her in a way that Caitlyn's did *not*. Somewhat wickedly, Caitlyn couldn't help wonder if Ash had picked up on that fact, and if so, what she thought about it. Maybe the skirt didn't need those extra inches after all.

"You sound surprised." Ash treated Caitlyn to a sly look that made its way to the tips of her toes.

"I kinda thought you wouldn't dress up," Caitlyn admitted. "It didn't seem like your style."

"I've gotta admit, I'm just as surprised to see you standing next to a Ford F-450." Ash's eyes darted between Caitlyn and the massive vehicle. "Are you big enough to drive it?"

"Yes." Caitlyn put her hands on her hips as Ash chuckled. "Our housekeeper's son loaned it to us until my dad's car gets fixed."

"Considering the Jag's track record," Ash pointed out, "not to mention your long commute, have you considered getting something a little more reliable?"

"I'll…" Until recently, Caitlyn's knee-jerk response would have been to say there was no need, as she would be heading back to New York soon. But the more time she spent in Boston, the harder it was becoming to picture going away again. "I'll have to think about that."

"Come on, guys," Sadie called out, leading the way toward the entrance to the outdoor museum as Ash's nephews chased after Happy like a couple of ducklings following their mama.

"You okay with them?" Ash asked Sadie when they were past the ticket booth.

"Of course." Despite both boys sticking to her like they'd been dipped in glue, Sadie gave an enthusiastic thumbs up. "They said they want hot dogs. Is it okay if I take them?"

"If you really don't mind." Ash dug in her wallet, handing over some cash. "Get yourself one too. Caitlyn, do you want anything?"

"No thanks," Caitlyn said. Sadie and the boys headed toward the food stand but Caitlyn held Ash back with a hand on her elbow. "Why don't we follow behind a ways and give them some space. It's no fun scarfing down hot dogs and sneaking candy from your trick-or-treat bag if you're afraid the grownups will catch you and you'll get in trouble."

"Good point," Ash agreed. After waiting a few seconds, they started off again at a leisurely stroll.

The neighborhood beyond the gates was filled with old houses from varying historical eras, all decorated for fall with pumpkins and wreaths made of leaves. There were no cars allowed, so kids could run free, making circles around a crackling bonfire or running enthusiastically along the dirt roads. Children were everywhere, carrying plastic sacks up to each front door in groups as the parents looked on. They'd scream trick-or-treat and bounce with excitement as museum staff in costumes filled their bags with candy.

"This place is amazing," Caitlyn said, trying and failing to recall the last time she'd gone out to celebrate Halloween. "It resembles the perfect New England small town from a movie."

"Safe too," Ash agreed. "It's like the old-fashioned Halloweens my mom talks about having as a kid. It's a great experience for the boys."

"For Sadie too." Caitlyn sought out her sister in the crowd, her heart lifting to see the girl laughing as the puppy in her arms licked her cheek. Ash's nephews were enthralled, and Caitlyn wasn't sure she'd ever seen so much happiness all in one place. Her gaze slid sideways, the feeling of fullness increasing as she caught a glimpse of Ash walking beside her.

It was one of those rare moments in life that couldn't possibly be improved.

"Why are you looking at me like that?" Ash asked as she busted Caitlyn sneaking a glance at her. It was actually the third time Caitlyn had done it, but there was no reason to come clean with that fact, nor to confess the tender thoughts she'd been thinking.

Caitlyn grasped for a cover story. "How did you find a Ghostbuster's costume that wasn't slut-ified?"

"Is that a word?" Ash gave her baggy jumper a pat.

"If it isn't, it should be." Caitlyn motioned to her own revealing costume. "When I went to the party store, this was the most tasteful thing I could find. And I'll have you know, that included a nun's costume."

"Scandalous." Ash laughed. "I guess I got lucky. I borrowed my brother's costume to wear tonight since he couldn't make it."

"How are he and your sister-in-law doing? And the baby?"

"Healthy, happy, and exhausted. The baby took her sweet time arriving, but Mom called me a few hours ago to say everyone's fine." Ash's expression was a blend of pride and contentment as she smiled, a reflection of how Caitlyn was feeling too. "Mom's going to bring the boys to the hospital tomorrow to meet their little sister, who luckily looks more like her mother than my brother, who I am duty-bound as a big sister to claim looks like a gargoyle."

Caitlyn snorted at the dig against Ash's brother, but couldn't help but smile too as she imagined the heartwarming family scene that would play out. Meeting Sadie in the hospital was about the only truly happy family memory she had from her own youth. "Are they excited?"

"Well, they *were* excited," Ash said. "But that was before they met your puppy. Now that's happened, they may want to negotiate for something more entertaining than a sister."

"Aw, I'm sure they'll be thrilled." Caitlyn's eyes misted enough that she had to blink to clear her vision.

"You're very softhearted for a cutthroat pirate." Ash was inspecting her in that way that made it fell like she could look straight through to Caitlyn's soul. It was wonderful, and terrifying, and made Caitlyn think thoughts that were not at all acceptable for a family place.

"That's pirate wench, thank you very much," Caitlyn shot back, working extra hard to keep up her humor shield. "Said so right on the package."

"I think it suits you." Ash gave Caitlyn another sidelong glance that went deeper than expected. "Reminds me of that red dress you wore on your first day."

Caitlyn lightly slapped Ash's arm. "Are you saying I looked like a slut?"

"Get with the program, Brewster. The politically correct term these days is wench, okay?" Ash pretended to shake her head in disgust. Caitlyn wondered if she was experiencing the need for a humor shield too. It was a fun thought. "Gotta teach you everything."

Caitlyn rolled her eyes in an exaggerated way. "So funny. Not."

"All I'm saying is part of me hoped the red dress would make an appearance tonight." Ash's cheeks were doing a good job of approximating the same shade as the missing dress.

"In your dreams. This is a family event," Caitlyn scolded. "I wasn't going to come dressed as a hooker."

Ash put her hands up defensively. "You said that part, not me."

"Trust me, that dress is hidden so far in the back of my desk drawer, it'll never see the light of day again." Caitlyn wagged a finger, even as she made a mental note to pull said dress out of hiding, just in case an opportunity to wear it arose.

"That seems very unfair," Ash complained.

They'd come to a stop beside a white picket fence. The sky was purple and pink in the twilight and the reflection of the sunset in Ash's dark eyes stabbed Caitlyn with a beauty that caused almost physical pain.

She swallowed, lowering her eyes to Ash's throat. "You know what I think is unfair?"

"No," Ash responded in a breathy whisper, as if the butterflies in Caitlyn's stomach were attacking hers too. "What?"

"That your jumpsuit is zipped all the way to your chin." Biting her lower lip, Caitlyn stretched out a trembling hand and grasped the zipper pull, easing it down an inch, and then another two. "That's better."

Ash let out a shaky breath. "Is it?"

Caitlyn studied the newly revealed expanse of skin, a tempting view that fell just shy of crossing any lines. "It's not the romper version of a Ghostbuster costume, but it will do."

Ash's brow creased. "What's a romper?"

"Picture khaki Daisy Dukes, only shorter."

Ash's eyes doubled in size, and there may have been a slight bit of drool pooling at the corner of her mouth. "I didn't know they could go shorter."

"Oh, they definitely do." The crowd around them empowering her to be a little more daring than if they'd been alone, Caitlyn ran her eyes up and down Ash's legs and let out a wistful sigh.

"I see," Ash said slowly, almost teasing. "You think I should have found one of those costumes instead of this sensible beige sack I borrowed from my brother?"

Caitlyn pulled in her cheeks to stop from grinning. "I think my legal counsel would advise me to assert my Fifth Amendment rights at this time."

"Uh-huh. Tell me, did they have a romper version of the pirate wench costume?" Ash made a show of checking out Caitlyn's legs, making the breath catch in Caitlyn's throat. Turnabout was, as they said, fair play, but that didn't mean Caitlyn's pulse didn't start ticking at double speed.

"You're looking at it." Caitlyn rustled the hem of her skirt like a can-can dancer. "I'm just so short you can't tell."

"If you were any taller and wearing that getup, you might get arrested." The hint of lust in Ash's tone nearly melted Caitlyn into a puddle.

Trying to play it cool, Caitlyn slanted her head. "What? No cracks about how I should've dressed like a Munchkin from *The Wizard of Oz* instead?"

"I would never make a joke like that." After keeping her composure for a moment, Ash snorted. "On second thought, I probably would. But for the record, I like your height."

A flash of heat engulfed Caitlyn's body, frying most of her brain circuits and leaving her a babbling fool. "I don't know, it makes it hard to reach cupboards, not to mention sometimes I—"

Ash clasped Caitlyn's shoulders with her hands as if to ground her. "You're perfect."

Caitlyn could barely hear from all the blood pounding through her head, but she'd been able to hear *that*, and the sentiment made her weak in the knees. "You mean my height is acceptable?"

"I stand by my prior statement." Ash drilled her gaze into Caitlyn's with a startling intensity that drove the breath from her lungs.

"Look." Caitlyn's voice hitched as she searched for anything to move the conversation to safer ground. "There's the kettle corn."

"Smooth transition," Ash teased. "At least you have your priorities in order."

"Kettle corn makes the world a better place." Though her heart continued throbbing harder than a grueling workout at the gym, Caitlyn offered a playful shrug and tried not to let on as they got into the line. "Should we get some for the boys?"

"Yes, unless you want to go down as the meanest pirate wench in history."

Caitlyn paid for two large bags of the salty-sweet treat, giving one to Sadie to share with the boys and keeping the second for her and Ash. It was still warm and the smell of sugar and butter was divine.

"They're showing a movie over there." Ash pointed in the distance to where several rows of hay bales had been set up and a children's cartoon was being projected onto the white wall of one of the buildings.

"Is it Wallace and Gromit: The Curse of the Were-Rabbit?" Sadie asked, her eyes sparkling. "I love that one. Come on, boys!"

Sadie led her merry band of trick-or-treaters, collecting candy from the houses along the way until they reached the makeshift outdoor theater.

"Your sister's a natural with the little ones," Ash said. "I feel like I should be paying her for entertaining my nephews all night. I was a little worried when I volunteered to take them, but this has been the easiest babysitting gig in history, thanks to her."

"Trust me, Sadie doesn't need the money—" Caitlyn clamped a hand to her mouth as she realized how her words might come across. "I didn't mean for that to sound the way it did, like we're a couple of spoiled rich girls."

"It's okay. I didn't take it that way." There was nothing but kindness in Ash's tone.

"What I meant was Sadie loves kids, so she's having the time of her life tonight." Caitlyn swallowed, tears stinging her eyes. "We're the only family we've got."

"Really, Caitlyn," Ash said softly. "I understand. No class warfare tonight. Or ever."

Caitlyn shot Ash a disbelieving look. "No more cracks about my Mayflower ancestry?"

"Considering there literally was a Brewster on the Mayflower, it's less a joke and more a simple statement of fact," Ash pointed out, but then shrugged. "Maybe I've finally figured out neither of us had it easy. You want to sit and watch the movie?"

"Do you mind standing instead? That rough hay would do a number on my bare thighs." Caitlyn led the way to a spot at the edge of the crowd, away from the wriggling children and parents who were starting to look frazzled as the evening wore on. They stood side by side, the rough fabric of Ash's costume brushing Caitlyn's bare arm. The simple awareness of how close they were was driving her wild. "Mind if I have some of that kettle corn you've been hoarding?"

"Here you go." Ash handed over the nearly full bag,

apparently in such a good mood she didn't even try to defend herself against Caitlyn's admittedly cockamamie accusation. "If you behave, maybe I'll buy you a candy apple before we go."

"What counts as behaving?" Caitlyn tilted her head cautiously, unable to stop the stream of tempting thoughts flowing through her mind. If she could risk one little thing, anything to relieve the pressure building like a dam about to burst. They were in public. It wouldn't be much. Just enough to preserve her sanity and avoid ever more dangerous thoughts.

"As I told the boys when we got out of the car, no kicking, biting, pinching, or spitting."

"What about this?" Pulse ticking faster, Caitlyn stood on her toes and placed a soft kiss on Ash's cheek. "Does that get me more points toward a candy apple?"

"That might get you a whole bushel of them," Ash said with a grin, looking surprised but pleased by Caitlyn's impulsive gesture.

"Good." Caitlyn snuggled closer to Ash, taking her hand and lacing their fingers together with a squeeze. "I do like to win."

Amazingly, her plan had worked. She felt better already. Surely it wouldn't be too difficult to continue like this until... A lump formed in Caitlyn's belly as she realized she had no idea how that sentence was supposed to end.

Until when?

Until she moved back to New York? Or Ash moved on to some new woman who wasn't a coworker, or was maybe taller, too... Until the sun went supernova and the earth exploded at the end of time?

Caitlyn closed her eyes, breathing in to stave off panic. Instead of the smells of candy and popcorn, it was the scent of Ash's soap that calmed her, engulfing her in its simple, no-nonsense comfort. Which it had no business doing, considering Ash was the source of her sudden existential crisis. But there it was.

CHAPTER NINETEEN

Sitting at her desk behind the day's pile of work, the hustle and bustle of the office a low hum in her subconscious, Ash ran the tip of her finger along her cheek. If she allowed herself to close her eyes, she would have been able to feel the exact spot where Caitlyn's lips had made contact. That memory would have filled her to the brim with the same fluttering excitement and anticipation she'd felt that night three weeks before.

She kept her eyes firmly open.

That didn't stop Ash's imagination from reliving that moment one more time, or for the feelings to flow like warm molasses through her veins.

"I need a vacation," she muttered to herself.

"Not today." Caitlyn's face peered through the open doorway, even more beautiful than it had been in the moonlight on Halloween. Which was quite a feat considering the terrible overhead lighting in the office.

Ash desperately needed to get a hold of herself before

these obsessive thoughts about Caitlyn drove her stark raving mad.

Caitlyn was studying Ash with a curious look, like she was expecting something other than the awkward silence that was all Ash seemed capable of producing. "It's almost time for the meeting with the Fosters and their attorney."

"Wonderful." Ash leaned back in her desk chair, closing her eyes to keep from drinking in the way Caitlyn's frame leaned against the doorjamb, her crossed arms doing wonders for—

Nope. This was neither the time nor the place, especially considering her overactive imagination was already responsible for her nearly being late for a client meeting. Ash was *never* late.

"It gets better," Caitlyn added as soon as Ash's eyes had opened. "Fergus Clark's family filed a wrongful death lawsuit this morning. They're claiming the negative environment created by Coach Dryden contributed to their son taking his own life."

At this news, Ash practically launched out of the chair, joining Caitlyn in the hallway. "Has the coroner's office determined cause of death yet?"

"Not yet." Caitlyn and Ash walked rapidly toward the conference room side by side. "But with a lawyer like Hank Kearns representing them, do you think that matters?"

"Hank 'Take No Prisoners' Kearns?" Ash stifled a groan.

"That would be the one."

"Fabulous." Ash's tone dripped with sarcasm. "And here I thought that mess couldn't get worse."

Caitlyn's jaw hardened. "I'd call him a no-good ambulance chaser if he wasn't so damned effective."

Dread weighed on Ash's frame, pulling her shoulders down. Hank Kearns was ruthless and known for getting big settlements. He'd be salivating to dig his hands into the deep pockets of the academy's endowment. "I should've known they'd end up with someone like him. The goal will be to get Moorehead to settle quickly and quietly."

"And for big bucks," Caitlyn added, confirming she and Ash were once again on the same wavelength.

"Hey you," Zach sidled up next to Caitlyn, catching Ash by surprise as if he'd materialized out of thin air. She immediately stiffened, not liking his ingratiating tone, which as far as she knew was the only one he had.

"Zach, buddy." For someone whose day was going to suck every bit as much as Ash's, Caitlyn managed to sound downright perky. It was a wonder how the woman managed it. Ash could never keep her true feelings hidden quite so deeply, but Caitlyn was a pro.

"I heard the news about the new Moorehead suit. Whatever you need, I'm your guy." He hooked a thumb toward his chest. *What a doofus.*

"I might take you up on that," Caitlyn replied.

At exactly the same moment, Ash said, "I think the two of us have that under control."

Ignoring Ash completely, Zach zeroed in on Caitlyn. "You just let me know what I can do."

"What's up with Zach?" Ash demanded as soon as

the fourth-year associate was out of sight. "Why is he being so friendly and helpful?"

"He's always like that. He's a—"

"Smarmy butt-kisser," Ash supplied, not trusting the guy or his intentions one bit. "I want to be straight with you—"

"Well, that's a shame." Caitlyn's tone was flirtatious, a teasing look in her eyes.

Ash's body tingled all over and for a moment her mind went blank. "What was I saying?"

"I have no idea." Caitlyn's smirk told Ash she knew exactly what effect her little joke was having.

"Oh, right. Zach." Ash took a breath, forcing herself to focus on something other than Caitlyn's shiny red lips. "I wouldn't trust him if I were you."

"You don't trust anyone," Caitlyn reminded her. "I wouldn't say I'm more trusting, but I know I have to give a little to make this job work."

"That's not true," Ash argued, referring to the first part of Caitlyn's statement. "I trust people."

She was about to add *I trust you*, but held back. No matter what signals her body was sending her—which were loud and clear in the *let's say whatever it takes to get this woman in bed again* variety—Ash's brain needed to keep a firm grasp on reality. Caitlyn was a colleague, which meant they were on the same side. But she was also the competition, every bit as much as someone like Zach. Just because she looked a hell of a lot better in a red dress didn't change the facts. The more Caitlyn shone, even if she had no intention of pursuing a partnership, the more it could detract from Ash's chances at the promotion.

Ash needed to do a lot more thinking about how to get what she'd worked so hard for in her career, and a lot less mooning over how soft Caitlyn's lips had felt against her cheek.

Caitlyn placed her hand on the conference room doorknob and turned it slowly, pushing the door open. A young man wearing a purple and gold men's rowing jacket from Williams College was flanked by a man and woman who appeared to be his parents. Another man, who was definitely an attorney, sat beside the father.

"Thank you for coming in," Caitlyn said in a breezy *everything's going to be fine* tone. And it would be fine—for Moorehead Academy and the law firm of McGill and Harding, that was—once the Fosters were confronted with what Ash and Caitlyn had dug up about Alex's less than exemplary behavior at school.

"Ready to settle?" the Fosters's attorney asked when Caitlyn and Ash had joined them at the table.

"You're dropping the suit?" Caitlyn countered with just enough snark that the other lawyer's expression flickered with doubt.

He let out an overconfident laugh but it was clear Caitlyn had made him sweat. Ash's chest swelled with an unexpected sense of pride. That woman was a marvel.

Meanwhile, young Alex looked as if he wanted to blast off into space, while his father had the look of a man who would like to bite the heads off of everyone in the room. The mother, however, wore a wary expression.

Ash caught her casting glances at her son in a way that didn't exactly exude confidence.

Finally, some good news. If the mother was having doubts about her precious son, the evidence they were about to present would go a long way to swaying her toward the modest settlement they would eventually propose.

"We've been talking to some of the students at Moorehead," Ash began, splitting her focus between Alex and his mother while ignoring the father and the attorney for now. "Know what we found out?"

The young man shook his head and Ash had to wonder if he was always so quiet, or if he'd been instructed not to utter a peep.

"I'll give you a hint," Ash continued, eager to see what reaction her revelation would receive. "It's about the junior varsity barbecue last year, and it's not that you're winning a merit badge for your hamburger grilling skills."

"Junior varsity?" the father growled. "Alex was a senior and co-captain of the varsity team. He wouldn't have been at some JV kiddie party."

"You'd think that, right?" Ash tossed back. The man's use of the word *kiddie* was priceless, considering what they were about to reveal. "In fact, Alex had no reason to be at the gathering, but we have several signed affidavits that he was, indeed, in attendance."

The father rolled his eyes. "So what? That's not a crime."

"No, it isn't. But"—Caitlyn tossed a stack of papers across the table, where the lawyer swiped them up—"we also have signed affidavits that Alex brought alcohol to the party."

The father looked angry enough to climb over the table. "That's—"

"A crime?" Ash suggested, shooting Caitlyn a bemused look. "I assume that's what you were about to say. Alex had, in fact, celebrated his eighteenth birthday shortly before this incident took place."

"Personally, I find it fascinating that one can both be under the legal drinking age and also be charged as an adult for supplying alcohol to minors, don't you?" Caitlyn asked. Alex's eyes doubled in size and his mother appeared to totter on the verge of passing out.

"I don't believe a word you're saying." The father crossed his burly arms over his chest.

"Mr. and Mrs. Foster." Ignoring the father's outburst, Ash moved her eyes slowly from one parent to the other, hoping to impress upon them the seriousness of the situation. "Last year, at the end-of-summer barbecue for the JV rowing teams, your son, who was eighteen at the time, snuck into the party uninvited. He poured alcohol into the punchbowl when no one was watching, and this resulted in many of the students becoming intoxicated, some to the point of illness."

The mom's head whipped toward her son. "You did that?"

"Don't answer that!" the lawyer shouted. "I'm sorry, ladies, but you just said there were no witnesses to this alleged punch spiking. How do you know it was my client?"

"Because he confessed, repeatedly," Ash answered.

"Bragged about it to anyone who would listen. We have seven signed affidavits supporting the accusation from students who witnessed his confession firsthand."

"Somehow," Caitlyn said, "this incident never made it into Alex's official school record. If it had, that would have been more than enough reason for an immediate expulsion."

"In fact," Ash added, "it's not too late to rectify that oversight, according to the Moorehead Student Handbook. Or we can refer this matter to the proper authorities. You should know, we're talking about a criminal offense that could result in jail time."

"Alex. Look me in the eyes and answer me." The mother didn't back down. "Is what they're saying true?"

Instead of answering his mother, Alex turned to his father with venom in his eyes. "I never wanted you to file this stupid lawsuit. I told you to leave it alone."

The father's arms slowly fell to his sides as he locked eyes on his son. "Answer your mother's question. Did you do it?"

Alex hung his head. "I didn't mean for anyone to get sick."

"What were you thinking?" the father bellowed.

"I thought it would be funny," Alex managed to choke out, tears filling his eyes. "I swear, that's not who I am anymore. I'm in college now. I know you might think I'm just saying this, but I've matured a lot. I feel terrible for the way I acted sometimes back at Moorehead."

"That school was a toxic environment for our son," Alex's mother pleaded.

"I'm not the only one who was an asshole at Moorehead," Alex insisted. "Mom's right. The environment there wasn't good for me, no matter what they say. Just take a look at those stupid gym rats, the ones sporting jackets with that dumb slogan. Something about dying."

"Do or die trying?" Adrenaline pumped through Ash's veins as she made the connection to Fergus Clark. On impulse, she turned to the Fosters's lawyer. "Your client is an adult. Any chance we could get Mom and Dad to wait outside for a few minutes and talk to just him? With you in the room, of course."

They had to get some answers about Fergus, and Ash's instincts told her that would be easier to accomplish with the parental units out of earshot. She gave a questioning look to Alex, who nodded slowly.

"I suppose that can be arranged," the lawyer replied begrudgingly. The parents tensed but didn't argue as they were shown to seats outside the conference room.

"What's this all about?" the lawyer demanded when the conference room door clicked shut again.

"I'm sure by now you've heard of the death of your former teammate, Fergus Clark," Ash began. "There's no question he was stiff competition your senior year. A rival."

The lawyer pounded his fist on the table. "Surely you're not trying to insinuate that my client had anything to do with Fergus's death."

"No," Caitlyn soothed, even as she shot an urgent glance in Ash's direction that said she had no idea what this unscripted detour was all about.

"Although," Ash said, drawing out the word. "I do remember one of the students saying you used to tell people you could murder someone and the coach wouldn't lift a finger."

"That was a joke," Alex said, his face contorted in terror. "If you think I had anything to do with Fergus—"

"Relax," Ash said, noting the sudden relief in Caitlyn's demeanor as well as Alex's. Apparently her colleague hadn't relished the idea of making crazy murder accusations at a guy who was still little more than a scared kid. "There's no reason for anyone to think you were involved in Fergus's death."

"I didn't care anymore about Fergus or the other gym rats once I was expelled," Alex insisted, trembling visibly despite Ash's assurances. "Even if they were cheating."

"Cheating?" Caitlyn leaned into the table. "How?"

"Those times they were posting were sick," Alex said. "I was top of the roster for a year, and all of a sudden Fergus and the others are riding my ass? You can't tell me it's simply from lifting weights."

"Are you saying they're taking steroids?" Caitlyn asked.

"No, those are banned. You get caught with that in your system, you lose out on being on a college team, for sure. I know Fergus had his eyes on a rowing scholarship, like me." Alex plucked at his purple and gold jacket for emphasis.

"What, then?" Ash asked.

"I've heard rumors?" Alex began with the tone of a question, his eyes shifting to his attorney. "I'm not into this at all. But some of the guys on my college crew have talked about this drug that's making the rounds."

"That's enough, Alex," his lawyer warned.

"It's not illegal," Alex insisted. "It's a prescription drug, for cancer or something. It's not on the list of banned substances, or not yet, so taking it wouldn't hurt your chances of getting onto a college team or making it to the Olympics."

"What's it called?" Ash asked, her breath growing shallow.

"It's a long Latin name," Alex said, screwing up his mouth as he thought. "Doxyla...something. I don't know. Guys just call it the Dox."

"Is there anything else you can think of?" Ash kept her tone steady even as her heart pounded. Whether the information Alex had provided about Fergus and his friends would turn out to be important in defending Moorehead against the wrongful death suit, she couldn't be sure. But at least it was one thing more than they'd known before.

Alex's lawyer cleared his throat. "Back to the matter at hand. I'm assuming you have something to offer to keep this underage partying story out of the press?"

Ash sighed, trying not to feel sickened by the realities of her job. Privileged private school kids took performance-enhancing drugs, another spiked the punch of underage students, and still they came out of it all ahead. "We do. Call the parents back in."

"Mr. And Mrs. Foster," Caitlyn said when they'd retaken their seats. "I'm sure by now you see the wisdom of keeping your lawsuit out of court. A jury would chew this up. But just to make the decision a little easier, the school is prepared to give you a prorated refund of tuition for Alex's senior year. That works out to forty-six thousand and eighteen dollars."

The amount for not even a full school term made Ash want to puke, but she was thankful for the bargaining tool. While the Fosters were much better off financially than many, they weren't the type who could turn down that much cash. Even so, Alex's father sat silently, clearly undecided.

"I just want this to go away," Alex pleaded with his father as the silence dragged on. "It doesn't matter anymore. I don't want to be judged all my life because of this—"

The father made eye contact with his wife, raising a brow. She nodded.

The lawyer answered for the family, "Looks like we have a deal."

The four of them filed out of the conference room, the mother speaking softly but firmly to Alex, who kept nodding a repentant head.

Ash let out a whoosh of air. "One potential Moorehead disaster down. One more to go."

"What was all that about that drug, the Dox?" Caitlyn asked when they were alone. "Do you think it's at all relevant to Fergus's case?"

"I don't know," Ash admitted. "But it could be. Looks like it's going to be a long weekend, trying to figure out what this drug is and whether it could have contributed to Fergus's death. Unless"—Ash paused, suddenly realizing the date—"I just remembered Thanksgiving is coming up next week. I think over half the office is departing for family gatherings in Connecticut and Pennsylvania and wherever else tomorrow afternoon. This place will be a ghost town come Monday. It didn't even occur to me to ask if you would be going—"

"You know what we call Thanksgiving in the Brewster household?" Caitlyn asked, pausing a beat before answering, "Just another Thursday. I don't have any plans."

Ash frowned, her heart heavy at this news. "You don't? But, Sadie…"

"Sometimes we go to Gilda's," Caitlyn said softly, almost like she could tell how hard Ash was taking this new evidence of their sad family life. "It's just, her sons are taking her to Florida this year for the holiday. I'm happy for her. She deserves it. I figured Sadie and I would just—"

"Come to my house." The words were out of Ash's mouth in a rush before she realized what she was saying. As soon as it sank in, her chest tightened, but it was too late to take it back. And deep down, Ash knew she didn't want to.

"You're hosting Thanksgiving dinner in that tiny apartment of yours?" Caitlyn arched a brow which, combined with the memory of exactly why the woman knew what Ash's apartment looked like, basically sent all of Ash's senses into free fall.

"I… uh…" Ash cleared her throat, desperately trying to pull herself together into the functioning adult she'd been mere minutes before. "It's my mom's house, actually. She's a great cook. My siblings will be there, plus Grant and Dylan. Oh, and the baby. There's a backyard. You could bring Happy…" Ash's voice trailed off as she belatedly recognized she was starting to ramble. She waited in agony for Caitlyn to reply, to shoot down her crazy suggestion, which was what the harebrained scheme deserved.

Instead, Caitlyn grinned. "Sadie and I would love to join your family for Thanksgiving next week. As for this weekend, Sadie's going to be at a friend's house until Sunday afternoon, so I'll see you bright and early Saturday morning. Looks like we'll have the whole office to ourselves."

Ash's heart pounded as she headed back to her desk, contemplating what had transpired. A weekend of working in the deserted office alone with Caitlyn was dangerous enough, filled with all sorts of temptations she would have to avoid. But Ash had also invited her—a *woman*, and an attractive one at that, whom Ash's mom was convinced she was head over heels for, no less—to a Tanner family gathering. And this wouldn't be just any introduction to the clan, which at the best of times was a trial by fire. Bringing her home at Thanksgiving, the granddaddy of all family holiday meals? Ash might as well be throwing Caitlyn into a fiery furnace. With lions.

What the hell had she just done?

CHAPTER TWENTY

"Do you have your sleeping bag?" Caitlyn glanced in the rearview mirror, taking stock of the pile of assorted items in the backseat as she pulled into the drop-off lot at Sadie's school.

"I've got it, and my toothbrush, and an extra change of underwear." Sadie offered up a questioning look. "Why the worry? It's just a sleepover."

Sure, it might be a run of the mill sleepover as far as Sadie was concerned, but she'd never had the Head of School call to say her sister was being taken to the ER because of a panic attack and wouldn't be allowed to return to the dormitories. That kind of experience changed a person's perspective.

"I just want to make sure you're prepared because I have a lot of work to do this weekend." Caitlyn could almost feel the reproach in her sister's eyes the moment she uttered the word *work*. "Before you start lecturing, yes, it's important. Besides, you're gone anyway, and

Gilda's grandson is taking care of Happy. Everyone's been accounted for."

"Except you," Sadie argued. "Another work weekend? That's all you ever do. Unless"—Sadie's lips curled into a sneaky smile—"is this your way of spending more time with Ash?"

Her belly squeezed tight like a surprised pill bug. Being on the spot rarely shook Caitlyn, but when it came to Ash, everything seemed to go lopsided. "Whaaaaaat?" Caitlyn would've preferred if her response hadn't included a high-pitched snort, but there wasn't much she could do about it now. "That's ridiculous. Ash and I are just coworkers." God, could she sound more cliché?

"I thought you said we were having Thanksgiving dinner at her mom's house." Sadie's tone said she could see right through her sister's nonsense, which was not a very respectful way to talk to her elders as far as Caitlyn was concerned.

"Yeah, well, we're friends too. We work together. We're… You know, this really isn't something I have to explain to you, young lady. Did you pack deodorant?" Caitlyn gripped the steering wheel as she pulled into a space, cursing her brain for its inability to stick to the script. She'd never had to explain herself to anyone when she'd lived alone in New York.

Of course, back then there'd been nothing that needed explaining.

As Sadie opened the car door, a detail from the day before popped into her head. "Hey, kiddo? Before you go, I wanted to ask you something."

"No, there won't be any boys at Taylor's house this

weekend." Sadie treated Caitlyn to an exaggerated roll of her eyes. "You've really turned into a buzzkill now that you're in your thirties, just so you know."

"Gee, thanks." Caitlyn took a composing breath, trying to picture how Ash would ask the question. She was so much better at getting Sadie to trust her than Caitlyn was. "I'm not worried about boys. It's actually more of a question for work—" Caitlyn put her hand up preemptively. "No more lecturing. I just need to know, have you ever heard anyone, maybe kids on the rowing team, talk about something called the Dox?"

The color drained from Sadie's face all at once. Her eyes darted around the parking lot and she lowered her voice to almost a whisper. "How do you know about that?"

That reaction wasn't something Caitlyn had anticipated and suddenly she was far more invested. She motioned for her sister to get back in the car but Sadie seemed too spooked to do anything but comply. "First, you're not in trouble, no matter what you tell me, okay? I just need to know what's going on." It took effort not to start listing all the things that it could be, wild speculations that Caitlyn knew would spiral out of control.

Finally, Sadie's shoulders dropped the smallest bit. She did lean in close, though, like they were in a spy movie instead of a near-empty parking lot. "Is it...?" Biting her lip, Sadie twisted the hem of her shirt between her fingers. "Is this something about Fergus?"

"It might be," Caitlyn answered honestly. "I'm not sure yet. That's why I need your help."

Sadie took a shaky breath. "I'm just gonna say first

that I've never taken it. As far as I know, nobody on the JV team has. Not yet. But, like, back before the Head of the Charles, some of the older boys were kind of, you know, pushing it, I guess? They said it would help us to win."

A light bulb snapped on in Caitlyn's head. "Is this what that conversation a few weeks ago was really about, when you were asking me how far I would go to win?"

Sadie nodded, her eyes downcast. "I know you're never supposed to take drugs and all that, but the varsity guys kept saying it was totally legal, you know, because it's a prescription. And—"

"Honey, before you say anything else," Caitlyn said, keeping her tone even and judgment free, "I need to explain something. Prescription drugs are not legal unless they've been prescribed to you."

Sadie frowned. "They're not?"

"No. Illegal possession of prescription drugs is a crime. If you've got pills that don't belong to you, I'll help you so you don't get into trouble."

"No," Sadie insisted, brows pressed tight together. "I was telling you the truth. I've never taken any and as far as I know, none of my friends have any. But are you sure that's true? I thought it was only things like, I don't know, cocaine or heroin that were illegal."

"I'm afraid not. Illegal possession of any Schedule III prescription drugs, like codeine, for example, can be charged as a misdemeanor with up to six months in jail. Having Schedule I or II drugs, like Ritalin, Oxycodone, or Fentanyl, can lead to felony charges."

"Felony?" A sweat had broken out on Sadie's forehead

and Caitlyn prayed she was telling the truth about not being involved in this stuff. For so many reasons.

"Do you happen to know what drug this Dox stuff actually is?"

"It's real name?" Sadie asked. "Um, it's called doxylacitromide."

Caitlyn's eyes widened. "That's a mouthful. How did you remember that?"

Sadie shrugged. "I'm good at chemistry."

Impressed, Caitlyn filed that information away for later, wondering if there was some kind of chemistry gift she could get the kid for Christmas. "Do you know where the guys are getting this doxylacitro...stuff?"

"There's a gym on Main Street," Sadie said. "It's a short walk from campus. They've got a big banner in the window that says *Do or Die Trying*. You know, that thing the guys are always saying, like Fergus and his friends. I think the trainer there gets it. But, um... if I don't head in soon, I'm gonna be late to class." While true, Sadie was now looking like she'd do just about anything to not be having that conversation anymore.

"Of course." Caitlyn turned her head toward the sleeping bag and duffle in the backseat. Her stomach knotted at the thought of her sister being out of her sight for a whole weekend after what she'd just heard, but there was nothing she could do. She'd have to let her go and trust Sadie to have good judgment. Hard as it was. "You going to be okay getting that inside by yourself?"

"Yeah," Sadie assured her, slinging the gear effortlessly onto her shoulders and back. "I'll be fine."

Caitlyn took a breath. *She'll be fine*, she reminded

herself. "Hey, Sadie? Thanks for telling me about the doxyla—"

"Doxylacitromide?" Sadie grinned.

"You think you could text me how to spell that?" Caitlyn gave a self-deprecating laugh.

"No problem," Sadie said, dashing off a text before grabbing her things. "Are you going to tell the police about what the varsity boys are into?" Her timidity when asking was a reminder to Caitlyn about Sadie's nerves and fitting in at school. The teams had been close enough in Caitlyn's day to know that Sadie would not want a reputation as a tattle-tale if this news spread. She didn't miss this age one bit.

"I don't know that it's a police matter quite yet," Caitlyn said, suppressing a groan at the thought of yet another legal mess for what she'd originally assumed would be an easy client. "I will have to talk to the Head of School about it, though. Drug abuse like this is dangerous as well as illegal. It can't be allowed to go on."

Sadie pressed her lips together before appearing to gather the courage to ask one more question. "Do you think Fergus overdosed on Dox? Is that what killed him?"

"Hard to know without all the facts," Caitlyn answered, her heart heavy. "But I'm going to do what I can to find out."

When Sadie had headed to class, Caitlyn picked up her phone and forwarded Ash the text from her sister before calling her at the office. "Hey, Ash? Did you see the text I sent?"

"The prescription name?" Ash asked. "I just assumed

you'd texted me instead of a pharmacy on accident."

"Look at it closer," Caitlyn directed. "Does it make you think of anything?"

There was an intake of breath. "Oh my God, is this the Dox?"

"Yeah, Sadie had some information about it that I think you'll find interesting. Don't worry, she's never taken it," Caitlyn added quickly, knowing Ash would feel the same way as she had when she discovered Sadie was wrapped up in all this, even if it was tangentially. "I'll tell you all about it when I get to work. For now, though, do you know anyone you could call at the medical examiner's office? We need them to add this to the list of substances they're screening for in Fergus's autopsy."

"Yeah, I've got a person I can call."

"While you're at it, maybe you can get an investigator over to the gym on Main Street?" Caitlyn turned the key in the ignition. "I should be at work in about forty-five minutes. In the meantime, see what they can find out about one of the trainers pushing Dox on the student athletes from Moorehead Academy."

"How's it going in here?" Caitlyn poked her head into Ash's office, taking in the minuscule space. She wasn't sure if it was any smaller than her own office, or if it was just an illusion because Ash's legs were longer and looked so cramped sticking out from the side of her desk. Still, Caitlyn supposed she was used to it, given the way her eyes scrolled down her computer screen with a level of concentration that seemed to leave her oblivious to her surroundings anyway.

"Oh, hey." Ash looked up, her lips forming a smile. There was a bumping noise as she stretched her feet and they smacked into her filing cabinet. It must've been commonplace because she didn't react, not even to make a face. "Ready for a piece of good news?"

Caitlyn's eyes lit up. It was around five o'clock on Saturday afternoon, the sun already set with the increasingly shorter days in late November, and she'd been grinding out work since eight o'clock that morning. She would take anything good she could get.

"You have cannoli and chianti?" she teased, unable to hold back a wink and loving how it made Ash blush.

"Damn." Ash laughed, a sound Caitlyn didn't think she would ever tire of, and which, regardless of whatever news her colleague had to impart, had already gone a long way toward brightening her day. "That would definitely be better than what I was going to say."

"Fine." Caitlyn gave an exaggerated sigh, enjoying the banter that seemed to come so easily now. If only the low hum of attraction always buzzing between them didn't complicate things, Ash would be the perfect friend. "What's your not-so-very-great-after-all news?"

"I just heard back from Brent at the medical examiner's office." Ash took a deep breath. "They ran the additional tests and found traces of doxylacitromide in Fergus's blood."

"They're working on a Saturday?" Caitlyn asked, frowning. "I know we do that all the time, but we're—"

"Insane?" Ash suggested.

"I was going to channel Sadie and go with losers who have no lives, but you know. Potato, pot-ah-to." Caitlyn flashed a silly grin, which Ash returned. The best thing about Ash was Caitlyn knew she could say something like that and the woman wouldn't take it the wrong way. They understood each other, especially when it came to their workaholic ways.

"Just between you and me, Brent sounded relieved to have the results back."

"Relieved?" Caitlyn frowned. "Why?"

"Because they've been struggling to figure out what the hell happened," Ash confided, her professional veneer slipping with the mild swear word, as had been happening lately when it was just the two of them. It tickled Caitlyn to see that side of Ash, both metaphorically and also literally, in several specific regions of her anatomy that made it hard to focus. "This has become a high-profile case with all the media scrutiny, and according to Brent, there just wasn't a good explanation for how a young, healthy athlete was alive one day and dead the next. No suicide note or any evidence of self-harm. The standard tox screens all came back negative. His heart just... stopped."

"The Dox killed him?" Caitlyn's own heart quickened as she thought of kids at Sadie's school taking the stuff, thinking it was harmless. All for the sake of better performance. "Did he overdose on it?"

"Too soon to tell," Ash cautioned. "But at least it gives them a new avenue to pursue."

Caitlyn nodded, glad to know there was at least

progress being made, even if they still couldn't be sure how much exposure Moorehead Academy had when it came to liability. Although if Caitlyn was honest with herself, she wasn't thinking about that as much as she usually would.

A young man—someone almost the same age as her little sister—had lost his life. It hit her in a part of her heart that usually remained separate from her work. At the end of the day, no matter who was at fault, Fergus Clark's time on earth was over. No amount of money or jail time could make up for that tragic loss.

"Are you okay?" Ash had leaped from her chair and maneuvered around her desk to put a hand on Caitlyn's shoulder before she realized she was crying. She nodded and tried to wipe the tears away but they continued to flow, harder and faster now as if acknowledging them caused the dam to burst.

"It's just such a waste," she managed to choke out. "He was so young, and he had his whole life..." As the sentence ended in a garbled cry, Ash wrapped her arms around Caitlyn and pulled her close.

"I know," Ash soothed, stroking Caitlyn's hair. Caitlyn's eyes stung, the sandpaper grit of exhaustion at war with her tears.

Her blunt nails lightly massaged Caitlyn's scalp, producing a calming sensation that spread through her entire body. Ash's blouse was open at the neckline, the bare skin of her chest warm against Caitlyn's tear-streaked cheek. The rhythmic ticking of Ash's heartbeat in her ear was more effective than the best meditation music as it slowly brought her back from the edge of her emotional onslaught and into a state of, if not serenity, something close to it.

How was it that Ash's presence and touch could do more good for Caitlyn's wellbeing than a day at the best spa? Caitlyn wished that time could stop, and that she never had to move from that spot.

"How do people do this?" Caitlyn's voice was soft and low, her arms clasped around Ash's back, refusing to let her go. Not that Ash was making any moves to escape. "How do they care about people, let them into their hearts, and take the risk of losing them?" She spoke into Ash's skin, unwilling to get the distance to see the effect her confession had.

"I don't know," Ash admitted, a hint of rawness in her tone. "I'm terrible at it. I work, and I work, and I tell myself it's because I love my family, but the more I've thought about it, the more I've realized it's a way to keep some distance. After my dad died—"

Ash drew in a trembling breath and Caitlyn dug her fingers into the woman's back, a physical reminder that she wasn't alone. It was possible Ash was shedding a tear or two of her own, but Caitlyn couldn't be sure because she had yet to remove her head from Ash's chest. "Losing your dad had to have been so hard."

"I told myself I went into law to avenge people like him, you know?" Ash rested her cheek on the top of Caitlyn's head, adjusting her arms but never coming close to letting go. The warmth of her embrace grounded Caitlyn, unwinding the spiraling panic over Fergus's death. "But let's be real. I mostly fight for companies with deep pockets. And I use the work as an excuse to skip spending time with the people I love because I'm afraid to let them in. I'm afraid to let anyone in."

It hit so damn close to home. The acid burn of the truth was something Caitlyn didn't have the strength to avoid anymore.

"I am too." Caitlyn swallowed hard, all the fears that had begun to overwhelm her since becoming her sister's guardian fighting to be free. "But with a sister like Sadie, and that damn puppy"—Caitlyn couldn't help but chuckle as she thought of Happy's ridiculous, fuzzy face—"there's no keeping them at arm's length." She took a deep breath, then added, "Or you, either."

"Me?" Ash sounded surprised, which made Caitlyn laugh some more.

"Yes, you." Caitlyn shook her head, which, considering she was still resting it against the woman's body, mostly resulted in her rolling her forehead around against Ash's cleavage. There were worse things in life. "You're literally the last thing from arm's length right now, in case you haven't noticed."

"I'm sorry." Ash made as if to let go of her, but Caitlyn held her tighter.

"Don't you dare." Caitlyn's heart skipped a beat as she realized she'd said it out loud, but now that the words were out there in the universe, she couldn't stop until she'd said everything she'd been holding back. "Can I trust you?"

"One hundred percent." Ash said it without hesitation, but it was hard to tell if she understood the gravity of Caitlyn's question or was answering with what Caitlyn wanted to hear.

"Do you promise?" Caitlyn raised her head and took in the searing intensity of Ash's dark eyes.

"Yes." It was clear in that instant she meant it completely, and while not a perfect guarantee the words were true, it would have to be good enough. It wasn't as if a pinkie promise would do anything in that situation.

Caitlyn inhaled slowly, drowning for a moment in the subtle scent of soap and shampoo that she associated with no one but Ash. She took a step back, putting distance between them. "In that case, I have a confession."

"Oh?" Ash raised an eyebrow but didn't say anything else, waiting for Caitlyn to continue when she was ready.

"I didn't really need to work this weekend." Caitlyn bit her lip, not sure how Ash would take this revelation and also uncertain how to explain. "I mean, I had work to do. It's not like I sat in my office all day playing games. But none of it was pressing. It was just, with Sadie away at her friend's for the weekend and no one at home but the puppy—who's great, by the way, but she can be a lot—and... and with me feeling this sadness inside with the Fergus thing, and... I guess I knew you were going to be here, and I just couldn't think of anyone else I'd rather spend the day with. But you had to work—"

"I didn't." Ash's shoulders shook in silent laughter. "I mean, I was the same. I had some work to do, but once you figured out the drug the kids were using, all my research was basically on hold until I heard back from Brent. But I knew you were going to be here today, so..."

Ash's words trailed off with a shrug and they both began to laugh at the absurdity of the situation.

"You mean instead of working, we could've... I don't know, gone whale watching, or something?" Caitlyn demanded between gasps.

"Whale watching?" Ash's face scrunched in disbelief. "That's really what you would've rather done today?"

"I don't know. Not necessarily that, but maybe—" Caitlyn stopped short, taking in the unmistakable look of lust in Ash's eyes, like she was about ready to ravage her right then and there. "Hold on, now. Don't get any ideas."

Caitlyn didn't know why she bothered to say that, as it was clear Ash already had the ideas, and equally evident from the rush of wetness between her legs, her body was on board, even if her brain was pulling its usual jerky move of trying to spoil the fun.

"What ideas are you talking about?" Ash teased, doing a terrible job of playing dumb. Especially as her tongue darted out to quickly lick at a bottom lip. Caitlyn felt her flush intensify.

"I think you know." Now that she'd protested, Caitlyn felt duty-bound to at least try to make a sound argument why this was a terrible idea. Even a client with a terrible case deserved a robust defense, right? "For one thing, this office is too small for shenanigans. There's barely enough room for the two of us to stand up, let alone..."

"I can think of at least a dozen things we could do standing up," Ash pointed out, immediately piquing Caitlyn's interest. *A dozen?* "But if you'd rather have room to spread out, there's always the conference room."

Oh. The office grew even smaller as Caitlyn came to terms with Ash's suggestion. Or maybe she was just becoming too hot to bear it. "Are you crazy? There could be *people*." Caitlyn's eyes were bugging out of her head at the thought of any of their coworkers making a surprise stop into the office and catching them *in the conference room*. Somehow that seemed a hundred times worse than just being overheard through a closed office door.

"Do you trust me?" The desire burned in Ash's eyes but her tone was cautious, reserved, as if leaving room for Caitlyn to make up her mind. This, from the woman who'd been hammering away at making partner no matter the personal cost. Ash was asking for something from Caitlyn and, understanding how much that offer meant coming from Ash, there was only one answer.

"Yes," Caitlyn whispered, her heart clenching at the frightening truth. What would it be like to trust someone again, truly trust, after so many years of guarding her heart? Would she even remember how?

Ash crept closer with all the dangerous grace of a hunter, but Caitlyn whirled around, shutting the office door and sliding the lock into place. At least now if anyone did come into the office, they couldn't walk in—just listen from the hallway to the sounds of debauchery Caitlyn was sure were bound to occur sooner or later.

Ash gave the lock a sideways glance. "This is a *really* bad time to find out you're a murderer after all."

"Shut up." Unwilling to let her brain come up with any more delays, Caitlyn slammed Ash against the door, kissing the woman hard. Her tiptoes pressed into the toes of her shoes as she lifted herself to get closer.

"Who knew being told to shut up could be this hot," Ash panted when Caitlyn let her up for air, though she caught her breath quick enough and began to nibble Caitlyn's earlobe.

"Sorry about that," Caitlyn said as she squirmed against the sudden overwhelming sensation of Ash's tongue on the side of her neck. The spot she was paying attention to seemed to be directly connected to the junction of Caitlyn's legs. "I didn't want to lose my nerve."

"You?" Ash ran her fingers through Caitlyn's hair, but instead of being relaxing, this time each stroke started a new fire in her core. "I can't picture you ever losing your nerve when it comes to getting what you want."

"When it comes to this…" Caitlyn's words trailed off in a moan as Ash cupped her breast from the outside of her shirt.

"It's not our first time." Ash let go of the breast so her fingers could get to work on the buttons of Caitlyn's shirt.

"It's different this time, because…" Caitlyn searched her frazzled brain for the right words but came up short. This wasn't a great time to make a speech. "Do you not feel it?"

Pausing in her efforts to gain access to Caitlyn's shirt, Ash cupped both of Caitlyn's cheeks. "I do. And it scares me too, if that helps."

"Oddly, it does." Caitlyn laughed. She undid the final button and let the shirt slide from her arms onto the floor.

They stared deeply at each other, Caitlyn unsure about the next step. Luckily, Ash—who had not been lying about having a dozen ideas for things they could do standing up—made the first move. Otherwise they might've been forever stuck in an epic stare down, or at least until their coworkers started to trickle in bright and early on Monday.

Ash took a few steps, positioning Caitlyn against the wood door with her arms pinned above her head. A shudder rippled down her spine at being held hostage to Ash's whims. Ash used her free hand to run her finger from Caitlyn's elbow to her shoulder, following the path she'd traced with her lips trailing a second or two behind.

"I really like kissing you," she murmured in Caitlyn's ear. As if to back up the claim, she took Caitlyn's mouth with hers, unrelenting with a passion that left Caitlyn burning even hotter with need.

It didn't matter that they were in the office. Caitlyn couldn't have stopped herself if she wanted to, not even if a hundred people had wandered in. She needed to be inside Ash, and to feel Ash moving inside her, too.

"Off," Caitlyn managed to growl as she freed her arms and undid the button and zipper on Ash's jeans with record speed.

Apparently, the need was mutual. Ash stripped off Caitlyn's pants in seconds, followed by her own bottoms and blouse.

Neither were completely undressed, both still wearing panties, but those thin layers of fabric were no real obstacle to determination. And God, was Caitlyn determined. With Ash's body against hers, Caitlyn slipped her hand beneath the elastic waistband, her fingers snaking toward their goal. Ash mirrored the same action, while kissing the soft spot where neck met clavicle.

Was Caitlyn really going to do this? Fuck Ash right here in her office?

Hell yes.

She dipped the tip of her index finger into Ash's hot wetness, pressing until she was completely inside.

"Oh, fuck." With a gasp, Ash did the same to Caitlyn, her finger long and sure. Both women grew wetter with each stroke.

Caitlyn's free hand reached around Ash, undoing the woman's bra with a precision that would've impressed the heck out of her under different circumstances, but this wasn't the right moment to take a victory lap. She had work to do.

Caitlyn pinched one of Ash's nipples, delighting in the way Ash's eyes darkened with unbridled desire. All for her.

As if to prove it, Ash added a second finger, pumping her wrist, biting Caitlyn's neck in the most sensual manner.

"Don't stop," Caitlyn pleaded, tears stinging her eyes. The fullness of Ash inside felt so good. How had they kept themselves from doing this for so long?

Both of them sucked in ragged breaths as they pressed on in pursuit of the ultimate goal. Caitlyn's wrist started to protest at the angle, but no way was she going to stop until Ash saw fireworks on the office ceiling.

She shifted to ease the pressure, adding a second finger. Ash let out a cry of approval before increasing the speed of her own strokes, moving in and out until Caitlyn's legs shook.

Unable to stand on her own but unwilling to stop,

Caitlyn dug her fingers into Ash's back for support.

Ash pressed harder against Caitlyn, locking the woman in position, not letting up, her fingers sliding in and out.

It took every ounce of determination for Caitlyn to keep pumping her own hand, but Ash's soft moans renewed her strength. They were both too close to stop.

Ash captured Caitlyn's mouth, their tongues tangling like swords in battle. Ash's wobbled a bit, but Caitlyn clutched the woman with one arm, doing everything to keep them upright until—

"Holy fucking lord!" Ash shuddered from head to toe.

Caitlyn would have welcomed the opportunity to crow about her accomplishment for a moment. After all, it wasn't every day the usually reserved Ashley Tanner screamed out something so downright obscene in the workplace. But there was no time. An orgasmic swell coursed through Caitlyn, threatening to spill at any moment. Ash had hardly recovered from her own moment of climax, but she apparently had no intention of shirking her duties. She continued plunging in and out of her until Caitlyn's sex quivered and tightened until Ash's hand was forced to still.

"It's... almost..." Caitlyn stuttered through clenched teeth.

Right when Caitlyn wasn't sure she could take anymore, Ash's finger crooked upward ever so slightly, hitting some secret, magical spot and releasing the full force of every desire and emotion inside her with an epic intensity. Clenching, Caitlyn's teeth closed on Ash's shoulder to keep herself from screaming at the top of her lungs. There might not have been anyone else in the office, but the way she was feeling, she was afraid they'd hear her in the next building over.

Finally spent, they sagged into each other, their chests heaving up and down together as they tried to catch their breath.

Caitlyn spoke first. "That was—"

"Amazing," Ash cut in.

"That was a vast improvement on what you said last time," Caitlyn teased, nuzzling her head into the crook of Ash's neck.

"Really?" Ash pretended surprise. "I feel like I should've taken notes."

"You didn't take notes?" It was Caitlyn's turn to joke.

"I did not," Ash confessed.

"In that case," Caitlyn said in a scolding tone, "I guess we're going to—"

"Have to do it again so I can make sure to get it all down this time? Let's get out of here." It was clearly difficult for Ash not to burst into laughter as she scrambled to retrieve her clothing.

"I just have one question," Caitlyn said, reaching for her own clothes as well while trying not to tangle limbs or bump heads with Ash in the limited space.

"What's that?" Ash looked suddenly nervous, like she feared a deep, emotional conversation she wasn't ready for.

Knowing there would be ample time for that kind of thing later, and not sure she was ready for it herself, Caitlyn grinned. "Is it faster to walk to your place, or drive?"

CHAPTER TWENTY-ONE

"Are you sure you're ready for this?" Ash had her hand on the doorknob as she glanced nervously over her shoulder at Caitlyn. She spoke just above a whisper so Sadie, who was still wrangling Happy out of the car in Ash's mom's driveway, wouldn't overhear.

"I think I should be asking you that question. You've gone a bit pale." Caitlyn placed a comforting hand on Ash's shoulder. "You aren't getting sick, are you?"

"If only," Ash replied, half joking. Regret was piling on her faster than paperwork to be filed at the courthouse. "My family can be a bit overwhelming."

Happy let out an excited yip as she finally freed herself from the car. Caitlyn responded to the sound by withdrawing her hand and letting it rest casually at her side. "All families are overwhelming. It's going to be fine. Just stick to the plan."

"Good idea," Ash said. "The plan. It's a solid plan."

The plan was, despite having spent the rest of Saturday night and all of Sunday together in Ash's bed and hoping to repeat this endeavor as soon and as often as possible in the near future, neither woman planned to tell a living soul. Not at work, and certainly not family, at least for now.

Bottom line? It was too complicated. At work, there was the fact coworkers dating was frowned upon, not to mention the whole partnership race that was entering the final stretch. As for family, both sides were likely to get a little too emotionally invested in the idea of their darling single members finally finding—well, it couldn't precisely be called love, or at least neither of them had called it that yet. Certainly not out loud. Maybe companionship was a better word.

Yes, that worked, Ash thought, refusing to acknowledge the small part of herself that felt like a balloon with half the air out. *Companionship*.

Ash's palm was slick as she started to turn the knob, forcing her to grip it extra tight, knuckles white against her skin. What Caitlyn didn't know was Ash had never brought a woman home before. Thanksgiving was stressful enough without tossing that into the mix, like someone announcing they were a virgin two seconds before doing the deed. No one needed that kind of pressure.

Goodness knew how her family was going to react to Caitlyn's presence. Yes, she'd warned her mom she was bringing guests, so it wasn't an issue of not having enough food—not that it ever would be since her mom cooked for an army on holidays. No, it was those crazy theories her mom had about Caitlyn being Ash's big crush, like they were destined to be soulmates or something. Her mom was likely to go gaga.

Because even though her mom had passed herself off as a cool, modern woman who respected independence and would never pressure her career-minded oldest daughter into marriage and family life against her will, Ash was beginning to suspect that had been an act. Or maybe an emotional defense mechanism, since Ash had never before shown the slightest inkling of being anything other than a perpetually single workaholic, and her mom hadn't wanted to get her hopes up.

But bringing home a smart, beautiful woman as her companion—and yes, Ash had already accepted this was a bullshit description for what she and Caitlyn were, but she was determined to stick with it for as long as she could—for one of the biggest family celebrations of the year, not to mention adding the extra enticements of the woman's adorable kid sister, and that fucking dog who was too cute to live? That went way beyond an inkling, and Ash knew it, even if she didn't want to face what it might mean just yet. Her mom would probably have ordered Ash a subscription to Bride magazine by the end of the night. And maybe Parenting magazine, too, for good measure.

So, no pressure or anything.

Ash remained frozen, the door unopened.

This was a bad idea. Bringing Caitlyn to meet her family at this point was too much, too soon. They should have picked up Chinese food and brought it back to Caitlyn's place. Why hadn't Ash thought of that before?

Hell, they probably still could do that, right? She hadn't knocked yet. No one had to know they were there.

Before Ash could put her brilliant new plan into motion, the door was wide open, but Ash hadn't done it.

"It's not locked, Princess." Mike wore his most brotherly of grins. In other words, he looked like a troublemaking pain in the ass. Another sign this had been a stupid move on Ash's part. His eyes slid from his sister to her *companion* and his face morphed into something akin to a private investigator on the hunt. "Well, hello there. You must be my sister's *friend*."

Crap. It had been less than two seconds and Mike already knew their friendly coworker cover story was bullshit. She was in for so much shit-talking at the table.

"Princess?" Caitlyn jacked up her eyebrows like she'd stumbled on a hidden trove of ancient treasure. "I think I need to know more about how your sister got that nickname."

"It's nothing, right, Mike?" Ash hoped her acid tone conveyed both that she would pay her brother a million dollars to keep his trap shut, and also send him to the bottom of Boston Harbor wearing cement booties if he didn't heed her warning.

Before Mike could say anything that might make Ash want to finally put into motion all those perfect murders she'd spent sleepless nights trying to plan, her two nephews came rushing toward her with unbridled glee. For the second time in as many minutes, Ash froze in place, a smile that was at least two-thirds pure terror plastered on her face. If they both hit her at once going that speed, she would end up in the hospital.

"Happy!" they cried as they got closer, breezing past her and straight to Sadie, their little arms encircling the yipping pup, who'd begun turning circles of pure excitement at their approach.

So, yeah. Apparently it wasn't good old Auntie Ash they'd been so overjoyed to see. Even if she had bought them an extra bag of kettle corn on Halloween. Ash hugged her arms to her chest. There was some gratitude for you.

"Well, who have we here?" Ash's mom asked, emerging from the kitchen as she wiped her hands on a dishtowel. Ash had been too busy feeling vaguely slighted over the forgotten kettle corn to notice her mom's creeping up on them, and now she was well and thoroughly trapped.

The point of no return.

"Mom," Ash cleared her throat, wanting to sink through the scuffed floorboards of the living room at the ungodly squeaking sound her throat had produced. She might as well be wearing a sign around her neck proclaiming herself so nervous she could die. "I'd like you to meet my coworker, Caitlyn, her sister Sadie, and this adorable fluff ball with them is Happy."

Ash put extra emphasis on the word coworker, hoping that would work like a Jedi mind trick to keep her mom's preternatural instincts from kicking into high gear and blowing the whole *just friends* cover story out of the water as Mike was already well on his way to doing.

Her mom lifted one eyebrow a fraction of an inch at

the description Ash had given, and Ash knew she was screwed. "Welcome. Grant, Dylan, why don't you show Sadie and Happy the backyard? I bet the puppy would love a chance to run around." When the youngsters left along with Mike and Sadie, her mom shook her head at Ash before turning her full attention to Caitlyn. "Ignore my daughter, dear. She's never done this before."

"Done what? Has she never had Thanksgiving at home? I wouldn't be surprised with how much she works." Caitlyn took a blissful inhale, her nose high in the air. Ash flashed her a smile of gratitude for trying to keep up the pretense, even though the jig was most definitely up. "It smells wonderful, by the way."

"Thank you," Ash's mom said graciously. "But what I meant was, you're the first woman Ashley's dated that she's ever brought home to meet the family."

"Is that right?" Caitlyn wore a flabbergasted expression as she swiveled to confront Ash with this tidbit, apparently too stunned to stick with that great plan they'd agreed on before their arrival. Ash wondered if Caitlyn was so wrapped up in the fact she'd learned that she'd missed how they were 'dating.' This was bad news. If Caitlyn had already been vanquished, the battle was all but lost.

"We—" All the years, from tween until now, of trying to shield this part of her life from her family were crumpled up and tossed in the garbage. What was the use? Her mom would never buy a denial at this stage. The next best option was distraction. "We brought a carrot cake from your favorite bakery in the North End, Mom."

Ash held the pink box up close to her chest, half wishing it'd turn into a sword so she could fall on it and escape the upcoming misery of a Tanner family "New Significant Other Roast." She'd been on the other side of them enough times to know it was gonna be brutal.

"Carrot cake? How nice!" Ash's mom exclaimed. She turned to Caitlyn, whose presence she had not forgotten despite the appearance of fancy baked goods. "I hope you weren't counting on pumpkin pie. I'm afraid we're not fans in this house."

"I'll be okay with anything as long as there are no raisins in it." Caitlyn spoke without a trace of humor in her tone. Which was just as well. Raisins in dessert was no joking matter.

"We're not Neanderthals!" Ash uttered with the disdain the shriveled brown lumps deserved.

"We have all the rest of the traditional Thanksgiving dishes," Ash's mom assured Caitlyn, chattering away like they were old friends. "Turkey, homemade gravy, two types of stuffing."

"Two?" Caitlyn's eyes were wide and Ash thought she detected some drool pooling in the corners of her mouth.

"Yes, we're a cranberry and Bell's seasoning family ourselves," Ash's mom explained, "but Felicia—that's my son Mike's wife. She's upstairs with the newborn right now, nursing. Oh, you should see the precious little thing! She's dressed in a onesie that makes her look like a turkey. Wait, what was I saying?"

"The stuffing," Ash muttered, her head a little woozy from her mother jumping between topics.

"Oh right. The stuffing. Felicia grew up with sausage stuffing, so now I make that one too." There was an almost imperceptible pause during which Ash's mom donned the slyest of looks. "You just let me know the kind you're used to and I'll make sure it's on the menu next year."

Next year? Ash did a mental double take worthy of a cartoon character—one of those spinning head, eyes popping out numbers. Was her mom serious with that?

"Mom, I think Caitlyn and I should—"

"How are you with a potato masher?" Ash's mom inquired, putting an arm around Caitlyn and leading her toward the kitchen without so much as acknowledging Ash had tried to speak.

"Can I pretend the potatoes are someone's head?" Caitlyn quipped.

"Depends. Is it Ash's? In that case, have at it. I do know how irritating she can be, and that might be a healthy way to get it out of your system. You'll have fewer arguments that way." Her mom glanced over her shoulder, not the least bit apologetic, and said. "Ash, go help your sister set the table."

"What if I want to mash potatoes?" Ash whined, earning her a scolding look from her mother that was definitely deserved, along with a snicker from Caitlyn, which, frankly, was beyond cheeky. Caitlyn hadn't even tried to stick to the plan, though at this point it would be futile. The universe, and her mother, were too headstrong to control. Instead, Ash made one last ditch effort at damage control. "Caitlyn, can I just have a quick word before you go help Mom?"

Caitlyn gave Ash's mom a look like she was asking for permission, which the older woman answered with a slight shrug before continuing to the kitchen alone.

"Don't yell at me," Caitlyn said preemptively before Ash could speak.

"You didn't even try to stay on script," Ash said in a tone that was absolutely not yelling despite the way Caitlyn hunched her head into her shoulders like a turtle trying to escape into her shell.

"It wasn't my fault," Caitlyn pleaded. "She overpowered me with some sort of mom magic. I didn't have a mom. I've never built up an immunity."

"She's going to pump you for information so hard you won't know what hit you. Be strong and just... try to be vague, okay?" Ash sighed, seeing no way this dinner would end in anything but complete disaster.

Her whole family was going to know about them, and Sadie too. Trying to sort out what she felt for Caitlyn under all that pressure was going to make it impossible to think clearly. Ash balled her fists, wishing she could stomp around and maybe kick something. Nothing alive, or hard. Just, like, a pillow or maybe one of Dylan and Grant's red rubber balls that they always lost over the neighbor's fence.

"Did you want to come into the kitchen and run interference?" Caitlyn offered.

"No can do," Ashley replied, having to acknowledge the fact Caitlyn could even suggest this backed up that whole not-having-a-mom excuse. "I have to go help Bree. Mom said."

As Caitlyn made her way back to the kitchen like a

prisoner walking to her execution—okay, maybe not quite like *that*, but Ash might have been feeling a little melodramatic at the moment—Ash went to the dining room where Breanna was doing her best to wrestle the oval table apart in the middle.

"You need some help?" Ash asked.

"Not as much as you probably will," her sister teased. "Now you know what it was like when I brought Jose around for Mom to do her own version of the Spanish Inquisition."

Ash's eyes darted around the room. "Where is he, by the way? Did Mom and Mike manage to scare him off?"

"No." Bree straightened up, her hands coming to rest on her hips. "He's gone to get the extra leaves for the table. And you should count yourself lucky."

"Lucky Mom didn't send me to the basement for the leaves?" Ash was puzzled. The fieldstone basement of her mother's house was icky and filled with cobwebs, but it wasn't like Ash would've said no to going down there. Especially if she could've taken Caitlyn, and then disappeared out the bulkhead door, hopped the fence, and made a run for it through the neighbor's backyard.

"Lucky because pretty soon Mom will be too distracted helping me plan my wedding to bother you and your new *girlfriend*," Bree said with a smirk.

The wheels all spun into place with the enormity of what had just been said. "Holy hell, Bree!" Ash couldn't say more because her sister's hand was suddenly plastered over her mouth.

"You can't say anything yet," Bree begged.

Ash made a series of grunting sounds to demonstrate that she literally couldn't speak. When Bree let go of her mouth, Ash demanded, "Are you engaged? Jesus, Bree! You've only been dating a few months."

"Nooo," Bree said drawing out the single syllable for several seconds. "Mom's only *known* we were dating for a couple of months. You're not the only one in this family with self-preservation, you know." *Huh.* Ash had to admit that perhaps Bree had a bit more common sense when it came to things than Ash had given her credit for. In her mind, Bree would always be the youngest, in dire need of guidance.

"Is he going to pop the question tonight?" If Ash had ever prayed for proof of the existence of a higher power, this might be the moment her prayers were being answered.

"Not until Christmas," Bree said in a harsh whisper, casting a warning glance toward the kitchen. "You're not off the hook tonight, Big Sis."

Ash wrinkled her nose, unsure she was convinced by the Higher Power's somewhat weaker than expected show of divine proof. Still, she could turn this to her advantage. "What'll you do for me to not start blabbing over the sweet potatoes tonight?" She waggled her eyebrows for diabolical effect.

"You wouldn't dare!" Bree seemed poised to say a good deal more, but just then Jose emerged from the basement door carrying three table planks. Bree smoothed the crazed look from her face, replacing it with something less likely to scare away her soon-to-be fiancé.

"Honey, you remember my sister, Ash. But why did you bring up three leaves? I told you we only needed two."

He leaned the leaves for the table against the wall. "Nice to see you again, Ash. Please, tell your sister we need all three. She won't listen to reason."

"The boys and baby aren't eating with us, so we need the usual number," Bree explained, doing an uncanny impersonation of their mother. She was well on her way to wifehood already. Ash kept quiet but found it difficult not to laugh inwardly at her sister's domestic squabble.

"There's Ash's guests," Jose countered, adding two fingers in the air.

"What—right. That's going to take some getting used to." Bree frowned, clearly having forgotten Caitlyn and Sadie were there. Ash should have felt relieved but instead was a little annoyed. Was it that hard to believe she had people who were important in her life?

"So, hey." Jose shifted on his feet. "You and your girlfriend are lawyers, right?"

She's not my girlfriend, Ash was about to argue, but then she sighed. What was the point? "Yes. We both are. Why?" She hoped he wasn't about to confess to a crime. That would put a serious damper on the Christmas plans.

Nervously, Jose skirted the table, which still didn't have the leaves put in yet, but that was typical of the Tanner family. Chaos. If you thought a job would take five minutes, it was imperative to add another fifty-five on top of that for interruptions, arguments, and jokes.

"Bree said I should talk to you if I got the chance."

Ash nodded. She was used to this, because when

people found out you were a lawyer, they immediately wanted free legal advice about landlords, parking tickets, or what have you.

"Okay," Ash began, about to ask him what the legal matter was when she saw a brilliant opportunity to rescue Caitlyn from her mother's clutches. "Say, Bree darling? I don't think it's fair to leave Caitlyn out of this free consultation you've suggested, so could you go get her from the kitchen, pretty please?"

"I—" Bree's protest dried up as Ash whistled the first few bars of the Wedding March. "I'll be right back."

"I had no idea you had such an aversion to getting your hands dirty when you were little," Caitlyn immediately said to Ash as she entered the dining room a few minutes later. A teasing grin lit up her face, making Ash realize with a jolt how much she'd missed Caitlyn's presence, even in the short time she'd been in the kitchen.

Ash made a growling noise, partially because of the teasing and partially because missing Caitlyn after a seven-second absence was totally unacceptable. She was going to have to do something about that. "I see Mike was regaling you with stories of our youth."

"He sure was, Princess." Caitlyn shot her a wink that would've turned her internal thermostat up to broiling if it hadn't been for the presence of her soon-to-be brother-in-law only a few feet away.

"We'll discuss that later." Ash's eyes narrowed in warning, though she had a feeling she would never live down that nickname for as long as she and Caitlyn were together.

Oh shit. Had she just acknowledged to herself that she and Caitlyn were together? This was the worst Thanksgiving ever. She was in so far over her head there wasn't a sign of life.

Jose cleared his throat, saving Ash from going deeper into an internal panic spiral. "I need some advice."

"Legal advice?" Caitlyn guessed, at once transforming from teasing girl—*not girlfriend, don't you dare think it*—to full work mode.

He shifted on his feet again, fingernails digging into his palms. "I'm a lead researcher for Rindge Biotech in Cambridge. I was promoted to the position earlier this year, and in going through my predecessor's files, I've uncovered data from a drug trial that went unpublished. Trial number seven. Frankly, that trial didn't reflect well on the product, although one particular positive finding was included in a research paper published two years ago which has been widely cited since."

"You think the negative trial data was buried on purpose?" Ash asked, a burning feeling beginning in the pit of her stomach that had nothing to do with hunger. When Jose nodded, she added, "What was the nature of these negative test results?"

"In a small but significant number of test subjects who were otherwise free of cardiac issues but who had been diagnosed with a Still's murmur during childhood—this is a heart murmur that's generally considered completely harmless and usually resolves by early adulthood—sustained use of the drug put patients at risk for serious cardiac complications." The internal conflict was evident in Jose's pinched face as he continued to explain.

"If you look at the test group as a whole, the cardiac side-effects were statistically insignificant. It only became noticeable because an abnormally high percentage of the subjects in this one trial had been diagnosed with the murmur and reported it on their intake forms."

"Any idea why that test group was different?" Caitlyn asked, using the soothing tone that always put Ash at ease and seemed to be having the same effect on Jose.

"My best guess is that all of those subjects had been recruited from one hospital, where the head of pediatric cardiology happened to be particularly diligent in diagnosing and making note of this type of heart murmur in the patient records, and had trained the doctors under him to do the same." Jose's shoulders bobbed. "It was just one of those weird idiosyncrasies you sometimes find. It shouldn't have made any difference."

"You said the heart murmur was harmless," Ash began, formulating possible counter arguments as she went. "Could your former colleague have overlooked the correlation, or dismissed it because of bias against seeing the condition as dangerous?"

"Yeah, I thought of that too." Jose's breath came out in an erratic rasp. "But then I found an internal memo addressed to him from one of the executives at our parent company, congratulating him for doing an excellent smoke-and-mirrors job on Trial Seven."

"That does sound a bit damning," Caitlyn said, putting into words what Ash was thinking. The burning in Ash's belly intensified.

"I raised my concerns, and my supervisors reassured me a hundred different ways. They kept saying, Jose, these are cancer patients. They're not out there running marathons, you know? But I don't know." He locked eyes with Ash, who acknowledged his doubt with a slow nod. "I believe we should be entering this information into the FDA's Adverse Event Reporting System—that's the main place where information on drug side effects is collected. But my superiors have said no, that it's not required. It's not like I can go to the company's lawyers. I'll get fired. I can't lose my job, but I can't sleep. What do I do?"

"You hold tight and let us look into this," Caitlyn was quick to reply. For once, the advice being asked for was meaty and would require a hell of a lot more than pointing a person in the direction of a lawyer who specialized in reducing speeding tickets. "We'll put a plan together."

Already, Jose appeared more at ease, his muscles loosening and his breathing not so tight. Ash knew Bree would be pleased, a fact she could leverage to get her sister's cooperation for the rest of the day in keeping her and Caitlyn from being roasted alongside the Thanksgiving turkey.

Turning her attention to the leaves that still hadn't been added to the table, Ash grabbed one and fitted it in place as she ran through the man's story for any details they might have missed. "That positive result you mentioned, the one that's been cited in other research. What was it?"

"Oh, yeah." Jose made a sour face as he helped her with the second leaf. "It found increased lung capacity and stamina among people who were treated with the drug. The company loved that one."

Ash sucked in her breath. She'd prayed for an intervention in her family's determination to embarrass her, but suddenly the universe seemed to be offering a different kind of assistance.

Caitlyn, who had been reaching for the final leaf, had frozen in place, wood piece only halfway slid into place. "Jose, what drug are we talking about?"

"It's called doxylacitromide," he replied, the complicated Latin name rolling off his tongue with ease.

"And the parent company you mentioned?" Caitlyn seemed to be at ease, but Ash knew her well enough to recognize she was doing everything in her power to remain calm while her insides were whirling.

"Parker Pharmaceutical," Jose answered.

Just then, Bree's voice came bellowing from the kitchen. "Jose? Is the table set yet or what? We need you to carve this turkey."

Jose wore a deer in headlights look as Ash said, "Go on. Help with the turkey. We'll finish the table."

"And we'll talk about this later," Caitlyn said, her eyes doubling in size the moment the man left the room. She turned to Ash, her mouth dropping open. "Did you just hear that, too, or was I having some sort of hallucination?"

"No, I definitely heard it." Ash's thoughts spun in her head like a dust storm was passing through. Jose's revelation was big on its own, but when added to what she and Caitlyn knew about Fergus Clark's death, it could be huge. Like, career-making huge. Partner-making huge.

"Holy shit." Caitlyn grinned as she clasped Ash's

shoulders, clearly thinking along the same lines. "This could be the biggest thing that ever happens to us."

"Yes, it could." Ash's hands trembled as she snapped the table together, grabbing the tablecloth from the top of the sideboard. "But if we don't get this set before my mom comes in here with the serving platters, we may not live long enough to see it."

CHAPTER TWENTY-TWO

Caitlyn tapped her pen on her leg as she hummed along with the Christmas tune streaming through her laptop. They were waiting for news from the medical examiner and Ash had been locked away in the dungeon that was her office, researching. It was Friday afternoon, and though the week back at work after the Thanksgiving holiday had felt like a million years, it was finally over. Now all she had to do was figure out how to get Ash to spend the weekend with her doing something fun instead of working because, Caitlyn had to admit, her legal brain was starting to feel blitzed. She was in the holiday spirit and after having a tantalizing taste of four days off in a row, she was ready for less work and more play, pronto.

"Holy baby Rudolph," Ash exclaimed as she entered through the open office door. "It's like the North Pole in here."

Caitlyn grinned as her eyes swept over the decorations that festooned every inch of space in her small office. Everyone was lucky she'd waited until after Thanksgiving. If it was up to Caitlyn, Christmas decor and music would roll out September 1st. "Don't tell me you're a Christmas hater. I've already gotten frosty looks from a few of the senior partners, and I'm not talking about the snowman variety."

Ash hunched down to take in the tiny tree on Caitlyn's desk, tapping one of the miniature gnome decorations that dangled from a branch. "No, I love Christmas, even if I don't get a chance to decorate much. Although I might if I had some of these little guys."

"Right?" Caitlyn let out a relieved sigh. Ash didn't know how close she'd toed the line of heartbreak for them both. "How can you not smile when you see gnomes?"

"Would that have been a deal breaker? Like raisins in carrot cake?" Ash gave her best *confess-all* stare, and Caitlyn wondered how anyone could resist its spell. She wanted to confess anything and everything if it meant being under it. And under Ash. Or on top. Both were equally desirable places to be.

"Hey. A girl's gotta live by her principles."

"In the interest of full disclosure, there's one part of the holidays I dread." Ash took a seat in the single tiny chair in front of Caitlyn's desk—this office being every bit as small as Ash's own—and poked at an old-fashioned red pickup truck with a tree in the bed sitting behind Caitlyn's monitor.

"Is it fruitcake?" Caitlyn gave a solemn and knowing

nod and Ash burst out laughing. Up until that moment, the Christmas music had been the best thing she'd heard all day. Now it was definitely Ash's laugh.

"I stand corrected. There are two things I dread. That, and shopping." Ash extended a long slender finger to punctuate her thought. It absolutely should not have been enough to make Caitlyn's mind go to places it didn't belong during the workday, but ever since they'd crossed the line that one Saturday night in the office, she'd been struggling with the ability to keep her naughtier thoughts switched off between the hours of nine to five.

"You're in luck." Caitlyn dragged her attention from Ash's hand, but not before a shiver raised goosebumps along her arm despite the office heat being set to Florida warm. "I happen to love Christmas shopping."

"Why doesn't that surprise me?"

"I'd hold your snark back—" Caitlyn teased, wagging her finger playfully.

Ash arched her brow. "You've met me, right?"

"Fair enough." Caitlyn placed both hands on her chest, relishing the way Ash's eyes took in the goods and the difficulty she seemed to have tearing them back to eye level. "Keep the snark to a minimum because I'm about to offer to go shopping with you tomorrow. We'll bring Sadie. She mentioned she needed to get gifts for some friends at school. And, if you keep the whining to a minimum, I'll get you a hot chocolate with crushed candy canes."

"Will there also be whipped cream?" Ash perked up

in her seat. Caitlyn knew she had Ash right where she wanted her.

"There's one thing you should know about me."

"You hate whipped cream, which means you hate life," Ash guessed, shaking her head like she'd been told a terrible secret. "It's probably best I learn this now, because—"

"I love whip cream and have a massive sweet tooth." Caitlyn said it like she was in a confessional.

"I knew there was something I liked about you." Ash grinned, probably the biggest one Caitlyn had personally witnessed on anyone. Whatever regret she'd been experiencing was gone, as another tidal wave of inappropriate thoughts threatened to drag her under.

You're at work, Caitlyn reprimanded herself. *Stay focused.* A borderline impossible task at this point.

Caitlyn's eyes fell to an envelope in Ash's hand. "What've you got for me? Office appropriate answers only," she warned at the naughty glint in Ash's eyes.

"Now who's a fun hater?" Ash asked with a pout. She opened the wide flap and pulled out the envelope's contents. "I have the report from the medical examiner's office for Fergus Clark."

All jokes about Christmas, thoughts of hot chocolate, and fantasies involving the conference room kindly shuffled to the back of her mind. Caitlyn leaned across her desk, folding her hands, as if Ash wouldn't guess how eager she was for the news. "Cause of death?"

"Sudden cardiac arrest due to probable ventricular fibrillation. The cause of the episode was marked as unknown, but they made note of the presence of a nonlethal quantity of doxylacitromide in his system at time of death." Ash set the report on Caitlyn's desk. "Meaning, not suicide, and not an overdose, intentional or otherwise."

"And therefore *not* Moorehead Academy's fault," Caitlyn added, a satisfied smile tugging at her lips. "Which is very good news for our client. Looks like Hank Kearns jumped the gun on this one. He'll have no choice but to back off."

"As much as I'm happy to be on the winning side of this, I feel terrible for the Clarks," Ash admitted, her eyes drifting to the floor and a melancholy tone coloring her words. "I imagine in a situation like theirs, it would be comforting to have someone to blame."

"Who knows," Caitlyn added thoughtfully as she considered the medical examiner's report. "There may still be someone to blame. Just not our client. At least, not yet, they aren't."

"What?" The sudden sharpness of Ash's tone caught Caitlyn by surprise.

"You know…" Brow creasing, Caitlyn bit down on her lip. "We talked about this on Thanksgiving. There's likely to be one hell of a class action if that buried trial data ever makes it to the light."

"I'm sure there will be, and I plan to have it make my career, just like we said." Ash searched Caitlyn's face with the type of intensity that went all the way to the bone. The conversation seemed to be veering in a direction Caitlyn wasn't comfortable with. "And here I thought I was rubbing off on you."

"What do you mean?"

Disappointment skirted over Ash's beautiful features and Caitlyn's heart sunk lower. "You can't possibly think *we* would be representing Parker Pharmaceutical."

"Then…" Caitlyn's voice trailed off, suddenly at a loss because that *had* been her assumption. She was about to ask *who* when it struck her with enough force to knock the breath out of her lungs. How had she been so thoughtless? "Oh, Jesus, Ash. Of course not. With your dad's history, the last client you would consider taking on is a company like Parker Pharmaceutical. I'm such an idiot."

"Was that really your first impulse? To try to sign those bastards?" Ash continued to study Caitlyn with a hint of distrust that made Caitlyn wish she could rewind the clock by a minute and start over.

"It wasn't based on any kind of moral reason," Caitlyn said, hearing too late how defensive she sounded. "I've been conditioned throughout my career to go for the deep pockets, and I think I learned early on how to bypass my own personal thoughts and feelings when I had to."

"I get it." Even though Caitlyn had no reason to doubt Ash was sincere, there was still a hesitation in the woman's tone that brought a panic to Caitlyn's insides.

"But you don't like it, and a little part of you doesn't like me right now because of it," Caitlyn guessed. It stung to say out loud, but she and Ash had become too good at reading each other for anything other than honesty. Which was, she realized, something she'd need to truly investigate later.

Ash's eyes darted to the hallway and she lowered her

voice. "Of course I still like you. And I do understand. We've both done a lot of things we're not proud of over the years, I'm sure. I just have a mental block when it comes to this particular case, because of my father."

"That's completely natural," Caitlyn soothed. "Granted, they're kind of the ideal McGill and Harding client, but—"

"But they deserve to have their asses handed to them," Ash interjected. "And I hate being on the losing side. Speaking of winning, gifts, you ready for some good news?" It was a peace offering, and Caitlyn was eager to snatch it up.

Caitlyn's eyes lit up. "You actually brought cannoli and chianti this time?"

"Damn. I've disappointed you again!" Ash managed a genuine laugh and the panic that had nestled in Caitlyn's stomach dissipated. "I'm not sure what I have to say will make up for that big a letdown."

"You really need to up your game, especially when I keep telling you what will make me happy." Caitlyn gave an exaggerated sigh, laying it on thick. "But fine. What is it you wanted to share?"

"I was doing some digging into that doxylacitromide stuff last night, and you wouldn't believe their ad campaigns. The TV commercials show all these runners, and rowers... just like the athletes who are taking this stuff like candy to enhance their performance."

Caitlyn rubbed her chin, trying to make sense of this news. "Didn't Jose say this is a cancer drug? What does running and rowing have to do with battling cancer?"

"Exactly. It's almost like encouraging people to abuse

this drug was the whole point of the ads."

Caitlyn went cold inside. "Even as they hid evidence that it could be dangerous to people with certain pre-existing conditions."

"Not if they weren't running marathons," Ash said with disgust, quoting what Jose had told them. "Only that was exactly what they were encouraging them to do."

"In some ways, this reminds me of the 1997 California lawsuit against RJ Reynolds where they ended up having to kill off that cartoon camel in their ads because it was an obvious ploy to get kids to start smoking."

"That was a $10 million settlement, if I remember correctly." Ash's eyes twinkled as she pointed this out, not that Caitlyn needed any more enticement to be brought around to her way of thinking. Defending Parker Pharmaceutical wasn't something Caitlyn wanted to do. She wanted to fight on the right side of this thing, and she had an idea of how to make that happen.

But first, priorities. Ash had risen to leave, and it was speak now or forever hold her peace.

"Hey, Tanner. The mall, tomorrow. You in?"

Ash sighed, her shoulders slumping as she groaned. Had she truly thought Caitlyn would forget? "I'm in."

Caitlyn clapped her hands in victory. It was almost as sweet as the hot chocolate she'd promised. "See you then!"

SITTING in her car and clutching the athletic forms Moorehead Academy had provided, Caitlyn surveyed the house where Fergus Clark's parents lived. It was a gracious home—two stories, distinctive architecture, with a three-car garage—in a neighborhood that screamed money. She hadn't called ahead. There was no way Janet Clark would've agreed to talk to her if she had. But with dusk approaching, there were lights on inside. Caitlyn was willing to take the risk.

Exiting her car, Caitlyn advanced on the front door, willing herself not to lose her nerve. She held her breath as she rang the bell.

A woman answered, and Caitlyn recognized her from photos in the news as Fergus's mother, though her frizzy hair and hollow eyes bore little resemblance to the person she'd been just a few months before.

"Mrs. Clark? I'm—"

"I know who you are and you have some nerve trying to talk to me without my lawyer here. Shove off." She tried to shut the door, but Caitlyn jammed her foot to stop it, the pain shooting up her leg.

"Did you know your son had a heart murmur?"

"What's that?" The woman's almost-dead eyes sparked with anger and roared back to life. "What's wrong with you people? Does no one at Moorehead Academy have a soul?"

Trembling, the woman hunched against the open door and began to sob. Caitlyn's chest squeezed tight and she couldn't help but remember Sadie breaking down as she spilled the news. "Please, Mrs. Clark," Caitlyn begged.

"Just listen for a moment. I'm not here on behalf of the school."

"Then who are you here for?" the woman growled.

"I'm… I'm here for you. I hope." Caitlyn tensed, expecting to be shouted at and turned away, but the woman remained silent, as if she lacked the strength to fight anymore. "I'm really sorry for your loss, and I know this is hard, but I think you'll want to hear me out."

"I shouldn't be talking to you without my lawyer here," the woman said warily.

"Hank Kearns?" Caitlyn did her best to keep her dislike of the ambulance chasing attorney out of her tone. Mrs. Clark had hired him, after all. "Has he not already called you?"

The woman's eyes narrowed. "About what?"

Caitlyn swallowed hard. The one thing she had not been counting on was having to break the news of Fergus's cause of death to his own mother. This was something law school didn't prepare you for, though experiencing what it was like to care for her sister gave her a slightly, if still woefully inadequate, understanding of what she should and shouldn't say. "Mrs. Clark, the medical examiner is ready to rule on the cause of death for your son. Honestly, I thought you would have been contacted by someone from their office, or by Mr. Kearns, already."

The woman responded with a strangled cry that pierced Caitlyn through to the depths of her soul. Caitlyn pressed her lips together and closed her eyes, trying to keep herself from breaking down. She wanted to offer comfort, but she was the last person this bereaved mother would accept it from, so she just waited, swaying slightly, until the worst had passed.

"Mrs. Clark?" Caitlyn said softly when she felt the woman might be able to respond. "Do you think we could go inside for a minute? It's getting cold out, and neighbors are starting to get home, I don't think you want them, you know, to see…"

Mrs. Clark nodded mutely, the prospect of being gawked at by neighbors terrible enough to penetrate her grief. She stood aside, waving Caitlyn in before closing the door. "It's all people do now. Stare. Whisper. That's the family whose son killed himself, they say."

"Only he didn't." Caitlyn braced herself—for what response she wasn't sure—but got a blank stare in return. She was committed to this now. "Your son's death was… well, the medical examiner is going to say it was natural causes, but that's not entirely right. But Fergus didn't take his own life, either."

The woman gripped Caitlyn's arm with shocking strength, a desperate look in her eyes. "He didn't?"

Willing herself not to flinch, Caitlyn shook her head. "No, ma'am. He didn't." Her words ended barely above a whisper. "It was his heart."

"You mentioned… the heart murmur." Mrs. Clark breathed deeply in and out, repeating it so many times Caitlyn feared she was on the verge of passing out. She continued to hold onto Caitlyn's arm, fingers like a vice, but no way was Caitlyn going to make her let go. The woman might end up on the floor.

"The school provided me with a copy of your son's records, including the paperwork the doctor signed off on when Fergus joined the rowing team in First Form." Caitlyn placed a hand gently over Mrs. Clark's before continuing. "It mentioned he had been diagnosed with a Still's murmur when he was a child, and that it was still detectable when the doctor did the exam."

"The doctor said it was harmless," the woman wailed. "I would never have let him play!"

"This is *not* your fault," Caitlyn assured her. "The doctor was right. Ordinarily, there's no reason to be concerned about that type of murmur. Your son was in perfect health to participate in any sports he chose. It's only… did Fergus ever mention a drug he was taking, doxylacitromide?"

"My son didn't get high. Never. What are you trying to claim, that he was some kind of druggie?" The woman grew agitated once more. "First everyone's pointing at us because Fergus died, then because they heard it might be suicide. And now? Now we're the family with the drug addict, I guess."

This wasn't going the way Caitlyn needed it to and she'd need to work hard to salvage it, fast. "Mrs. Clark—"

"Do you know what it's been like living in this neighborhood since Fergus died? Filled with these judgmental, holier-than-thou types who pretend to be your friends when everything's going great, when they think you'll donate to their charity or give their brother a job at your company. But they're all just waiting for some juicy gossip as soon as something goes wrong." The woman continued to rail, paying no attention to Caitlyn's attempt at redirection.

Caitlyn took a moment to sweep a quick glance at her surroundings. Only the living room light on, and Halloween decorations were still in sight despite the Christmas season approaching. It was as if everything had stopped in this house the moment they'd learned about their son's death. Imagining what the upcoming holidays would be like, Caitlyn's heart clenched. She was even more determined to nail Parker Pharmaceuticals to the wall for what their greed had caused.

"I can only imagine it's been a living hell," Caitlyn answered truthfully.

"We just want to move." A desperate quality had crept into Mrs. Clark's tone. "Fergus was our youngest. His older sister lives in Ohio. We just want to sell this house and go there, but we're not as rich as some of the families at Moorehead. My husband has to work to pay the bills. I thought maybe with a wrongful death settlement… but now you're saying no one's at fault?"

"No, ma'am. That's not at all what I'm saying." Caitlyn set her jaw, determination coursing through her veins. "The makers of the drug your son was taking, that they were knowingly marketing to young athletes like him while hiding studies suggesting it could in rare cases have dangerous side effects, are most certainly to blame."

Mrs. Clark put her hands to the sides of her head as if to steady herself. "What was this drug you keep talking about? He wasn't on any medications. I don't know where it could have come from."

"It's a prescription drug, for cancer," Caitlyn

explained. "Most likely he was getting it at the gym near school. Several of his teammates appear to have been taking it, and it's all the rage with some athletes right now because it's not a banned substance and no one's testing for it in competitions."

"Cancer?" Mrs. Clark blinked a few times and shook her head. "I don't understand."

"It was developed for cancer, but one of the things it does is improve cardiovascular strength. I have reason to believe the manufacturer, Rindge Biotech, was aware of this, and also knew about potential heart-related side effects if used by highly active people with a certain type of heart murmur. The type your son had."

"But, how?" The woman still looked confused, and Caitlyn couldn't blame her. "I don't understand how the boys would even know to take such a thing."

"Well, there's more. I believe the parent company, Parker Pharmaceutical, was also well aware of both the cardiovascular strengthening properties of the drug and the potential for dangerous side effects if misused. Despite this, they signed off on a marketing campaign to sort of subliminally push the drug for off-label use as a performance enhancer for endurance sports, like running and rowing."

"Parker Pharmaceutical?" Mrs. Clark's eyes grew large. Understanding began to settle on her grief-stricken face. "They're... huge. You'll excuse me for saying, Miss... I'm sorry, I never got your name."

"Caitlyn Brewster."

"Ms. Brewster..." The woman frowned. "That firm you work for, McGill and Harding, isn't it? It seems like

Parker Pharmaceutical is more your type of client, not someone like me."

This statement hit like a blow to the gut, because it was exactly what Ash had pointed out too. And they were both right. The firm she'd gone to work for right out of law school, that her own uncle had helped to found, was not one of the good guys. At least, not often enough. But that was going to change, even if Caitlyn had to go directly to her Uncle Bertie to plead her case.

"You're completely right," Caitlyn admitted, sensing truth was the only way to keep Mrs. Clark listening. "But I believe in *this* case. I think Parker Pharmaceutical is responsible for your son's death. I want to help you sue the bastards. It won't bring Fergus back, but you might be able to save another family from the pain you're going through."

There was silence. Long enough Caitlyn's mouth went dry.

Caitlyn was prepared to count to twenty, after which she would turn around, walk through the door, and head back home in defeat. When she reached nineteen, Mrs. Clark let out a long, thin sigh.

"What do you need from me?" Her tone, while reluctant, was soft.

Caitlyn's heart pounded. Was it possible she'd won the woman over? "Right now, I just need to ask some questions."

The woman nodded, looking tired but like there was a slight ray of hope where only darkness had been before. "Okay. But I'm not agreeing to anything yet. Just talking."

"I understand." As Caitlyn followed Mrs. Clark to the living room, she struggled to keep her joy in check. It wasn't the time or the place. But once the Clarks were officially on board, she couldn't wait to share the news.

Ash was going to be so proud of her once she knew. But for now, Caitlyn wanted to keep it a surprise.

CHAPTER TWENTY-THREE

"I just need one more thing from Newbury Comics," Sadie declared, pausing beside the entrance to the mall's food court to sort through the multiple shopping bags dangling from her wrists.

"Newbury Comics?" Ash set her own assortment of bags onto the tile floor with a groan. "Wasn't that all the way back down by Macy's on the first floor?"

"It won't take long." Sadie said this with the energy that only humans under the age of twenty possess.

Ash turned to Caitlyn, who was holding at least three of Ash's bags and wore a despondent expression that matched how Ash felt. That, at least, allowed for a brief flicker of schadenfreude. "Go on. Go without me." Ash said this the way a narrator in a documentary might read a letter home from a Civil War soldier. "Tell my mother and the children I fought as bravely as I could."

Caitlyn rolled her eyes. "Buck up, soldier. That café I was telling you about is right around the corner. Why don't we go get some hot chocolate while Sadie walks ten miles in the snow, uphill both ways, to finish her shopping."

Ash perked up considerably at this prospect, grabbing her bags from around her feet. "Do I get extra whipped cream?"

"Only if you stop whining," Caitlyn told her, giving Ash's hip a bump with her own as they carried their bags through the crowded food court. This restored Ash's spirits, which became even brighter as she noticed the café had several open tables and fewer people than the main area they'd just plowed their way through.

"Thank God. I thought I might die." Ash collapsed onto a chair, cramming all the shopping bags into the corner before sprawling out with her limbs in front of her. Now that she was seated, every inch of her body ached. "I'm not sure I will ever be able to get up again."

"Too bad, Princess. You have to place your order at the counter." Caitlyn put her hands on her hip, intent on staring her down. Ash responded with a whimper, her lower lip jutting out in a well-practiced pout, making Caitlyn's determination waver. "Fine. You sit here and I'll take care of it."

"You're the best." Ash flashed a grateful smile, surprised by just how deeply she meant it. Caitlyn was the best thing that had ever happened to her, and Ash honestly wasn't sure how she'd gotten so lucky. Except, maybe, that for once, she'd let down her guard and allowed another person to have access to the parts of herself she usually kept locked away.

Who knew that would turn out so well?

As she turned her feet in circles, wiggling her toes

inside her boots to keep the circulation going, one of Ash's favorite holiday songs filtered through the cacophony of shoppers. She found herself humming along. She, Ashley Tanner, was in a mall, doing Christmas shopping for her family—actual presents that she might even wrap, as opposed to stopping at a grocery store on Christmas Eve and selecting gift cards from a picked-through display near the register.

And she had one beautiful, tiny Elle Woods look-alike to thank for it. Ash could never have predicted her life would bring her to this moment, and yet here she was. With the holiday looming, Ash had made up her mind. She was inviting Caitlyn and Sadie to join her family for the annual Christmas Eve giant deli tray and early gift opening extravaganza, and they were going to spend Christmas Day together too. And no more pretenses about being friends from the office. She was going to tell her whole family the truth.

Fortunately, Ash already knew her announcement, however unprecedented, would quickly be overshadowed by her sister's engagement news, and therefore the timing couldn't be better. She just had to find the right time to talk about it with Caitlyn.

Caitlyn carried a tray from the drink counter, cautiously weaving through the tables before pulling up short to avoid being wiped out by a man on his phone, shouting as if the world was ending. Caitlyn sported a devious smile that instantly made Ash both curious and a little nervous. She hoped this wasn't Caitlyn's way of breaking the news that she, too, had forgotten a gift for someone and had to go traipsing back through half the mall to find it. They'd been shopping for what seemed like an eternity, and Ash had emphatically crossed the last name off her list with a promise not to step inside another store until she died.

Of course, Ash had yet to buy anything for Caitlyn or Sadie—not like it was easy to do when they'd been with her all day. It was fine, though. Ash was fairly sure she could handle another shopping trip on her own. They would be worth it.

Caitlyn still wore that mischievous grin.

Ash's tummy did a flip. "What gives?"

"Since you didn't come to the counter with me, I took the liberty of ordering you one of my favorites." Caitlyn set the tray down on the table. "Extra whipped cream."

Ash could hardly believe the three mugs in front of her. Chocolate flakes were scattered like tiny twigs along a snowy hill of whipped cream. Some type of white frosting with red and green sprinkles hung down the sides of the glass mugs like garland. On the plate were crushed peppermints and red and white balls of… actually, Ash wasn't sure. As if that wasn't enough, a full candy cane stuck out of the top of the drink.

"I may have miscalculated on that extra whipped cream. When you promised me a hot chocolate, I had no idea it would be…" Words failed Ash.

"I think the word you're looking for is masterpiece." Caitlyn rubbed her hands together in obvious glee. "It's like a Christmas miracle in a mug."

"I don't even put sugar in my tea." As arguments went, Ash knew it was a losing one. And Caitlyn looked so pleased with herself. It was time to lay off the snark, even if that was her go-to form of communication, and opt for something at least as sweet as the sugar-laden (diabetes inducing) holiday offering her beautiful girlfriend—that's right, *girlfriend*, and she wasn't even going to try to walk it back—had brought her. "I love it."

"You do?" Caitlyn's eyes lit up like it was already Christmas morning and she'd just caught a glimpse of all the goodies under the tree. Then a text arrived on her phone, stopping her mid-thought. Caitlyn glanced at the screen, her face clouding.

"What is it?" Ash's stomach tightened. She didn't like how quickly the joy had drained from Caitlyn's face. "Everything okay?"

"There's just a... complication at work. No big deal. I can deal with it... later." Caitlyn forced a smile that failed to reach her eyes. "I'll bring Sadie home and then head into the office later on tonight."

For "no big deal" Ash couldn't help thinking it sure looked like a big deal. Caitlyn's perky holiday mood was gone, and even the abomination of sugar in front of her failed to restore it as she took a sip. What was Caitlyn working on that could cause such a plummet?

"Whatever needs taking care of, I can do it," Ash volunteered. "I live fifteen minutes from the office. There's no need for you to go in."

"I... I think this is something I need to do on my own." Caitlyn's eyes flickered with a cageyness that was unexpected given how close she and Ash had been working, not to mention their budding relationship outside of work. Ash tried to shut the alarms in her mind off.

"Tell you what. I've already got the Zipcar for the day

and I'm nowhere near using all the miles. I'll take Sadie home once we finish shopping." At almost the same moment, Sadie came into the café, waving when she spotted Ash and Caitlyn.

"You wouldn't mind?" Caitlyn blinked, and this time when she smiled, it looked genuine. "You're a lifesaver!"

"What's going on?" Sadie asked as she sat down and proceeded to knock back a good portion of her hot chocolate in one go. Ash could almost feel the sugar rush in her own veins.

"I need to make an unexpected detour to the office, but Ash has volunteered to take you home," Caitlyn explained. "I shouldn't be gone too long."

"Again?" Sadie's narrow shoulders bent as she slumped over her mug. "I thought you said you weren't going to work so much."

"I know…" Caitlyn's lips pressed into a line.

"I really can't help with it?" Ash pressed, curiosity beginning to stretch its claws.

"No," Caitlyn said, "but tell you what. I'll make up for it by ordering from Mama Maria's when I get home. Ash, you're more than welcome to stay—if you don't have to get the car back, that is."

"It should be fine," Ash assured her. "You know how I feel about their pizza."

What she really meant was *you know how I feel about you*. Anything she could do to make Caitlyn's life better, and any way she could spend more time with her and Sadie, Ash was up for it. Recalling Sadie's earlier disappointment, Ash made a mental note to get Caitlyn to take her promise not to work so many weekends seriously.

She'd get the woman to take some time off, even if it meant having to make the same pledge herself.

Wasn't it about time?

Ash had been working six or seven days a week from the day she walked through McGill and Harding's door. With the partnership announcement less than a month away, there couldn't possibly be anything left for her to prove. And what was the point of finally making it to partner if she couldn't let her foot off the gas a little and enjoy her life? She'd earned it, and she finally had someone she wanted to spend the time with.

Ash's gaze drifted from Caitlyn to Sadie, a feeling even sweeter than her hot chocolate blossoming in her chest. Make that a couple of someones, and a curly-haired mop of a puppy too.

"Okay, I'm off. Thanks again, Ash." Caitlyn grabbed up her things. "I... I really appreciate it."

Ash let out a breath. For a moment, she'd been certain Caitlyn was going to say *I love you.* Which would've been some pretty weird circumstances for saying such a momentous thing for the first time. But even as she nodded and waved Caitlyn on her way, Ash couldn't help feeling a little sad, because the truth was, she'd wanted to hear those words.

If you want to hear them, a little voice said in her head, *you might try saying them yourself.*

Ash sucked in her cheeks to hold back a laugh. That damn voice in her head was probably onto something. Maybe she'd do exactly that. Tonight, after pizza was done and Sadie had left them alone to go play whatever games on her computer she liked to do with her friends, Ash would tell Caitlyn exactly how she felt.

Ash's entire body threatened to clench into one giant stress ball but she forced herself to relax. Just because she'd never said *I love you* to anyone before didn't mean she needed to stress about it, right?

Ash lifted the mug of cocoa to her lips, grimacing as soon as the syrupy hot liquid hit her taste buds. Yikes. She slid it toward Sadie, who had apparently already finished hers and was looking bereft. "You want the rest of this?"

"Yes!" Sadie slid the mug over with an expression of total happiness. "Before we head home, do you mind if we go to just one more store?"

Ash held back a cry of despair. After all, she was supposed to be the grownup, and Sadie really was a good kid. She deserved to enjoy the holidays. Ash took a fortifying breath and nodded. "Sure. One more store."

The overjoyed clicking of paws on a bare wood floor greeted them the moment Sadie opened the front door to her house. Laughter bubbled up in Ash's chest as excited yips echoed in the entryway. With as much time as she'd been spending lately with Caitlyn, Sadie, and the puppy, it almost felt like Ash was coming home.

It was a comforting feeling.

"I think he missed you," said an older woman with bright red hair, whom Ash somehow hadn't managed to meet yet. Yet the woman lit up with instant recognition. "Are you Ash?"

"I am." Ash's stomach fluttered, absurdly nervous standing in front of this woman who was the closest person Caitlyn had to a mother. What if she took one look at Ash and didn't approve?

"I'm Gilda. It's so very lovely to finally meet you." The woman didn't put her hand out to shake, but it wasn't because any of Ash's worries had proven true. Instead, she pulled Ash into a full-body embrace, the kind only plump grandmotherly types could truly pull off.

Instead of being put off by the crushing hug, it made Ash smile. Not simply because the housekeeper smelled of freshly baked sugar cookies and peppermint like her body had been sculpted from a Christmas candle. It was because Ash recalled that in the not-so-distant past, Caitlyn had said she'd seen razor wire with edges less sharp.

Look who's lost her edge.

Ash's smile turned slightly frown-like as she pondered that thought. It hadn't exactly turned out how she'd intended, seeming to suggest she'd lost her drive. Would people start to think that? It couldn't be further from the truth. Just because she wanted to slow down a little and spend more time with Caitlyn didn't mean she was going soft.

"It's lovely to meet you too," Ash mumbled into Gilda's bakery-scented apron, glad no one had been able to catch her momentary crisis of confidence.

"Would you two like some hot chocolate to warm up?" Gilda offered after releasing Ash from her embrace.

"No thank you," Ash was quick to say, pretty certain she'd never drink another hot cocoa in her life.

"You seem like more of a black tea gal, minus the sugar," Gilda declared, her rosy cheeks making her look like Mrs. Claus, at least if Santa's spouse had suddenly decided to spruce up her white locks. "Come on into the kitchen."

Ash gaped as the woman turned and started down the hall. "How—?"

"It's one of Gilda's many magical powers," Sadie whispered. "Don't question it."

Sadie picked up one of Happy's toys and tossed it down the hallway, the dog's nails once again doing a number on the floor. Ash followed Gilda to the kitchen as requested, pondering whether the woman truly did have magical powers, or whether Caitlyn had mentioned her tea preference in conversation enough times for it to stick.

In which case, Caitlyn must talk about her an awful lot. Ash wasn't sure whether the fluttering she felt was due to pride or nerves.

"Where's Caitlyn?" Gilda asked as she filled the kettle with water.

"Work, naturally," Sadie answered, joining Ash near the island. Ash didn't miss the note of bitterness. "Where else would my sister be?"

"You'll understand some day." Gilda flicked the kettle on.

Sadie crossed her arms and looked unconvinced. "You'd think her uncle wouldn't make her work so hard."

"Her uncle?" A warning claxon sounded in Ash's

brain, taunting her with a deep sense of dread even before Sadie could answer.

"Oh, you know. Uncle Bertie." Sadie said this like it was common knowledge, but Ash's insides went cold. "You must have met him since you work at his firm too."

Ash tried swallowing, but couldn't, given the lump forming in her throat. "Are you saying you're related to Cuthbert Harding?"

"Not me." Sadie, not seeming to detect Ash's distress, laughed. "The relationship is only on Caitlyn's mom's side. Her grandmother and old Bertie were brother and sister."

"I... had no idea," Ash managed to squeak out, sounding much like the toy Happy was busy destroying. Her mind scrambled to make sense of what she was hearing.

"That doesn't surprise me," Gilda said, squinting a bit as she looked at Ash, seeming to pick up on the shock Sadie had missed. "Caity doesn't like people thinking she didn't work hard to make it on her own. She always tries to win."

Sadie said, "Not that one time, though. Whoever it was, she must've really felt sorry for them." Before Ash could question this assertion, Sadie picked up the toy Happy had dropped at her feet and tossed it down the hallway again.

Gilda popped a teabag into a mug and poured hot water over it.

Ash could barely breathe. Thoughts tumbled around faster than shirts in a clothes dryer. How had she been so stupid?

Caitlyn Brewster was a liar.

A hard worker? Please. She was just like all the rest.

No wonder she'd been hired with such haste, being related to Uncle Bertie. It didn't get much more special privilege than that. While Ash had worked her buttocks off to win the opportunity simply to get her foot in the door, all Caitlyn had to do was pick up the phone and say, "I want to work in Boston." Why had she even bothered entering that stupid mock trial competition in the first place when her family legacy had been guaranteed?

Ash nearly choked as a possibility occurred to her. What had Sadie said about not winning *that one time*? And *feeling sorry for them*? Which time? And who?

Ash wanted desperately to chase the girl down and demand an answer, except she really didn't want to know. The answers that were fighting to click into place in her head were enough to spin Ash's world off its axis.

"I just remembered!" Ash made a show of bonking her forehead, much harder than necessary, but somehow the pain felt good. A bit of reality in what was fast becoming a nightmare. "I have to get the Zipcar back to Boston in an hour."

Gilda frowned. "Are you sure you can't get an extension? I thought Sadie said you were staying for dinner."

"Afraid not. There's going to be a massive fine if I don't go right now. Can you explain to Caitlyn?" Ash made to leave, not sure she could stave off the tears threatening to spill long enough to make it back to the car. She needed to get out before she fell apart.

"What a shame. Let me at least make your tea to go, to keep the chill off on the road." Gilda opened a cupboard, and it took ages—or approximately five seconds—to locate a silver travel cup with *See You Later, Litigator* written on the side and a sketch of an alligator. This tiny detail confirmed that Ash must be trapped in a terrible dream. That couldn't possibly be real.

Ash was already speed-walking down the driveway when Sadie called out from the front door, "Where are you going? Don't you want pizza?"

Ash knew she really should stop and answer, but if she did, she'd have to go back. And if she went back, she'd have to give Sadie a hug, and pet Happy on that adorably fuzzy puppy head, and understand exactly how much she was losing. And if she did that, her heart would break even more than it was doing now.

Ash picked up speed, pretending not to hear.

CHAPTER TWENTY-FOUR

It was a dreary Monday morning, a sprinkle of rain having turned most of the pavement in the greater Boston area to ice, as Caitlyn balanced her coffee mug on top of a binder and tried to open the office door without having to put her bag down in a puddle. Wind whipped her hair around her face, only making things worse.

"Let me help!" Zach rushed up behind, taking the mug and folder into one hand, and opening the door with the other. "This isn't chauvinistic, is it? Men can still do this?"

"People can always help their coworkers." Caitlyn hadn't intended to sound so snappish, but she hadn't slept well the previous night—scratch that, the past two nights—and was in no mood for Zach's flirtations, no matter how harmless or lame.

As they walked side by side to the elevator, Zach eyed the binder, which Caitlyn had labeled near the top corner.

"Parker Pharmaceuticals, huh? That's a whopper of a whale. Did you sign them?"

Immediately regretting her neatness and efficiency—she could have left the binder unlabeled considering she knew exactly what was in it—Caitlyn practically ripped the research material and extensive handwritten notes from his grasp. "Maybe. Maybe not."

It was a childish retort, but considering Zach hadn't skedaddled from her sight yet, her mood wasn't exactly improving with each passing second.

"I'm thinking you haven't, but it's in the works." He continued tailing Caitlyn from the elevator and down the hall to her office, chattering like he thought she cared about his opinions and theories when all she wanted was silence and a little space as she hung up her coat and settled in. "If I can be of any assistance as you're putting together your proposal, all you have to do is ask." Zach flashed his pearly whites, and Caitlyn experienced an almost irresistible urge to douse him with scalding hot coffee. Sadly, what was left in her travel mug—her *second* favorite because Ash had absconded with the best one when she'd ditched Caitlyn on Saturday night with zero explanation—wasn't all that hot anymore after the long drive through Boston morning gridlock.

"You'll be my first call if I do," she said, mostly to get the guy off her back. She put her bag on the hook next to her coat and slipped the binder into her desk drawer. "But the highway was a skating rink and I'm running late to a meeting, so I've really gotta run."

"Gotcha." Zach did that annoying double-index-finger-gun-maneuver thing guys always felt compelled to do, including a clicking sound as he pointed each finger at her in turn. Reason four hundred ninety-two why Caitlyn preferred the company of women. Not that they didn't present a whole other host of issues to contend with, but in all her experience, not a single one had done that stupid finger pistol move. "Let me say one last thing. If I help you land the Parker account, can I be second chair? I went to school with the grandson of the owner."

Why wasn't she surprised to hear this? But that was a potentially useful nugget of information and Caitlyn stored it away in her mental file.

"Second chair, hm? That's an idea." Not a good one, but Caitlyn didn't think she needed to say that part. Though they'd been careful to keep their romantic relationship under wraps, by now everyone in the office must have noticed that she and Ash were the hottest legal team in town. At least, they had been until Ash had rushed off on Saturday without so much as a word of explanation. Gilda and Sadie had been mystified. Tamping down a sense of foreboding, Caitlyn was determined not to worry. She and Ash were the dynamic duo, better together than they were apart.

But it was possible Zach hadn't gotten that memo because he grinned, apparently taking her statement at face value, and then ran off after Larry Cooper, most likely to do some more high-level butt kissing. If Zach spent more time actually practicing law instead of ingratiating himself with favors, he just might make something of himself on his own merit. Too bad it would never happen. A guy like Zach had been conditioned since birth to rely on family connections and deals made with a handshake at the country club. Caitlyn knew because she'd grown up in that world too. She'd just had the good sense to realize early on that she could do better.

In some ways, Ash had helped her with that since the very first day they'd met.

But speaking of Ash, Caitlyn did need to get to the bottom of whatever was going on. Was Ash feeling ill, or had an emergency come up in her family? Caitlyn had been worried sick ever since she'd arrived home to discover Ash was gone with no explanation. And the woman hadn't returned one message since.

She started down the long hallway toward Ash's office. The light was on, meaning she wasn't sick, or at least not serious enough to stay home. Caitlyn's lips curled into a half smile. Knowing Ash, she would have to be on her deathbed to stay home, and even then, she'd probably insist on working remotely.

"Knock, knock," Caitlyn sang out in a cheery tone, lightly tapping her knuckles on Ash's door.

Ash shot daggers at Caitlyn with her eyes, turning Caitlyn's blood to stone. She stopped in her tracks.

What the hell was going on?

Belatedly, Caitlyn regretted not taking the time to grab a second cup of coffee, extra sugar, before stumbling into whatever battle this was, which she was about to have whether she liked it or not. It was way too early on a Monday morning for this. Especially seeing as she was completely unprepared.

"What happened Saturday?" Caitlyn asked,

approaching Ash with caution, like she was a fire-breathing dragon.

"Saturday?" The temperature of the office dropped at least five degrees from Ash's tone alone. "As I recall, you had to bail because of some mysterious work-related business." The stiffness in Ash's body was closer to their bleak first few weeks working together.

"But you didn't seem at all upset by it at the time," Caitlyn argued, even though she sensed arguing with Ash when she was in such an oddly foul mood was in no one's best interest. "I expected you would stick around until I got home. I brought pizza *and* cannoli."

Ash remained rigid in her chair, not responding even to the magic word *cannoli*. Something was majorly not right with this situation, but Caitlyn was at a loss about what it could be.

"You missed out," she added timidly, praying something, anything, would snap the woman out of her funk.

"I have work to do." With that proclamation, Ash returned her attention to her laptop, making it clear Caitlyn had been dismissed.

Hell no. Caitlyn was not about to put up with *that*. Maybe her father could get away with going emotionally distant and disappearing from her life, but not Ash. That was *not* going to happen.

"Not until you tell me what's going on." Caitlyn closed the office door quietly to give them privacy, keeping one hand on the knob in case she was overwhelmed by the need to run, because damn, Ash's expression was scary. "You haven't returned a single one of my messages in more than a day. I even tried *calling.* You know how much I hate talking on the phone."

"You answer the phone all the time." Ash delivered this observation in a cool monotone. Though she might live to regret it, Caitlyn wished the woman would get good and riled up, and just tell her what was wrong so they could fix it already and move on.

"For work, yes." Relaxing her grip on the doorknob, Caitlyn balled her fists. There would be no running. She was committed to staying for the fight. "I don't call *people* people."

Ash blinked, still doing her best impression of a robot in a human suit. "Is that what I am? *People* people?"

"I don't know what you are right now." Caitlyn punctuated her sentence with a stomp that sent a shock of pain from her foot to her knee.

"That's odd, because I know what *you* are." Ash paused like she was taking aim, but Caitlyn wasn't sure what the incoming bomb was going to be. "Or should I say who you are?"

"What does that mean?" But already Caitlyn was awash in dread.

"How's Uncle Bertie?" There was nothing remotely warm in Ash's dark eyes, not even the molten anger that Caitlyn had seen in them too many times to count. How she wished she were seeing that now, instead of this. "No one around here has seen him in quite some time, but I'm betting you have."

A rush of adrenaline hit Caitlyn so hard that it had the opposite effect nature had intended. Instead of bolting, she couldn't move a muscle. "I can explain."

Ash steepled her fingers under her chin waiting like an executioner who had asked if the condemned had any last words. Caitlyn got the sense she could talk all she wanted, but as soon as she finished, the ax would fall nonetheless.

"Can you not do that?" Caitlyn pleaded.

"Do what?"

"Look so intimidating." Caitlyn pressed her lips together tightly.

"This is how I look. If you're intimidated, maybe the issue is you, not me." Even now, Ash wasn't showing outward forms of anger. That was bad news. It had to be. Caitlyn's brain was in a tailspin trying to figure out what she could do to get the woman to react normally, by having a fit and then getting over it.

The only plan she could think of was telling the truth.

As plans went, that was shit.

Caitlyn sat down in the chair next to the desk anyway, determined to tell Ash everything and hope for the best. "It's nothing sinister. You already know I've never wanted to cash in on my family connection. That's all it was, laying low and putting in my time like everyone else."

Ash laughed out loud, but not the good kind of laughter. It was the type that made her look a little unbalanced. "Sure. And when you needed to come home for Sadie, you didn't pick up the phone and ring dear old Uncle Bertie?"

She couldn't possibly expect Caitlyn to feel guilty over that! Not when she knew how awful the situation with Sadie had been. "That was different. Sadie was in trouble." Caitlyn crossed her arms, perturbed by the unfairness of the accusation. Ash would have done the same, called in any favor she could, if one of her own siblings was in trouble. She had some real nerve to judge Caitlyn for doing what she would have done in a heartbeat. "What's really bothering you, huh? That I'm working here now at a position you don't think I earned with enough blood, sweat, and tears? Or that I didn't confide in you about who my grandmother's brother happened to be the minute I stepped off the elevator, back when you were determined to pretend you didn't even remember my name?"

"I think I could've gotten over the lie of omission," Ash said softly, and for the first time, a note of pain sang through, sharp enough to pierce Caitlyn's heart and leave her trembling.

"Could have?" That implied Ash hadn't, or wouldn't, or there was something else. Basically, it left Caitlyn feeling she was screwed.

Ash sank back into her chair, pressing her palms into her eyes. A look of near defeat if ever Caitlyn saw one and it chilled her to her core. "I mean, yes, it hurt that you had kept it from me, even when there were times later on, once we'd gotten to know each other—trust each other—better, that you could have told me. But after I went home on Saturday, I spent a lot of time ruminating." The hands dropped into her lap, but Ash didn't look any less worn.

"That never goes well." Caitlyn tensed as her attempt to lighten the mood fell flat.

"I figured out your other secret, Caitlyn."

"What other secret?" Caitlyn asked in a hoarse whisper. Flipping through her mental database at top speed, she couldn't come up with anything else. What did Ash think she'd done?

"The one about me. And the mock trial, six years ago."

Oh. That secret.

Caitlyn felt everything she and Ash had built over the past several months teeter, threatening to come crashing down. She couldn't let that happen.

"Ash, I don't know what—"

Ash stopped her with a raised hand and a scowl. "I didn't need your pity back then, and I certainly don't need it now."

"W-what?" Caitlyn stuttered. "I'm not following."

Ash pressed on. "I never understood, considering the very first night we met you talked such a big game, critiquing everyone in the room, how you made a rookie mistake at the end. I chalked it up to nerves getting the better of you, but that wasn't it. Was it?"

Caitlyn didn't reply, just squeezed her eyes shut to keep tears from spilling out. Ash was right. It hadn't been nerves. But no one was ever supposed to know.

"I'm not sure what's worse"—Ash's tone remained steady but there was a seething quality right below the surface that threatened to dissolve Caitlyn into a million tiny pieces and wash her away—"the fact you didn't think I could beat you fair and square, or that you thought I was some charity case."

"That wasn't it," Caitlyn argued, even though it kind of was, if she stopped to think. "I never took pity on you.

I only thought it was unfair of me to try to win a prize I didn't need."

"Look me in the eyes and say that." Ash's jaw tensed. "You can't, can you? A prize you didn't need? I mean, why even enter? And for fuck sake, not a single other asshole in that competition needed that prize any more than you did. Just me. That's no reason to throw the fucking game."

For Ash, that had been a monumental number of swear words within office walls. Caitlyn was stunned.

"Ash… this is ridiculous." Caitlyn grasped for something, anything, to fix this mess she'd caused. "You're upset about something that happened six years ago. It shouldn't even matter anymore."

"Right. How could I be upset by having you hand me a victory? Spoken like a woman who's had everything handed to her on a fucking platter." Ash straightened. "If you don't mind, I need to get back to work."

"What…?" Caitlyn cleared her throat, thickened with emotion. "What does that mean for us?"

"Honestly?" Ash closed her eyes, like all the energy had drained from her battery, leaving her unable to go on. "I'm not sure. I just don't have the bandwidth to deal with it right now."

Caitlyn counted to five before leaving Ash's office, in hopes the woman would say something else. Not one word, unless you counted the angry pounding on her laptop.

Leaving the office, Caitlyn started down the hallway, which seemed miles long, when Zach headed right for her. She couldn't. Not after that.

"Whoa, there, little lady—"

Caitlyn's teeth clenched. "Fuck off, Zach."

His eyes grew wide and Caitlyn realized her error.

"That came out wrong. What I meant was, opening a door for a colleague is fine, calling me *little lady*—not so much. Okay?" This was the one time Caitlyn was thankful she was related to the firm's founder, because if Zach reported her to HR for how she'd spoken to him just now, she would abso-fucking-lutely play the uncle card.

"I was only teasing." He placed a hand over his heart, not that he could easily be mistaken for someone who made a habit of being sincere. "I thought of something that might help you land Parker."

Like she gave two fucks about Parker, although, if Caitlyn managed to sue the shit out of the evil pharmaceutical company, maybe Ash might forgive her for the past. Or at least thaw a degree or two. Right now, it had been hard to tell Ash apart from an abominable snow monster.

Disliking the guy but knowing he might be useful, Caitlyn linked arms with Zach. "Tell me everything you know about Parker Pharmaceutical."

"I think the best way to land them—"

"No," Caitlyn interrupted. "I don't want to work with them. I'm thinking of suing them."

He laughed as if she'd said the funniest thing he ever heard, which he followed up with, "Don't be ridiculous. Parker gets sued all the time. If we can bring them onboard, the firm would be rolling in it. And you can bet our bonuses would be sweet. I mean, especially if we make partner, am I right?" He wasn't going to get it. He was like all the rest of them—like she'd been—chasing after the approval and the promotion.

"You know what, Zach? I really don't care." Caitlyn left the stunned fourth-year associate to ponder this sentiment and hurried back to her office, intent on what was truly important: fixing things with Ash.

CHAPTER TWENTY-FIVE

Ash stared at the calendar on her desk, convinced for a moment that time had been running backward. It was finally Friday, but this may have been the world's longest week and she only had herself to blame.

No. Caitlyn was to blame, Ash reminded herself. Only her heart wasn't in it anymore.

Did it really matter who was at fault when the result was the same? A week's worth of days that fluctuated between furious spurts of energy and hours of staring blankly at the walls, each night spent tossing and turning in sleepless misery.

Ash had been so certain her relationship with Caitlyn was meant to be, she'd been ready to announce it to the world—or at least to their families—until Sadie had revealed the secret Caitlyn had been keeping. It had knocked the wind out of Ash, and wounded her pride deeply to confront the truth of the mock trial win Ash had built her career on.

On the other hand, was it really worth the pain she was causing herself not to at least try to work things through? Especially when her life, which had seemed fine before, now felt painfully empty?

But she lied about who she was, a voice in Ash's head reminded her. *And she didn't think you were good enough to win on your own.*

That was the part that hurt the most. As miserable as she felt, she wasn't sure she could ever get over the psychological damage inflicted by knowing Caitlyn was just one more person she would always have to prove herself to.

Ash poked at her mouse with her index finger, not quite ready to start the work day. She was contemplating another cup of tea despite having half a cup left when Jenna rushed into her office, a hurricane in heels.

"Who in the heck are you wooing?" The paralegal's face was flushed.

Wooing? Was Jenna trying to imply that she'd heard a rumor about Ash and Caitlyn? If so, the timing was abysmal. They hadn't so much as spoken to each other since Ash had given Caitlyn the cold shoulder on Monday, and if she were being honest, she wasn't sure they'd ever speak again. That wasn't Ash's choice, just a fact. The evidence to support it was right in front of her, in the form of the hot tea that still partially filled her mug.

Hot tea.

Ash gulped down a sob. The entire week, the kettle had been left alone. Her sandwiches went undisturbed. Her pens... Okay, Ash had never figured out what mischief Caitlyn had done to her pens but she'd replaced them all with a new box and hadn't asked questions. Regardless, it seemed a safe bet the pens were fine this time around too. Caitlyn wasn't enacting petty revenge for Ash's mistreatment of her. Not this time.

There was only one explanation Ash could find for it. Caitlyn had given up.

"Jenna, what are you talking about?" Composing herself, Ash put the cap back onto her pink highlighter. "I haven't been on a date in years."

Was this a lie? After all, she and Caitlyn had never officially called the time they spent together a date.

"Why would I care about your pathetic lack of love life?" Jenna chided, waving her comment away. "I'm talking about whatever whale of a client you've got on the hook."

Ash's brow furrowed. "You lost me."

"Oh, come on now." Jenna found a comfy spot on the corner of Ash's desk to make herself at home, settling in to dish out the juicy gossip. "Every equity partner in the office is being called on to help wine and dine them, whoever they are. I haven't seen Mr. Cooper this excited since—well, since Caitlyn Brewster showed up in that red dress, but that's probably not a great example."

"That didn't clarify at all," Ash scolded. Worse, it had put the image of Caitlyn in her red dress front and center in Ash's head.

"Stop pretending, will ya?" Jenna was giving Ash that *we're buddies* look. "You know I won't tell. Once the information is in, I'm a locked safe." Jenna even went through a ridiculous mime routine of locking her lips shut and tossing the "key" over her shoulder.

"Have you lost your mind?" Ash stared at the paralegal. "Jenna, you're good at your job, don't get me wrong, but the fact that you're in here telling me about a potential big client that's being kept hush-hush is proof that lock on your safe is easily picked."

Jenna started to speak, but then gave Ash a scrutinizing look. "You seriously don't know what's going on? I was sure this was your doing."

All at once, Ash remembered Jenna stating on the very first day Caitlyn arrived that she was some sort of legacy of the firm, but Ash had let that detail slip her mind. A huge mistake. Her carelessness had caused her to get crushed. Who knew heartache hurt this much? Ash pressed her palm to her chest, hoping it might dull the pain some.

"I seem to be the last to know about everything," she said quietly.

"Well, shit." Jenna's outburst put Ash on the edge of her seat.

"What's wrong?" She wasn't sure she could take much more bad news.

"It's just, the way the guys are kicking up their feet like a bunch of roosters, this potential client is a big one. I overheard Mr. Cooper and Mr. Lamont crowing about how this sealed the partnership race for sure." Concern lined Jenna's forehead. "That's why I assumed it was you, because you were clearly in first place before when it came to anything measurable. I thought they were saying this was putting you over the edge."

Over the edge? Ash swallowed. She might be about to go over the edge of a cliff from the sound of it. But if she wasn't the one who was responsible for the whale, who was?

Before she could react to Jenna's disturbing revelation, Caitlyn came charging in like she was on the attack.

"Who the hell do you think you are!" The tiny woman was absolutely terrifying in her rage, so much so that Ash shrank back into her chair. For a brief moment, she contemplated scrambling under her desk.

Jenna must've had a similar reaction because she'd begun slowly slinking her way out of Ash's office, closing the door behind her as soon as she'd reached the relative safety of the hallway.

"Nicely done," Ash said, trying to slide her cold veneer back in place to hide her total shock. "Jenna's not known for being discreet. Everyone in the office is going to hear about that outburst."

"Good." Flames were shooting from Caitlyn's eyes. "I hope everyone hears what a two-faced backstabber you are."

Ash sucked in a deep breath that ended with a sharp pang in her chest. Was it too much to hope her heart was about to stop and put her out of her misery?

"Where is it?" Caitlyn growled.

"What are you talking about?" Ash focused on a spot on the wall above Caitlyn's mercifully short head to help keep her calm.

"My binder." The woman looked ready to burst.

"A binder?" Ash's brain spun. Was it possible Caitlyn was losing her frigging mind? "This isn't high school,

Brewster. You can go buy yourself another Trapper Keeper."

"High school?" Caitlyn's eyes had a wild quality to them, like a horse ready to bolt. "No, this is way more like college. You're like my evil ex all over again."

"Are you totally nuts?" Ash pushed her chair back from her desk, honestly becoming a little concerned for Caitlyn's well-being. She was starting to talk nonsense. "I know we've had a bumpy patch this past week, but what could I possibly have done for you to compare me to that woman?"

"You stole my notes on Parker Pharmaceutical." Caitlyn paced the postage stamp of an office, breathing heavy, looking ever more like a caged animal as the seconds ticked by. "God, you really would do anything to make partner, wouldn't you? You're even more cold-hearted than I gave you credit for."

"Parker Pharmaceutical?" Now Ash was seeing red. "I can't believe you would think for one minute I would have any interest in that company. But if I did, I would damn sure use my own research to land—oh, shit. It's *you*."

"What's me?" Caitlyn's eyes darted around the room, like she was searching for a place to shoot more of her rage but had momentarily lost sight of the target.

Ash's head spun and she cradled it in her hands as the depth of this betrayal sank in. There was a lot she'd struggled with regarding Caitlyn over the week, but that had never crossed her mind. "You're the one who's bringing them in. The big whale. All that talk about understanding where I was coming from because of my dad's death was complete garbage, just a way to throw me off the scent while you reeled them in and stole my partnership in the process."

Caitlyn's rage transformed to bewilderment as one second of silence followed another, until finally she said, almost pleadingly, "Ash, what are you talking about? What's happened?"

Ash crossed her arms close to her chest, only instead of creating a barrier, it felt more like hugging herself to stay safe. "Like you don't know." Only it was starting to occur to her that maybe Caitlyn really didn't know and something else was going on.

"I truly don't." Caitlyn sat down in the chair next to the desk, clasping her hands in her lap so hard the knuckles were white. "Last I knew, Fergus Clark's family was on the verge of retaining McGill and Harding to pursue legal action against Parker Pharmaceutical."

"Not sure how that's going to work." Ash pressed her lips together, struggling to work out a picture that was shifting like grains of sand in the wind. How would Fergus's family even know to consult a lawyer for a lawsuit? Jenna's news was certainly not that, though. Ash felt it in her gut. "I don't know this for certain, but I would be willing to stake my reputation that Parker is about to come on board as the firm's newest client."

"Yeah, no shit." Caitlyn let out a frustrated cry. "I said that like two minutes ago. They're signing on because you... only it wasn't you, was it?"

Ash couldn't help but release a short, bitter laugh. "You think I would put aside over twenty years of vowing to bring down the types of bastards that basically killed my father because we had some stupid fight over a little contest more than half a decade ago?"

"I..." The shadow of a smile flitted across Caitlyn's lips. "You admit the fight was stupid?" Now she sounded all lawyer, going in for the kill.

Ash tilted her head to one side, the sudden switch of emotions leaving her off-balance. "Why does that matter?"

Caitlyn's eyes watered. "Because maybe it means there's a chance we can get past it? When I thought you'd stolen my notes and gone after Parker just to show me up, to embarrass me the way Bridget did in college, I was convinced there was no hope. But now, I mean…is there?" Oh. She hadn't been going in for the kill. She'd been building her defense. Ash's stomach knotted.

"Are you honestly saying that someone in this office stole your notes, went after one of the biggest prospective clients in this firm's history behind your back, ruining a prospective class action lawsuit you were working on in the process, and what you're focused on right now is whether or not I'm still *mad* at you?"

"Um…" Caitlyn swallowed before locking eyes with Ash, the pain and hope in them impossible to hide. "Yes?"

"This has been the worst week of my life." Ash leaned closer as Caitlyn's shoulders slumped, as if all hope had been removed. "Not because I found out you were a Harding, or because of the mock trial, even if I'm not thrilled with that one."

"Then why?" Caitlyn spoke in a hoarse whisper.

"Because none of it matters more to me than you."

Ash's heart pounded as Caitlyn's chin snapped up, hope restored like a beam of light shining from deep inside. She'd missed her so fucking badly the moment ached, bitter and sweet.

"Does that mean it's not over?" Caitlyn bit her lip, clearly nervous but not breaking eye contact as she waited for Ash's reply.

"I don't want it to be," Ash confessed, the hair on her arms standing up as tingles ran along her spine. "Not if you don't want it to be."

"I don't," Caitlyn choked. "I really, really don't."

Ash swiveled in her chair but before she could stand, Caitlyn had made it around the desk and was launching herself into Ash's lap, arms clasped behind Ash's neck as she covered every bit of exposed skin she could find with warm, slightly salty kisses. Ash pulled her close, not certain she would ever be ready to let go.

"I'm sorry," Caitlyn whispered. "I'm so sorry I hurt you."

"I know you didn't mean to," Ash whispered back, clinging to Caitlyn.

Dissatisfied with her ears and neck getting all the attention, Ash slanted her head to claim Caitlyn's lips with her own, feasting on them like she was half-starved until finally they both seemed to remember they were in the office—not the most private place—and slowly pulled apart. Caitlyn rose on unsteady feet and did her best to smooth her clothing back into place. Her lips were still kiss-swollen, though, and Ash couldn't wait to get back for more.

"I thought I had lost you for good." Caitlyn closed her

eyes as a new wave of pain hit her. "If you had actually betrayed me the way I thought, it would've killed me."

"I could never do that," Ash vehemently promised. "But someone did. Who else knew about the research you'd been doing?"

"Two people. You and me." Caitlyn got an oh shit look on her face before smothering it with a palm and speaking through the cracks of her fingers. "And Zach. He saw the label on the binder and started bragging about how he went to school with someone in the Parker family."

Ash's jaw clenched. "Zach's not bright enough to sign a client this big on his own."

"I don't know. You told me not to trust him." Caitlyn's shoulders drooped. "I should have listened."

Ash remained perfectly still and quiet, trying to formulate a better plan to find out what was really going on than to march into Larry's office, guns blazing. "Zach's calling in all the big shots on this one to back him up. There still might be time to head this off."

"How?"

"Your uncle." Ash's lips curled into a wicked grin.

Caitlyn frowned. "What about my uncle?"

"He's still the last word around here. If you can win him over, explain how signing Parker isn't the right choice for the firm—"

"I know I'm related to him," Caitlyn argued, "but it's not like we're close."

"We have to do something, though. The Clark family and others who have been hurt by those opportunistic assholes at Parker are depending on us."

"Us?" Caitlyn grinned like Ash had just handed her a gift.

Ash's cheeks tingled under the intensity of Caitlyn's adoration. "Just call your uncle, please?"

Caitlyn tapped a finger to her chin, eyeing her phone with distaste. "What's the temperature?"

"Metaphorically?" Ash was baffled. "Do you want to know how people in the office feel about signing Parker?"

"No." Caitlyn gave Ash a look she might give when Happy ran so fast she slid into a wall without stopping. "It's a Friday afternoon. I literally want to know how warm it is outside."

"Okay," Ash said as if she was following. "It's currently fifty-one degrees, with a six mile per hour north-easterly breeze."

Caitlyn clapped her hands together. "Perfect."

"It is pretty nice for this close to Christmas, especially after that freezing rain earlier in the week, but what the fuck does that have to do with our current problem?"

"It means I know exactly where my uncle is right now and have a much better way of talking to him than on a phone." Caitlyn put her hand on Ash's doorknob and lifted an eyebrow. "You coming?"

"Where?"

"Belmont Country Club, naturally." The evil gleam in Caitlyn's eyes made Ash's pulse quicken. "The course will be closed for the season, but with weather like this, the driving range will be open to members. As will the bar. Uncle Bertie wouldn't miss either one. So, you in?"

"Why the hell not?" Uncertain Caitlyn's plan would work but willing to show a little faith in her, if only to prove she was still capable of it, Ash gripped the arms of the chair to heft herself upward. "As long as you're driving."

THE NARROW ROAD to the country club was lined with trees that would provide a green canopy of shade in the summer, but offered only bare limbs and glimpses of sapphire-blue sky on this unseasonably warm December afternoon. They'd driven mostly in silence for the twenty minutes it took to get from the center of the city to the suburb of Belmont. Ash had stared out the window most of the way, almost afraid to speak, in case the fragile peace between her and Caitlyn was broken. Instead, she tried to absorb as much of the familiar closeness of the woman, knowing now how she'd taken it for granted before.

As if expecting them, Caitlyn's uncle was standing in front of the club as they pulled into the parking lot, squinting one eye, looking toward the heavens.

"Did you call ahead?" Ash asked, unable to conceal her shock at seeing the founding partner of her firm seemingly waiting to greet them, wearing baggy golf pants and a brightly colored, almost garish, sweater-vest. A wool cap covered his thinning white hair.

"No." Caitlyn's hands tightened on the steering wheel. "What am I going to say to him?"

Ash's eyes widened. Caitlyn had marched out of the office with such confidence, Ash had assumed she had a plan. Taking a risk, Ash put a hand on Caitlyn's shoulder, grateful when the woman leaned into the touch and didn't pull away. Maybe the rift between them really could be repaired. Ash prayed that was the case.

"Just explain why taking on this company as a client is a bad idea," Ash encouraged. "Your uncle's a shrewd businessman as well as a savvy lawyer, and representing Parker Pharma is as bad for McGill and Harding's reputation as it is for the bottom line."

"You think he'll listen?" Caitlyn covered Ash's hand with her own, holding onto it like it gave her strength.

"Only one way to find out." Ash dipped her head to plant a quick kiss on Caitlyn's knuckles, elated at how natural the gesture felt. In time, she felt certain things would be back to normal between them.

"Uncle Bertie!" Caitlyn waved as she exited the car, repeating the words a bit louder when the man didn't make a move.

"Is that you, Patty?" The man broke into a wide grin, but Caitlyn visibly stiffened, slowing her gait.

"No, it's Caitlyn, Uncle Bertie."

"Who's Patty?" Ash whispered.

"Patty was my mother," Caitlyn replied under her breath while offering her elderly uncle a wide smile.

Ash's heart fell. "I think we know why he hasn't been in the office lately."

"That's what I said, silly girl," her uncle replied. He had a mischievous sparkle in his eye, making it hard to determine if he was simply being combative because of the loss of his mental capabilities, which Ash had suspected for quite some time, or if he was simply being impish with his niece. "Would you and your friend like to come into the club for a Shirley Temple?"

Ash held in a groan. Had Cuthbert Harding really just offered a child's drink to his grown niece and a fifth-year associate from his own firm, whose name he hadn't even tried to recall? This was worse than she'd imagined, and any hope she'd held of the founding partner being able to right the wrong of pursuing Parker as a client quickly vanished.

"Uncle Bertie," Caitlyn said gently, her soft manner hinting she had reached a similar conclusion to Ash's but was going to carry on with her mission anyway, just in case. "I need you to listen. If Larry is thinking of signing Parker Pharmaceutical, it's a mistake. They're going to face a class action that'll be damaging to their reputation. The public won't like it."

"Since when did we start caring about the public?" He seemed bored with the conversation already, or perhaps he'd had his own heart set on a Shirley Temple and was frustrated at being denied.

Caitlyn quickly changed her tactics. "One of the junior associates at the firm went through the files I had prepared for a lawsuit against Parker Pharma, and is using my hard work in this ill-conceived bid to bring them on board."

He nodded, seeming to finally understand. "I see. You want to make sure you get the proper credit for landing the account and get put in charge of it. Smart girl."

"No." Caitlyn spoke with a forcefulness that seemed to catch her uncle by surprise, dispersing the last of the cloudiness in his eyes. "I want McGill and Harding not to sign them, because I'm in the early stages of a class action lawsuit that will reduce the company to rubble if I have my way. It'll be worth millions."

Cuthbert Harding stroked his chin, sharp and focused at last, as he considered his niece's request. "Seems to me, if you've spotted the opportunity for a class action suit against them, you won't be the only lawyer to do so. We sign Parker, they'll keep us busy fighting off these suits for years. That should keep you in a lifetime of bonuses, my dear."

"This isn't about money, Uncle Bertie," Caitlyn argued. "This is about being on the right side. This company caused harm to countless numbers of people. A boy is dead, and there could be others."

"Sounds like Parker really needs us," the man said, showing no sign of coming around. "Oh, there's Larry now." He waved to a car that had just pulled into the driveway. He turned his attention away from them as he watched the car pull into a space, and it became clear to Ash he'd been outside waiting for Larry this whole time, no doubt to discuss the very deal she and Caitlyn had come here to oppose.

"But... it's not right." Caitlyn looked to Ash for back up, but Ash couldn't think of anything to add. There was no point. Ash loved Caitlyn for trying, but there would be no changing the mind of a man who was mired in the past and set in his ways.

"Right and wrong doesn't pay the bills, Patty." It seemed the once-sharp lawyer was already starting to slip back into the haze. "I'm proud of you, but I'm going to side with Larry and Zach on this one. Better luck next time, pumpkin."

"There won't be a next time." Caitlyn's voice was firm and loud enough to make Ash jump. "I quit."

Caitlyn's uncle frowned, a look of confusion on his face. "Is that right?"

"Yes." Caitlyn stood up straighter, squaring her shoulders. "Yes, it is. I resign, effective immediately."

After staring, uncomprehending, for a moment, the old man finally shrugged. "I need to find Larry. Where did he go?" He wandered off muttering, and Ash got the sense he hadn't processed Caitlyn's sudden resignation at all.

But Ash had, and she stared at Caitlyn with a sense of awe. "Are you sure you want to do that? McGill and Harding is your family firm, and you're a shoo-in for a partnership."

"Even if that were true, and I don't think it is"—Caitlyn led the way to the car without a backward glance—"I can't do this anymore. You've reminded me of what's really important, Ash, and I can't continue with business as usual any longer."

Ash's stomach twisted as she considered how else to respond. "That's admirable." She wanted to be brave, to stand up for her principles as Caitlyn had done. But the risk was so great, and she'd worked so hard…

With shame and trepidation, she said, "I wish I could do the same, but I don't think I can."

CHAPTER TWENTY-SIX

Caitlyn killed the engine of the Jag in the parking lot of the strip mall that stood at the address the realtor had provided. She hunched over the steering wheel to check out the surroundings, uncertainty sparking inside her as she surveyed the drab two-story building. It was a far cry from the high-rise where she'd worked in New York, or even the sleek waterfront offices of McGill and Harding that she'd called home until less than twenty-four hours ago when she'd shocked herself by quitting her job.

Had that really happened? Caitlyn's stomach knotted at the memory. Only the fact she was sitting in this parking lot right now, waiting on a realtor to show her a possible office space for her as yet nonexistent new law firm, made the possibility seem like it must be a crazy dream brought on by too much chianti.

Not that Caitlyn could use that as an excuse for what she'd done. She'd been stone-cold sober when she'd given Uncle Bertie her notice, not even a Shirley Temple to cloud her judgment. It had come out of the blue, bursting from her like an overfilled water balloon. A gush of emotion. Yet it felt right in a way she was still trying to come to terms with. She was warming, the earth thawing in spring.

The only thing that would make it more so was if Ash had decided to leave with her.

Don't dwell on that now, she urged herself.

"This is… different," Ash said, observing the scene from her spot in the passenger's seat and offering her assessment in a cheery tone that didn't bother to hide her misgivings.

Before either of them could exit the car, an unmarked white van pulled into a spot on the far side of the lot. The side door opened and at least ten people poured out in a rush, donning aprons as they raced through a plain door with no sign. Caitlyn shivered, imagining all sorts of nefarious explanations for what she'd witnessed. "What do you think that's all about?"

Ash scanned the parking lot, clearly on edge, until suddenly she relaxed into a laugh. "There's a restaurant on the other side. That must be the entrance to the kitchen."

"That's a relief." Caitlyn started laughing too. "I was picturing some kind of human trafficking story. Although, I guess I do need clients, so maybe I shouldn't be so glad to find out it's nothing to worry about." Along with not dwelling on Ash's refusal to quit, Caitlyn was working overtime to not panic over her now-clientless docket.

"What time is the realtor supposed to meet you?"

Ash asked, the use of the word *you* instead of *us* leaving Caitlyn slightly hollow. Not that she could let on. It reinforced the fact that though Ash was along for support, Caitlyn was embarking on this insane and totally spontaneous journey alone. There were no family-name connections in her back pocket for real now.

Which was totally reasonable. Ash had worked five years to climb the ladder at McGill and Harding. She had family obligations to worry about, and a career that was ready to take off. There was security to be found there that made swallowing the bullshit tolerable. Meanwhile, what could Caitlyn offer? To answer that question, she had only to refer back to her recent assessment of her new endeavor: insane and spontaneous.

"I think that's her now," Caitlyn said, spotting a dark Toyota that had pulled into a space a few cars over from them. A woman dressed in slacks and a stylish wool coat had just gotten out, clasping a folder to her chest and looking totally at ease despite the grass growing up through the surrounding cracks in the asphalt. "Ready to go check out the new digs?"

"Absolutely," Ash said with the breezy confidence of someone who had no personal skin in the game.

Meanwhile, Caitlyn was such a nervous wreck she could barely introduce herself to the realtor without throwing up the three Frappuccinos she'd had in lieu of breakfast. Which, in retrospect, may have been an even bigger miscalculation than hurling her resignation at her uncle in his beloved country club's parking lot. She couldn't tell if her heart was racing because of panic or a caffeine and sugar megadose, but it thudded against her ribs like a jackhammer.

They entered via a glass door that the realtor held open for them, chattering about something to do with building security and swipe badges. They made a left down one hallway, and then a right to a separate hallway, pausing in front of a wooden door that still had the marks of double-sided tape on it from where the previous tenant had removed their sign.

"This will be your reception area," the realtor said as she unlocked the door, swinging it open to allow Caitlyn and Ash to step through. The lights weren't on, and given the drabness, that was probably for the best.

"The listing said a small lobby and two offices?" Caitlyn asked, trying but failing to reconcile the reality of the space with the grand dreams she'd had in her mind. It was hard to tell with barely any furniture in it, but the rooms seemed tiny, even by comparison to the miniscule offices she and Ash had been shoved into as associates at McGill and Harding.

Caitlyn let out a small sigh, unable to hide her disappointment. Maybe she'd been too hasty in quitting, and foolish to follow up her verbal resignation—which her uncle probably wouldn't have remembered considering the frail shape he was in—with a written confirmation to all the equity partners. There was no going back now, and she felt a small jolt of relief that Ash had been sensible enough not to jump on the great resignation bandwagon.

Even if it did sting a little.

"Now where is that switch?" the realtor muttered.

There was a snap, followed by the flicker of fluorescent bulbs overhead. "There we go. What do you think?"

The realtor had that overly enthusiastic tone people used when they wanted to trick you into joining them in being excited about something that didn't deserve it. Her ploy wasn't going to work. What Caitlyn *thought* was that she had been right before in believing illumination wouldn't improve the surroundings. The walls reminded her of the dormitories at Moorehead Academy, which had been painted a dull beige, though not any time recently. Possibly not within the past five decades. There were scuffs around the baseboards, too, although the carpet, despite having a print that screamed 1980s, looked relatively new. That was something, anyway.

"It's, um..." *The only office space offering a monthly lease in the right price range within a thirty-mile radius,* Caitlyn reminded herself, forcing a smile. "It's got potential."

"Plants," Ash whispered, offering a look that almost masked her horror behind a thin film of positivity that mirrored the realtor's. "Nice green ones will brighten this place up."

"Exactly my thought." The realtor beamed. "What a clever business partner you have."

Caitlyn's smile faltered. Ash was, indeed, clever, and if they were entering into this arrangement as business partners, Caitlyn could tackle any challenge, even the world's most boring office space, with confidence. But that wasn't the case, and she couldn't keep letting herself get her hopes up that Ash would change her mind.

One thing was for sure, the current state of this office

wouldn't do anything to sway her. Everything about it said run away as fast as you can.

"Do you think we could look around for a few minutes alone?" Caitlyn needed a break from the over-eager realtor's perky commentary on how great this clearly *not* very great space was. For all her earlier impulsiveness, now was the time for Caitlyn to give what she was doing some serious consideration.

"What do you think?" Caitlyn asked when the realtor had left. "For real."

Ash turned her head slowly, taking in all the details with an expression of careful consideration. "It's not so bad. There's room for a receptionist's desk in this first room, and the office itself is more spacious than it looks. There's a big window, even if the drapes the old tenant left behind make it feel dark and small. Maybe some new blinds, though…"

Caitlyn tried to see the space again, with less distress and pessimism. Yes, it was small, but Ash reminded her there were things that could be done.

"And a fresh coat of paint," Caitlyn added, taking a deep breath as she sized up the work needed. Maybe it wasn't so bad after all. At least Ash hadn't advised her to jump ship and come slinking back to Larry and the rest of the partners with her tail between her legs. Caitlyn didn't think even the infamous red dress could make them take her back.

"You should call the temp agency McGill and Harding uses and see if Emily's available," Ash commented. "She's temped in about every law office in Boston and would be a great assistant."

"Wow." Caitlyn boosted her eyebrows. "You think I should hire staff already?"

"And order some new furniture." Ash rapped her knuckles on a beat-up steel desk that was the only item in the room that might soon be Caitlyn's new office, most likely too heavy to make it worth the former tenants taking it with them. "Unless that's too... permanent?"

Caitlyn frowned. "What do you mean?"

"It's just..." Ash bit her lower lip, worry forming lines across her brow and around her eyes. She searched Caitlyn's face like she was looking for a sign, and Caitlyn's stomach knotted over whatever she was going to say next. "Sadie seems to be doing really well now."

Caitlyn tilted her head, not seeing the connection between her sister's mental health and this empty office space. "That's upsetting you?"

"No, not at all," Ash rushed to say. "I think it's great Sadie's doing so much better. I mean, she might even decide to move back into the dorms next semester."

"I can't see her leaving Happy," Caitlyn commented, still not seeing where the conversation was going but feeling vaguely uneasy at the thought of Sadie deciding to leave home again. She'd only just gotten there, and was settling in so well.

"What if she was able to take Happy with her as an emotional support animal?" Ash pressed, an idea that wasn't completely outside the realm of possibility considering the school's own counselor had suggested as much. "You came back to Massachusetts because Sadie needed you. If she doesn't need you here anymore, you would be free to do whatever you wanted. Like go back to New York, for instance."

Caitlyn's pulse gathered speed as she pieced together what was really driving Ash's speculation. She took a step closer to Ash, wrapping an arm around the woman's waist. "I don't have any plans to move back to New York." It truly had not crossed her mind, not even when she'd melted down in the shower that morning over her decision to jump off a ledge without looking first.

"Why not?" There was a tremor in Ash's voice, like she wasn't sure if she wanted an answer. "There are plenty of firms there to choose from that would salivate at the opportunity to have you and your class action suit against Parker Pharma come—"

Caitlyn pressed a finger to Ash's lips, stopping her before she could finish. "Because I don't want to be in New York. I want to be here. With you." She removed her finger from Ash's lips and used it to brush a stray piece of the woman's dark hair behind her ear.

"It's as simple as that?" Ash croaked, sounding like she could barely believe it was true.

"Nothing is ever simple," Caitlyn said, tracing a path with her fingertip behind Ash's ear and down along her neck to her collarbone. "This past week has taught us that. But I like what we have. The other day, we could have said truly hateful things—"

"I'm pretty sure I did," Ash said, squeezing her eyes shut, but whether from the pain of the memory or because Caitlyn's finger had tickled that sensitive spot above her pulse point wasn't clear.

"Yeah, I probably did too." Caitlyn scooted the collar

of Ash's shirt to one side, standing on her toes to press her lips against the exposed skin. She breathed in deep, Ash's scent both calming her and making her heart race at the same time. She pressed a kiss to Ash's ear before whispering, "I need you to listen to what I'm about to say and please don't interrupt."

Ash nodded, swallowing hard. Caitlyn could almost feel the shivers running through her as she waited for what Caitlyn needed to tell her.

"I love you." Caitlyn wrapped her arms around Ash, holding her tight. "I want to be with you. I don't know how all of these changes with work are going to go yet, and it's terrifying, but the one thing I know for a fact is that I've fallen madly in love with you."

Ash's breath caught but she didn't speak.

Caitlyn relaxed her grip so she could look into Ash's eyes, searching for a clue as to how she was taking this news. Total silence and motionlessness lasted for several seconds that felt like an eternity.

Finally, Caitlyn quirked one brow. "Are you going to let me hang there like this?"

"You told me not to interrupt." Ash's voice was breathy, her pupils large and dark. Caitlyn swallowed a chuckle.

"You can go ahead and speak now," Caitlyn urged.

Ash had the look of someone who had been run over by a large truck, like the one Caitlyn had driven to trick-or-treating. "I don't know what to say."

The blood drained from Caitlyn's face and her knees went wobbly.

"About work," Ash added in a rush, her eyes widening

as she seemed to realize the way her statement had come out. "Damn it. I totally screwed that up. Of course I love you."

Caitlyn burst into laughter, relief and tenderness tickling her from the inside. "You're an original, that's for sure."

"This is new territory for me." Ash tugged on her collar. "Is it suddenly roasting in here?"

Still giggling, Caitlyn pressed her lips to Ash's, keeping her urges under control as she recalled the realtor who was waiting on them in the hallway. "Let's look at the rest so we can go back to my place and do this properly."

"Sounds good to me," Ash said with a grin. "So, this other room, are you thinking a conference room? Or maybe a break room?"

"I'm not entirely sure." Caitlyn cast a glance at the office on the right, nearly identical to the one on the left that she'd already claimed as her own. "I have a… hope." It was a hope that was currently breaking free of a chrysalis, and she needed to help it out. After all, if the hope couldn't stretch its wings, there was no chance of flight.

"Are you thinking of poaching someone from the old office?"

Caitlyn wiggled her brows, wondering how long it would take for Ash to figure out what she was saying. "I want to."

"If you say Zach, I'm walking out that door and never returning."

"I never want to see that worm ever again." Caitlyn

rolled her eyes. "I know we kinda touched on this yesterday, but it was in the heat of things with my uncle, so I wanted to make it clear. There's no pressure, and I know there's a lot at stake, but I'm hoping at some point in the future, you'll consider joining me. I only want to work with the best, and you're the very best, Ashley Tanner."

Ash took a step back, and Caitlyn wondered if a feather could literally knock Ash off her feet. "You really believe that?"

"I always have," Caitlyn said softly. "Despite my actions to the contrary six years ago. I know you might not be ready, but the office will be here, waiting, if..."

"It's a big jump"—Ash's body tensed like she was literally standing at the edge of a cliff—"and I've worked so hard to make partner that I just don't know if I can do it, no matter how much I wish I could."

"I totally get it." Caitlyn took Ash's hand, swallowing her disappointment. At least she'd been clear in communicating what she wanted. For now, that was the only thing she could do. They both deserved for things to be front and center, with as little room for misunderstanding as possible. "It's a huge risk, and I know it's scary because I woke up at three this morning wondering if I'd lost my mind."

"And I've been tossing and turning, too, wondering how I can keep working at that place when you're being so brave and going after what I always thought I would —" Cutting herself off before she could launch into a full monologue, Ash sniffed. "Do you smell egg rolls?"

Startled, Caitlyn inhaled deeply. Sure enough, the mouth-watering scent of hot oil and cabbage tickled her senses. "I think I do. Isn't that a sign of brain damage, or a stroke, or something?"

"I don't think it's a stroke," Ash said, sniffing again. "It's got to be the Chinese restaurant downstairs."

"Oh my God, I love the smell of egg rolls," Caitlyn declared, her stomach beginning to rumble. "Are you as hungry as I am?"

Ash nodded. "That smells divine."

"It does, and I'm taking it as a sign from the heavens," Caitlyn said with a grin. "Now to find the realtor and finalize the lease. After that, we're having Chinese food for lunch, courtesy of the Law Office of Caitlyn Brewster, Esquire."

Ash gave Caitlyn's shoulder a nudge with her own. "It has a nice ring."

Caitlyn agreed. Not as nice as the Law Offices of Brewster and Tanner, but not bad.

CHAPTER TWENTY-SEVEN

The holidays passed in the blink of an eye. For the first time in her life, Ash brought a woman —and not "just a friend", but an official *girlfriend*—home for Christmas with her family. Plus Sadie and Happy, of course. They were a package deal after all, a whole little family Ash was quickly coming to think of as her own. Ash endured the good-natured ribbing from her siblings, which passed as quickly as she'd hoped when Jose proposed to Breanna on Christmas Eve.

It all went by in such a blur that when Ash woke with a start, bolting upright in bed, she wasn't sure of the day, or even the year. Had the new year already arrived? Ash had a vague memory of champagne toasts… but nothing more. As she waited in the darkness for her eyes to adjust, for a moment she couldn't remember where she was.

"What's wrong?" Caitlyn stirred in the bed beside her, hair sticking up in spots to form a silhouette in the dim light of an adorable bird with feathers that were out of control. From the feel of the bedding and the position of the windows, Ash concluded she was at Caitlyn's house, but her nerves were still shaken.

"Bad dream, I think. I'm not sure anymore." Ash took several deep breaths, willing her pulse to slow. Finally, it sank in. Today was the day. It was the first day back to the office after New Year's, and the day the partnership offer would be announced. From all the rumors swirling around the office, there would be only one. In a few more hours, she would know her fate, and if all the hard work she'd put in had been worth it.

Her stomach threatening to revolt, she pulled her knees in tight.

"It's going to be okay, Ash." Caitlyn rubbed Ash's back.

"What if I don't get it?" Ash's voice trembled. It wasn't that she didn't have other options. Going to work with Caitlyn, for one. But if she wasn't selected after everything she'd sacrificed, would it mean she wasn't good enough? Logically, she knew the answer was no, but in her heart, it was another matter. After giving it her all, working twice as hard as anyone else around her, if she didn't win, how would she ever be able to believe she wasn't destined to be second best for the rest of her life?

"The firm would be foolish to choose anyone but you." Caitlyn tugged on Ash's shoulder, urging her back under the covers where their naked bodies could twine between the soft sheets.

"Be honest." Ash snuggled closer to Caitlyn, letting her fingers drift lazily up and down the woman's back, eliciting tiny sighs like the purring of a contented cat.

"Are you secretly hoping they don't give it to me so I'll come work for you?"

"*With* me, as an equal, remember? But, no. I'm cheering for you, I promise." Caitlyn snaked her fingers through Ash's hair and dragged her head closer to claim her lips with velvety kisses. "I wouldn't want to win that way."

"What if I *do* get the partnership?" Ash fretted, unable to turn off the part of her brain that kept offering up things to worry about, no matter how much her body wanted to sink into Caitlyn's embrace and forget anything else existed.

"Then we will hit the town tonight to celebrate." Caitlyn draped one leg across Ash's hip, her pubic hair tickling Ash's pelvis in a way that was almost tempting enough to put all other thoughts aside.

Almost.

"What if Larry wants me on the team that's working to sign Parker Pharma?"

"Considering I've just brought the Clarks on board as clients, you'll have to come clean about our relationship," Caitlyn said, a fact Ash already knew and that filled her with dread. Telling the family was one thing, but letting her coworkers in on her private life was a totally different story. Especially as, with Caitlyn's dramatic exit, it would be quite the office scandal for a while. "It's a pity, though. Facing each other on opposite sides of the bench could be kinda hot, in a way. We could battle it out all day in court and then work out the tension when we get home."

Caitlyn ran a hand along Ash's thigh, working her fingers into the crevice between Ash's legs by way of demonstrating exactly what method of work out she had in mind. Temptation swelled from a whimper to a roar, but for now, Ash kept her thighs pressed together, blocking full access. She was simply too stressed to relax and let herself go, even with the promise of something that would feel so good.

Caitlyn's hand stilled. "Are you hoping they don't give it to you?"

"It would make my decision easier," Ash was shocked to hear herself admit. "Albeit, it's a cowardly way out, letting others determine my future. Not brave, like you."

"Stop thinking that way," Caitlyn pleaded. "You're not a coward. With as much as you've done to help your family, you're one of the bravest people I know. One of the most stubborn too." Caitlyn wiggled her fingers between Ash's legs to drive her point home.

"You just had to throw that one in, didn't you?" Even as she said it, Ash rolled so she was flat, sliding her legs apart in submission to Caitlyn's insistence.

"It's one of the things I adore about you." Caitlyn climbed on top of Ash, taking full advantage of the opportunity to run her hands along Ash's torso, stopping to massage her breasts. "Even when your stubbornness works against me, I do like that you're always you."

Ash sucked in a breath as Caitlyn drew a nipple into her mouth. "That's what I'm worried about."

"What do you mean?" Caitlyn asked as she peppered Ash's chest with kisses, working her way to the other side.

"I want to be brave. I want to fight for the little guy. I want to make a difference in the… ah!" Whatever else

Ash had been about to say was lost as Caitlyn's hot mouth located its intended target, drawing the other nipple in with an increasing suction Ash could feel all the way in her belly.

"Just remember," Caitlyn said when she'd had her way with the second breast and had come up for air, "if you become partner, you'll have greater freedom to sign clients you'll be proud to represent. It's not all black and white." Spoken as if Ash hadn't been standing right beside her when Uncle Bertie put money first and foremost in the firm's priority list.

"You're such an optimist." Ash's chuckle turned to a groan as the alarm sounded, just as Caitlyn was slithering downward with the promise of chasing away all Ash's tension, at least for a little while. "Please don't tell me it's time to get up already."

"Is Ashley Tanner really begging to stay in bed late on a workday?" Caitlyn teased, nipping Ash's inner thigh playfully, showing no more inclination toward getting out of bed than Ash did. "I mean, it would be a shame if you missed your big moment."

"I couldn't agree more." Ash pressed her hand to the top of Caitlyn's head, urging her lower, crying out as the woman's eager tongue made contact with her yearning clit. Sure, the partnership announcement would be life changing, but that wasn't the big moment Ash was focused on right now. "Exactly why I don't want to get out of bed yet."

Despite hitting the snooze button not once but three times more, and braving a packed commuter train ride into the city that reminded her of the downside of staying at Caitlyn's place on a work night, Ash still reached the office before most of her colleagues. All but a couple offices along the long hallway were dark, but the lights were on in Caitlyn's office. Ash's heart beat faster, her spirits lifting as they always did when spotting that light on in the early morning, until she remembered it was no longer Caitlyn's office, and the person she wanted to see wouldn't be waiting inside.

In fact, what Ash did find waiting inside—a shiny pair of Italian dress shoes perched on the desk—caused her body to respond in exactly the opposite way as it would have if Caitlyn had been there. She recoiled in horror, unable to take her eyes off the gritty dirt that coated both soles.

"What are you—?" Ash's blood boiled as Zach, feet up and head lolling back, bounced a stress ball off the ceiling. "Why are you in Caitlyn's office?"

"Didn't you get the memo?" Zach tossed the ball again, a resounding thwack shaking white dust from the ceiling tiles onto the shiny desktop, mingling with bits of sand that had dropped from those completely unhygienic shoes. "Caitlyn was fired. This is my office now. At least until they make my promotion official."

Ash's eyes narrowed, her hands tightening into fists against her thighs at the man's unbridled hubris. His promotion? Was he serious? Or did that mean he'd heard something… There was a lot to unpack in what Zach had said, but Ash decided to start with the most important point. "Caitlyn Brewster wasn't fired. She quit to start her own firm."

"Well, then, she's an idiot." His feet fell to the floor, leaving a coating of debris in their wake. Ash hoped if Zach ate his lunch off that desk, as most everyone in the office did, that he'd contract a disease. It was disgusting. "Hey, by the way, I want you as my second chair on the Parker case."

"Second chair?" Ash resisted the urge to laugh in his face, but only barely. And only because the implications struck fear in her heart. He had to be joking, right? "Have they even signed yet?"

"No, but they will." Zach served up a cocky grin. "Larry's going to let me call the shots on this one, seeing how I rescued the firm from Caitlyn's poor judgment on the matter."

"Yeah, well, we'll see." Ash left the office in a fury, nearly stomping down the hall. Had Zach really been given Caitlyn's office, and was he going to be put in charge of a client as important as Parker Pharmaceutical? If so, he was probably right. The partnership was all but his. After he'd stolen research and gone behind Caitlyn's back. Who needed hard work when you had a penis and a defiantly gray moral code?

Ash was still fuming about this, her anger blinding her to her surroundings, when she nearly rammed into Larry just outside her office. Ash chomped down on her bottom lip to keep herself from exploding in a fit of ill temper.

"Just the person I was looking for." Larry clapped Ash

on the back, apparently not noticing her flushed face and dagger eyes.

Ash simply nodded, not trusting herself to speak as she desperately tried to rearrange her face into an expression that didn't look like she was ready to commit a murder. She should have gotten pointers from Caitlyn long ago. If he was here to break it to her that Zach was about to be promoted instead of her, someone was going to need to tie her down to keep from losing her shit.

Larry looked Ash in the eyes. "I want you on the Parker case. First chair."

As her head spun from the rollercoaster quality of this offer, coming so quickly on the heels of Zach claiming the client was all his, it was everything Ash could do to hold in what was certain to be maniacal laughter if it escaped her control. Had the entire office gone mad?

"Larry, I—"

"They're on the verge of signing," Larry interrupted, saving her from becoming a babbling idiot. Ash had no idea what she was going to say. "Just in time, too. Rumor has it there's a big lawsuit from the family of that dead rower coming down the pipe any day, although I'm not sure which law office will be handling it. We need our best on this. And look, I know you and Caitlyn are buddies. Do you think you can talk her into coming back? What I really need is my dynamic duo in action again."

The thought of calling Caitlyn her "buddy" was almost as hilarious as the idea that Ash would ever, ever work in Parker Pharmaceutical's favor.

"She seems committed to striking out on her own,"

Ash managed to say. And to think she'd worried at one point that her and Caitlyn's relationship would be fodder for office gossip. Clearly, no one had a clue. And speaking of clueless, it appeared Caitlyn was continuing to fly under the radar when it came to representing the Clarks, let alone the half dozen other people she'd contacted to join the suit.

Because they were out there. Families who'd experienced acute and traumatic loss without knowing what had happened.

"Yeah, I think you're right." Larry's shoulders slumped. "I hear she has an office already."

Ash's heart beat a little faster at this revelation. They might not have caught on that she and Caitlyn were having sex against the office door after hours, but in certain things, news traveled fast in the world of law. If they knew about the office space, the rest would come out soon.

"Anyway, I'll see you at the big meeting today," Larry said as he continued down the hall. "One o'clock!" As he walked away, Ash realized she hadn't had a chance to turn down First Chair, in part because... God, was she really still torn on what to do?

Exhausted before the day had begun, Ash sank into her desk chair. She was experiencing whiplash from the competing thoughts in her head. Clearly, Larry wanting her on the Parker case was strong evidence she'd cinched the partnership. Why else would he mention it, and ask her to try to win Caitlyn back instead of telling her he wanted her to team up with Zach? As for the fourth-year associate and his arrogance, the thought of him being stuck as her second chair would've made her laugh if it didn't also make her nauseous.

And when it came out that Caitlyn was opposing council for the Parker suit, and she and Ash were dating, would that put Ash's position with McGill and Harding in jeopardy?

If that was the case, was she better off walking?

Ash had headed into the office hoping for some clarity, and already she was more confused than she'd been when she'd woken up petrified in Caitlyn's bed. She stared at the ceiling, wishing for a sign. Was she better off staying at the firm, swallowing her morals even as she accepted the reward for all the hard work she'd put in? Or should she jump ship and join Caitlyn, going after the bad guys and fighting for the defenseless as she'd pictured herself doing ever since her dad had died with no one to fight on his side?

She waited, but nothing happened. When it came to offering signs, the Head Honcho Upstairs was really falling down on the job.

Jenna's head appeared in Ash's doorway. "What's the plan?"

"I wish I knew," Ash responded with glum aplomb, before realizing it was unlikely the paralegal had the mindreading skills necessary to have discerned Ash's inner turmoil, let alone be questioning her about it. "I mean, plan for what?"

"When you make partner, of course." Jenna strolled into the office displaying way more confidence on the outcome of this topic than Ash herself felt. "Everyone has their money on you."

"What about Zach?" Ash cast a wary glance in the general vicinity of Caitlyn's former office, where there was no telling what completely unhygienic activities that overgrown frat boy was engaging in now. Probably picking his nose.

"I think that'd cause an uproar, don't you?" Jenna asked. "Do you know he's never tried a case in court?"

"What?" Ash sat up straight, stunned at this revelation. She kept track of a lot of information about her rivals, but somehow this gem had slipped through the cracks. "He's a fourth year. How is that even possible?"

"He's got a gift for last-minute settlements," Jenna replied. "Which is great, except not exactly what the firm needs in a partner. So, congratulations, Ashley Tanner. No way will it be anyone's name but yours that they announce at the meeting today."

She should have been elated, but instead, the moment Jenna had left her alone with this news, she felt ill. Was her curdled belly the sign she'd been looking for from up above? Or was it just a sign she needed a stiff drink and a vacation? Unable to focus on work, Ash passed the time leading up to the meeting by watching the second hand on her office clock make its way around the face time and time again. Each time, it seemed the answer to her dilemma moved further from her comprehension.

"Ash!" Reappearing in the doorway some unknown number of clock revolutions later, Jenna shouted through cupped hands. "Earth to Ash."

"What?" Ash dropped her pen and tore her eyes away from the still-ticking clock.

"It's time."

"It can't be." She looked back at the clock she'd been staring at for who knew how long, realizing she'd had no idea of the time. It was two minutes until one. For the first time in recent memory, she—the person voted most likely to arrive in the conference room first—was running late. The most important meeting of her life, and she was going to be in the standing room only section in the back.

"I hope you brought your appetite," Jenna chattered as Ash speed walked beside her down the corridor. "I hear they've brought in a nice spread."

"I'm not in the mood for cheese," Ash grumbled, still unable to comprehend how anyone could be so obsessed with free food.

"Who doesn't like cheese?" Jenna demanded, as if Ash had attacked her religious views or said something unkind about her grandmother. "You've been acting peculiar all day."

Ash was about to respond, but as she opened her mouth and took a breath, she was engulfed in a familiar scent she couldn't put her finger on at first. It filled her with a sense of both peace and longing as it tickled her nose.

"What is that smell? Ash asked, breathing in another lungful of the delectable air. "Is that… egg rolls?"

"I told you they were bringing in a topnotch spread." Jenna dove for a plate and made a beeline for the Chinese buffet that had been set up along one wall of the conference room. She looked questioningly at Ash, who remained rooted in place smack dab in the middle of the conference room doorway. "Aren't you coming?"

"Actually, no." After so many days of uncertainty, Ash

had never felt more confident of anything in her life. Of all things, the simple smell of egg rolls had given her the kick she needed to stop being an idiot. Becoming aware of someone behind her, Ash turned to find herself face to face with Larry Cooper. Kismet with a side of duck sauce, it seemed. "I'm sorry, Larry. I quit."

He stared. The large features of his face twisted and contorted as they ran a marathon, with comprehension at the finish line. "What?" Larry's eyes bugged and he spent a moment sputtering. "Funny joke, Tanner. Now let's all sit down so we can get started."

"I'm serious. I quit." Elation bubbled in Ash's chest like freshly uncorked champagne. "I don't care who gets the partnership. I don't care which big whale just got signed. I'm done."

She started down the hallway as Larry called after her, "Where do you think you're going?"

"To get egg rolls," Ash called back, picking up speed so she could catch the elevator that had just arrived on the floor. Now that she finally knew where she needed to be, she didn't want to waste another minute getting there.

CHAPTER TWENTY-EIGHT

Adjusting the bandana covering her head, Caitlyn dipped her roller into the tray of sky-blue paint. She'd been working since nine in the morning, ever since the fifth call to local painters confirmed no one could get around to painting her new office space until March at the earliest. That wouldn't do. Caitlyn had meetings lined up with several potential clients the following week and she needed to give the appearance she was running a classy establishment, not some fly-by-night scam. So, she'd done what any independent small business owner would do. She rolled up her sleeves and did it herself.

Caitlyn tilted her head to one side and then to the other, stretching the screaming muscles in her neck and shoulders, hoping to convince them to work a little longer. There was one room to go for today and her back was threatening never to forgive her, but it had to get done. There was still furniture to put together, pictures to hang on walls, and she needed to make a trip to the garden shop over the weekend for those plants Ash had sworn would bring life to the space.

A sense of melancholy invaded Caitlyn's spirit at the thought of Ash, with a glance at the door that led to what should have been her office. It was the one room Caitlyn hadn't begun to tackle, not seeing the point. It was piled high with furnishings and supplies right now, and the door would be closed when clients came in. A storage room, nothing else.

How much more enjoyable would this day of painting have been if Ash had been doing it with her? The hours would've flown by. As she rolled paint on the wall, watching the lighter blue stripes begin to cover the darker first coat of paint that was already dry, she choked back a lump in her throat.

You've gotta stop dwelling on it, she told herself in the sternest of tones. After all, Ash had worked so hard for this partnership, sacrificed so much, and she deserved for it to pay off. Being recognized as the best by one of the top law firms in the country was important to Ash in a way it wasn't to Caitlyn. And that was okay. As much as she loved Ash, Caitlyn could never truly understand how damaging it was to have society assume she was less-than because of life circumstances beyond her control. If Ash needed to be a partner at McGill and Harding to give her the type of legitimacy that Caitlyn, with her family legacy and Ivy League degree, had the privilege of taking for granted? Well then, it was Caitlyn's job to support her in that pursuit.

Leaving her roller in the tray, Caitlyn peered out the window in what would soon be her office, trying to judge what time it was from the amount of light left outside. The sun was about halfway down, making it close to two-thirty, or possibly three o'clock, though it felt darker with the clouds that engulfed the sky like a thick gray blanket. Snow weather. As if reading her mind, a scattering of tiny flakes began to fall.

Larry would probably be announcing the partnership any minute now. Maybe he already had, although knowing him, he would have dragged out the suspense as long as possible with several boring speeches in which he repeatedly stated the obvious while not sharing the one piece of information everyone cared about.

A smile teased her reluctant lips at the realization she would never have to sit in on a meeting like that again as long as she lived. This new undertaking may not have shaped up exactly as she would've liked, but never having to arrive seventeen minutes early to jockey for a position in an office full of barracudas was a solid consolation prize for not getting to work with Ash every day. Though she'd always wish she could have both, because there was a lot she and Ash could do in a conference room if given seventeen minutes.

After wiping a paint splattered hand on her t-shirt, Caitlyn picked up her phone. No word from Ash. Caitlyn's stomach knotted with the stress of not knowing. Setting the phone down again, she picked up her roller. There was nothing more calming to an anxious mind than laying on a fresh coat of paint. With the way Caitlyn was feeling right now, she might end up repainting the whole house.

She's going to get it, Caitlyn repeated in her head as she moved the roller up and down. She just had to. As much as Caitlyn wished Ash had chosen to come work alongside her, that didn't mean she wanted Ash to fail. No way. Her uncle's firm would be insane not to choose Ash. And when the news came that they had, Caitlyn was going to be the best girlfriend ever. They would get dressed up and go out for a nice dinner. There would be champagne. They would celebrate in style, even if deep down, Caitlyn's heart would be breaking just a tiny bit. She'd get over it, because Ash was worth it.

"What are you doing?"

Caitlyn let out a startled yip. There was Ash, standing in the office doorway, staring quizzically from the paint roller in Caitlyn's hand to the bandana on her head. Caitlyn quickly scanned around her to make sure there'd been no errant drops of blue. Whew. The tarp she'd used to cover the floor had done its job.

"Baking a cake. What does it look like—?" Caitlyn's eyes fell to the bottle of champagne in Ash's hand. Her heart lurched but her belly warmed with pride. "You got it!"

Ash shrugged but didn't confirm or deny Caitlyn's statement.

"Don't act modest," Caitlyn scolded. "This is a big fucking deal." She began to run the numbers in her head —how long it would take to finish this wall, pack up the paint supplies for the night, get home to wash and dress—

"I thought you were hiring painters." Coming closer, Ash set the bottle down on top of the step ladder, the only flat surface in the room that wasn't covered in plastic tarps.

"I tried, but nobody was available. Can you believe the soonest anyone could fit me in was—?" Caitlyn gave her head a vigorous shake as she realized she was getting sidetracked. "Who cares about that? My girlfriend just made partner at McGill and Harding. Let's pop that cork. I picked up plastic cups for the water cooler yesterday, if I can find them under all the junk in the other room."

"We're going to need to get this other office cleaned out," Ash remarked, following as Caitlyn opened the door to the spare room, revealing an impressive mountain of shit.

"Don't remind me," Caitlyn said with a groan. "I've got four days left to get this place client-ready, but at least I don't need to rush on tackling this storage space until later."

"Then where the hell do you expect me to work?"

"You're going to get a big, fancy office at—"

Caitlyn's pulse quickened as her brain struggled to make sense of what had just been said. And what Ash hadn't said since she arrived. "Where you'll work...? Wait, are you saying...?" Blood rushed in her ears and Caitlyn's body felt ready to pop from hope just like the bottle of bubbly they were about to consume.

A grin spread across Ash's face, her eyes dancing with mirth. "Do you know what we need to go with the champagne?"

"Ash, stop fucking around and just tell me," Caitlyn growled. "What are you saying? Did you get the partnership or not? If those bastards passed you by, I swear I'll—"

"Whoa, tiger." Ash put a hand on Caitlyn's shoulder. "Let's not go on a rampage!"

"Ash!" Caitlyn stomped both feet, one after another.

Ash held up both hands defensively, using one to draw a cross over her heart as she said, "I swear to you, I don't know."

"What?" Caitlyn's nose crinkled. "Did they delay the announcement or something?"

"Not that I know of." Ash locked eyes with Caitlyn's, stopping her breath. "I didn't stay for it."

"Why not?" Caitlyn whispered, trying her hardest not to get her hopes up and failing miserably.

"Because it doesn't matter. I don't want to be there." Ash swallowed, blinking eyes that glistened with unshed tears. "I want to be here, with you."

Jaw dropping, Caitlyn covered the lower half of her face with her hand.

"Did you know your hand is covered in paint?" Ash laughed.

Caitlyn couldn't hold in an elated giggle. "Do you mean it?"

"About the paint? Oh yeah. It's everywhere." Ash made a face as Caitlyn swatted her shoulder. "And now it's on me."

Caitlyn's hands went to her hips. "I'm serious, woman. Are you honestly telling me you quit your job to come work here with me, and you didn't even stick around to find out if you'd made partner?"

"Absolutely," Ash swore, once more tracing her index finger over her heart.

Caitlyn leaped in the air, clapping her hands. "Brewster, Tanner, and Associates, here we come!"

"Associates?" Ash's brow furrowed. "We have associates? We'll need a bigger office."

"We don't have any yet, but I'm dreaming big. Although I did confirm that temp you suggested, Emily, for Monday." Caitlyn's countenance sobered as the enormity of what Ash had done sank in. "Are you absolutely sure?"

"I've never been so sure about anything in my life," Ash promised.

"We should get changed," Caitlyn said with an eye to her paint-soaked attire. "We're going out on the town tonight."

"Are you crazy?" Ash gestured to the messy storage room. "I've got an office to get ready."

"Don't you want to celebrate?" Caitlyn asked. "I don't want us to fall into old habits, working so hard all the time that we fail to take time for what's really important."

"I agree," Ash said, tenderness in her eyes. She took a step toward Caitlyn but stopped short, eyeing paint-covered fingers. "But there are only two things I want right now. Egg rolls, and you."

Caitlyn arched a brow. "Egg rolls?"

"Definitely," Ash confirmed. "And you."

They stood frozen for a moment, close but not touching. Finally, with a roll of her eyes and a hearty laugh, Ash swept Caitlyn into her arms. Ash planted a kiss on her mouth, long and sensuous. When she pulled back, there was a dot of blue paint on her nose.

"Oh no," Caitlyn cried out. "The paint! I got it all over you, and your suit too."

"I don't care." Ash kissed her again, Caitlyn's insides melting. "But since my best suit's ruined now, maybe it's a good time to discuss going business casual?"

"Whatever you want," Caitlyn declared, meaning it to the bottom of her heart. Whatever Ash wanted, Caitlyn would happily give her, as long as it meant they could be together from now on.

SNOW FELL STEADILY on the expansive lawn behind Caitlyn's house, but inside the glass conservatory with its heated inground pool, steam coated the windows with a thick fog. Potted palms and tropical flowers thrived like it was Florida instead of Massachusetts, and the sounds of laughing, splashing, and barking filled the air as birthday balloons and streamers fluttered in a light breeze from the ceiling fans.

"Oh my goodness!" Caitlyn ducked behind her hands as Sadie tossed a toy into the water and Happy went bounding after it. It was no use. Water sprayed up from the pool and drenched her on the chaise. Somehow Ash, lounging in the chair beside her, remained dry. "I can't believe she's actually following through with teaching that dog to dive."

"And I can't believe I only figured out last week that

you had an indoor pool at your house." Ash stretched her arms above her head and her ab muscles, on display thanks to a bikini that didn't leave much to the imagination, rippled in a way that would be playing on a loop in Caitlyn's dreams for weeks.

"Technically, it's my dad's house, which explains the pool." Caitlyn grabbed a towel to dab away the droplets from her legs and chest. "That man's never been in the same room with the word subtle."

Or with his younger daughter on her birthday, she thought, although she kept herself from voicing it. As much as so many things in her life had changed for the better recently, some things never would. There was no point in bringing attention to it and spoiling the day.

"You know what I can't believe?" Ash's mom piped up from where she sat at one of the glass patio tables with Felicia, who was rocking three-month old Tatiana—whom Ash insisted on calling Tater Tot—in her arms. "I can't believe Ash is *hosting* a family get-together." This was punctuated by the whoops and cheers of Ash's brother, nephews, Breanna, and Jose all splashing and swimming with Happy.

"Caitlyn's the host," Ash argued, turning an apologetic look toward Caitlyn. "I'm afraid now that my nephews know you have a pool, they might move in with you."

"Sadie loves having them here," Caitlyn replied. "She couldn't sleep last night, like it was Christmas instead of her birthday eve."

"Birthday eve?" Ash raised a questioning brow. "Is that a Brewster tradition I need to be aware of?"

"No, but I think it should be." Caitlyn laughed at the horror that crossed Ash's face. "Don't give me that look. Your birthday comes next, so you stand to benefit more than I do."

"Do I get to open a gift?" Ash's eyes twinkled with mischief.

"It depends if you're on the good list or the naughty list," Caitlyn teased. Considering the way her girlfriend looked in her swimsuit, Caitlyn had her hopes set on the naughty list, and planned to be the one doing the unwrapping. But why wait until Ash's birthday? They had all weekend, thanks to a strictly enforced new office policy that limited overtime to one weekend per month.

"Ash! We need more beer!" Surfacing at the deep end of the pool, Mike pointed to an empty beer bottle near the ledge.

"Get it yourself, your majesty," Ash called back, even as she rose and walked to the cooler to fetch her brother a fresh bottle.

"How do you put up with all that sass?" Bree joked, swimming up to the edge of the pool.

"It's a mystery," Caitlyn replied, rolling her eyes. But it really wasn't. Ash's sass, as her sister referred to it, was half the attraction. As for the other half? Caitlyn's gaze drifted to the polka dot bottoms of Ash's suit, coming up with an answer that rhymed with *sass*.

"Don't try scaring this one away," Ash's mom warned, making a shooing motion with her arms at Bree and Mike. "Your sister may never find anyone else who can put up with her."

"Mom's got a point." Bree stuck her tongue out at

Ash, who was returning to the pool with her brother's beer, before ducking under the water—most likely to avoid her older sister's retaliation.

"I could get used to this." Mike took a healthy slug from the fresh bottle. "Haven't I always told you, you're my favorite sister?"

"Please. All you do is give me sh—ugar," Ash corrected as her eyes darted to Dylan and Grant, who were paddling around the shallow end in brightly colored pool floaties.

Caitlyn craned her neck to look at the table behind her. "Mrs. Tanner, Ash tells me you're retiring soon?"

"How many times have I told you to call me Bev?" Ash's mom wagged a finger at Caitlyn, which had the odd effect of making her feel more like she belonged than that she was getting in trouble. "And the kids keep pressuring me to, but I've said time and again, I'll retire when I have *four* grandchildren. That's the deal."

"Don't look at me!" Mike protested. "Felicia and I have done our part." This was reinforced by the look of terror in Felicia's eyes, as if contemplating even the idea of another pregnancy and child would have her running for the hills.

Mrs. Tanner looked hopefully to Bree, who held up her hands, including the one with a diamond ring shining prominently from its ring finger. "Slow your roll, Mother! Jose and I aren't even getting hitched until next October, and I want it to be just the two of us for a few more years. I teach little kids at school all day, and unlike my dear sis, I don't want to bring my work home with me."

At the mention of their older sister, both Mike and

Bree turned to look at Ash. Caitlyn could almost feel the panic rolling off her in waves as her face took on the look of a feral cat who was about to get thrown into the pool. But before Ash was forced into a reply, she was saved by a blast of cold air as the door to the outside opened and Gilda came in with a huge sheet cake with seventeen candles on top.

"Time for cake!" Gilda exclaimed as she set the homemade masterpiece down on the patio table and reached into her front apron pocket for a box of matches to light the candles.

"Hold on just a minute. I need to go put on a robe." Caitlyn turned to Ash. "You want to come with me?"

Ash raised an eyebrow but followed after her into the small shower and changing area on the far side of the conservatory.

"Did you ask me back here for a quickie?" Ash teased, waggling her eyebrows to hilarious effect. "We'll have to hurry. You should see how fast my brother polishes off cake."

Caitlyn's tummy fluttered as she gathered up her courage. "No, I wanted to talk to you about something."

Horror skirted over Ash's gorgeous features. "If this is about babies, I will push you into the deep end and hold you under," Ash declared.

"Ashley Rachel Tanner!" Caitlyn's hands flew to her hips. "That is a pathetic excuse for a murder plan. There are nearly a dozen witnesses. You'd be arrested in seconds."

"Especially since most of my family would probably side with you, now that they've seen this pool," Ash agreed with a smirk. As Caitlyn refused to break eye contact, Ash's expression grew serious. "Sorry. What did you want to talk about? But seriously, not babies. We don't even live together."

"Not yet," Caitlyn said, swallowing another round of nerves. "Which is what I wanted to talk to you about."

"What do you mean?" Ash's eyes were wide, her tone hesitant but in a way that gave Caitlyn hope to press on.

"You spend most of your nights here," Caitlyn said, as though building a case in front of a jury. "And when you do stay at your place, you have to take a commuter train to the closest station and then Uber into our office. Or I have to pick you up."

"Isn't it cake time?" Ash made a show of checking her bare wrist.

"Yes, but we're not done with this conversation," Caitlyn warned, knowing if she didn't make it to the end of her list now, she never would. "In addition to not being convenient, you pay a fortune for an apartment that could literally fit inside the pool. We could pay a part time assistant with that money."

Ash let out a nervous laugh. "I think it'd cost more than my rent to hire someone."

Caitlyn fixed Ash with an intense stare. "You're missing the point."

Ash leaned into Caitlyn's ear and whispered, "No, darling. You're missing the part where you list loving me and wanting to spend time with me as the reason I should move in with you."

"I—" Caitlyn gasped. In all her careful planning to appeal to Ash's rational nature, she'd somehow managed to leave out the most important part of her argument."

"Well, of course I do."

"Then I guess we'd better put on our robes and go tell my family they're going to be spending a lot more time at Auntie Caitlyn and Auntie Ash's pool." Ash looped her arm around Caitlyn's waist, holding her tight. "Unless there's no cake left, in which I reserve the right to reconsider."

Bubbling over with joy, Caitlyn nodded vigorously. "That's only fair," she said, grinning from ear to ear.

EPILOGUE

The hotel suite's French doors stood open, pleasantly warm spring air wafting in gently from the balcony that overlooked the sea. As Ash hung the last of her suits inside the antique wardrobe in the bedroom, the pop of a champagne cork shattered the silence, followed by Caitlyn letting out a celebratory whoop. Ash jumped several inches backward, nearly sending her tumbling onto her ass. Recovering her balance, she scurried into the adjoining sitting room to discover Caitlyn with one hand over a deep green bottle, the other grasping for a tall crystal flute as fizzy liquid bubbled from the top.

"What on earth are you doing?" Ash demanded, rushing to help Caitlyn with the glasses before any more of the precious golden liquid hit the floor.

"Oh, no. You can't be a grump tonight." Caitlyn managed to fill both flutes without further mishap, handing one off to Ash and keeping the other for herself. She clinked the rim of her glass against Ash's. "Cheers."

Ash took a sip, her taste buds delighting as the champagne danced over her tongue. "Jesus, that's good. What type is—actually, no. Don't tell me. If I find out it costs thousands of dollars, I may spit it out in shock, which would be a waste."

Caitlyn mimed zipping her lips shut and Ash inwardly groaned. Not that they couldn't afford to splurge on a decent bottle of bubbly—business in the little over a year since they'd struck out on their own had exceeded all expectations—but Ash didn't even know why they were celebrating. They were attending a three-day Women in Law symposium, not going on a vacation, despite the sunshine and tempting beaches.

"What's the special occasion, anyway? It's not like we're rubbing elbows with royalty this weekend," Ash said, pausing to savor another sip of champagne. "Is this because Happy won the diving competition two weeks ago? Or is this just some sort of Pavlovian response to being back in your grandmother's old house? Am I going to wake up to you calling out for the butler to bring you tea on a silver platter in the middle of the night?"

"I see class warfare is back on the menu." Taking a seat on the couch near where Ash was standing, Caitlyn batted her long dark lashes, setting off an immediate spike of longing, even as the woman's half-smirk suggested Ash's teasing would not go unpunished. "I'll have you know, the only reason Willis ever brought me a silver tray was so I could ride it down the main staircase like a sled."

"What I wouldn't give to have witnessed that." Sinking into a plush velvet sofa, Ash took in the room, still unable to fathom how anyone could have lived in a place like this and found it normal. Though the furnishings and décor had been updated when the mansion was turned into a hotel, the deeply carved moldings and glittering chandeliers were a reminder that Caitlyn's childhood and her own had been worlds apart.

"You seem troubled." Caitlyn shifted closer, setting her glass on an end table so she could rest her hand on Ash's knee. "Is everything okay?"

"I feel about as much of a fish out of water tonight as the last time we were here for the mock trial," Ash confessed, feeling foolish that, as a grown woman, she was still unable to shake her sense of not belonging. For all the growth she'd experienced since striking out on her own—well, with Caitlyn—there were still some deeply-rooted insecurities that felt as if they'd take a lifetime to diminish. "What has it been, eight years now?"

"Almost to the day. But don't forget"—Caitlyn's eyes shone with encouragement, the pride in her tone filling Ash with warmth—"we're here because of you. We didn't get this nice suite because my grandma used to own this place. We got it because you're the keynote speaker. Over a hundred women traveled here from around the country to hear the inspirational story of how you're avenging your father's death by fighting against a pharmaceutical giant—and winning."

"We haven't won yet," Ash cautioned, though she did allow herself a celebratory sip of champagne as she recalled with a thrill how the latest motion in the class action suit against Parker Pharma had gone their way. "There's a long way to go until Fergus Clark's family and the others get the justice they deserve." A familiar knot in her shoulder and twinge at her temple made themselves known. Waiting on the motion had been a nail-biting experience.

"You tense up every time you talk about it." Caitlyn crooked a finger. "Take your top off."

"Not the direction I thought this was going," Ash remarked, though she wasted no time in following Caitlyn's orders. Goosebumps raised along her flesh in the cool air, but the fire that ignited in her core kept her from getting cold.

"Sit with your back toward me."

Ash frowned. That was not the command she'd expected. "Now you've got me confused."

By way of reply, Caitlyn kneaded her fingers into Ash's shoulders, setting free a moan. The tight muscle ached in the best possible way. "You really should see a professional massage therapist."

"There you go, talking like a rich person." Ash's teasing ended in a whimper when Caitlyn really dug her fingers in, the flash of pain and relief commingling. "Why would I pay someone when you're doing such a fantastic job?"

"What if we got a couples massage?" Caitlyn suggested. Ash felt one bra strap slide off her shoulder, followed by the other. "We could book it here at the spa for tomorrow after your speech."

"Or, we could do our own." Ash's voice was husky as the possibilities flooded her imagination. "I'll rub yours while you rub mine."

"Are we still talking about backs here, or did you have

some other body parts in mind?" With a laugh, Caitlyn placed a soft kiss on the back of Ash's neck. "For the record, no spa I've been to has done a massage like that, couples or otherwise."

"I'm not sure if I think that's a shame, or a relief." Ash slanted her neck to the right, giving Caitlyn access to an earlobe.

"Now it's time for your present," Caitlyn whispered, breath sending delightful shivers racing down Ash's neck. Her nipples tightened in response.

"It can wait—Uh, wait." Belatedly, the meaning of Caitlyn's words registered in Ash's brain. "What present?"

"Your anniversary gift."

Maybe Caitlyn's massage had turned Ash's brain into goop, but nothing about that statement made a lick of sense. "I wasn't aware we even *had* an anniversary."

"Of course we do. We just talked about it." Caitlyn paused as if waiting for Ash to make the connection. When that didn't happen, she said, "The mock trial, remember? Eight years ago, almost to the day."

"Eight years..." Quickly doing the math on her fingers, Ash's brow settled into a deep crease. She turned to face Caitlyn, noting with satisfaction the way the woman's eyes flitted to her bare breasts the instant they were within her view. "You're off by a full month."

"I said almost," Caitlyn replied, a hint of petulance in her tone as she pried her gaze off Ash's tits and managed to establish eye contact. "I know it's not exact, but since we were going to be back where it all began, I wanted to make it an occasion."

"That explains the champagne," Ash remarked with belated comprehension. Despite Caitlyn's obviously shaky grasp on dates, Ash felt like a schmuck. She'd never stopped to think about whether they had an anniversary, let alone planned a way to celebrate one. Considering she and Caitlyn had been together officially for more than a year now, this really should have come to her attention earlier. "I'm afraid I didn't get you anything for our anniversary."

"If you can keep your whining about upper class American society to a minimum while we're here," Caitlyn said with a dramatic roll of her eyes, "it will be present enough."

"If my gift is a Rolls Royce or something, you can take it back. One thing I've learned from dating you is that fancy cars are a pain in the ass to maintain."

"You caught me." Caitlyn gave her fingers an exaggerated snap. The next moment, she'd slid from the couch onto one knee.

Ash's heart clenched. Was Caitlyn about to propose? She couldn't! Ash was topless. How would she ever be able to tell her family how it happened if Caitlyn popped the question while Ash's boobs were running free?

Caitlyn burst out laughing. "Your face is priceless right now, and I think you've gotten the wrong end of the stick. I'm not proposing."

"I didn't think you were going to," Ash mumbled, crossing her arms over her chest. She was way too aware of her shirtless state all of a sudden and cast a wistful glance at the top she'd tossed halfway across the room.

Still on her knees, Caitlyn reached under the sofa and

retrieved a rectangular box from its depths. It was wrapped with shiny gold paper and tied with a red satin ribbon. "Given your expectations, I think this is going to be a dud."

"What is it?" Taking the box, Ash gave it a shake, listening intently at the muffled sounds that came from within. Ash eased the lid off, her trembling fingers revealing that seeing Caitlyn on bended knee had left her more shaken than she'd let on. She ran a finger along the silky black fabric inside, lifting it out with a smile. "It's a robe."

"You mentioned needing one." Caitlyn gnawed at her lower lip with an uncharacteristic lack of confidence. "I mean, it's not much, I guess."

"That's okay," Ash quipped. "It's not really our anniversary, either."

Caitlyn let out a burst of laughter. "How did I fall madly in love with such a curmudgeon?"

Ash grinned. "I like that. Can I get it embroidered on my robe?"

"Curmudgeon?" Caitlyn arched her brow.

"Yes. I'd like it in gold thread, please."

Caitlyn took the robe and held it out by the shoulders. "Stand up and slip it on. See how it feels on your bare skin."

"I'm thinking there's something else I'd rather feel against my bare skin." Ash swept her eyes along Caitlyn's body, leaving no doubt what she had in mind.

"Oh really?" Caitlyn undid the top two buttons of her blouse, letting the neckline fall open so Ash could enjoy a better view. "And what was that?"

"Well, I hear this swanky establishment has some super high thread count sheets." With a not at all subtle glance at the bedroom, Ash stood and put a hand out for Caitlyn. "What do you say, Brewster?"

Caitlyn hopped to her feet. "Yes."

"Not I do?" Ash joked.

"We'll see about that," Caitlyn teased as she followed Ash to the bedroom.

As they climbed under the silky-smooth sheets, Ash couldn't help but sneak a peek at the nightstand drawer, her pulse ticking faster. Sometime this weekend when the time was right—probably when they were both wearing shirts, though that wasn't a hundred percent guaranteed—Ash would reach for the small black box she'd hidden inside, the one with the vintage diamond and sapphire engagement ring exactly the same shade as Caitlyn's eyes.

Eight years, almost to the day, since they'd first met in this place that held a special spot in both their hearts. Well, minus a month, but still…

As if Ash hadn't thought of her own way to mark the occasion and make it special. She was pretty sure by the time she was through, Caitlyn would never call her a curmudgeon again.

A HUGE THANK YOU!

Thanks so much for reading *Devil's Advocate*! Miranda and TB have cowritten so many books now and we're often asked how we manage to work so well together. What many don't realize is Miranda and TB go way back. How far back? We were actually born in the same hospital, just nine weeks apart, although TB keeps insisting it was seven weeks because math... While we may quibble about plot points, we're often laughing as we do.

For example, while working on this story, Miranda said to TB, "Please stop mentioning cannoli in every book we write." You may have noticed we mentioned cannoli many times in *Devil's Advocate* because Ash lives in the North End and, according to TB, it's a North End law stating cannoli must be mentioned in all stories set in that lovely neighborhood. Miranda's still checking the statutes to determine if TB made this fact up, but we're talking about cannoli. TB takes that deadly seriously.

If you enjoyed *Devil's Advocate*, we would really appre-

A HUGE THANK YOU!

ciate a box of a dozen cannoli, but since that's kind of hard to ship, and messy, a review on Amazon, Goodreads, or your favorite book review site would be almost as sweet. Even short reviews help immensely.

TB has published more than thirty novels, and she still finds it simply amazing people read her stories. When she hit publish on her first book back in 2013, she had no idea what would happen. It's been a wonderful journey, and she wouldn't be where she is today without your support.

If you want to stay in touch with TB, sign up for her newsletter. She'll send you a free copy of *A Woman Lost*, book 1 in the A Woman Lost series, plus the bonus chapters and Tropical Heat (a short story), all of which are exclusive to subscribers. And, you'll be able to enter monthly giveaways to win one of her books.

You'll also be one of the first to hear about her many misadventures, like the time she accidentally ordered thirty pounds of oranges, instead of five. To be honest, that stuff happens to TB a lot, which explains why she owns three of the exact same Nice Tits T-shirt. In case you're wondering, the shirt has pictures of the different tits of the bird variety because she has some pride.

Here's the link to join: http://eepurl.com/hhBhXX

And, if you want to follow Miranda, sign up for her newsletter. Subscribers will receive her first book, *Telling Lies Online*, for free. Also, she runs monthly giveaways, including paperbacks, ebooks, and audio, that her readers love. For cat fans, she shares adorable photos of her felines, who are sisters and tag-team to destroy everything in Miranda's house. Their first Christmas was a particularly trying time, and about half of the ornaments survived. Luckily, they're adorable. Seriously, you don't want to miss out on Miranda's heartfelt and funny newsletters. Here's the link to join: mirandamacleod.com/list

Thanks again for reading *Devil's Advocate*. It's because of you that we are able to follow our dreams of being writers. It's a wonderful gift, and we appreciate each and every reader.

TB & Miranda

ABOUT THE AUTHORS

TB Markinson is an American who's recently returned to the US after a seven-year stint in the UK and Ireland. When she isn't writing, she's traveling the world, watching sports on the telly, visiting pubs in New England, or reading. Not necessarily in that order.

Visit TB's website (lesbianromancesbytbm.com) to say hello. On the *Lesbians Who Write* weekly podcast, she and Clare Lydon dish about the good, the bad, and the ugly of writing.

Originally from southern California, Miranda MacLeod now lives in New England and writes heartfelt romances and romantic comedies featuring witty and charmingly flawed women that you'll want to marry. Or just grab a coffee with, if that's more your thing.

Before becoming a writer, she spent way too many years in graduate school, worked in professional theater and film, and held temp jobs in just about every office building in downtown Boston. To find out about her upcoming releases, be sure to sign up for her mailing list at mirandamacleod.com.

TB and Miranda also co-own *I Heart SapphFic*, a website for authors and readers of sapphic fiction to stay up-to-date on all the latest sapphic fiction news. The duo won a Golden Crown Literary Award for *The AM Show* in 2022.

Printed in Great Britain
by Amazon

14033117R00246